The Editor

DENISE N. BAKER is Professor of English at the University of North Carolina, Greensboro. She is the author of *Julian of Norwich's Showings: From Vision to Book* as well as numerous articles on mysticism and other topics in medieval literature and culture. She is the editor of *Inscribing the Hundred Years' War in French and English Cultures.*

A NORTON CRITICAL EDITION

Julian of Norwich
SHOWINGS

AUTHORITATIVE TEXT
CONTEXTS
CRITICISM

Edited by

DENISE N. BAKER
UNIVERSITY OF NORTH CAROLINA, GREENSBORO

W · W · NORTON & COMPANY · *New York · London*

W. W. Norton & Company has been independent since its founding in 1923, when William Warder Norton and Mary D. Herter Norton first published lectures delivered at the People's Institute, the adult education division of New York City's Cooper Union. The Nortons soon expanded their program beyond the Institute, publishing books by celebrated academics from America and abroad. By mid-century, the two major pillars of Norton's publishing program—trade books and college texts—were firmly established. In the 1950s, the Norton family transferred control of the company to its employees, and today—with a staff of four hundred and a comparable number of trade, college, and professional titles published each year—W. W. Norton & Company stands as the largest and oldest publishing house owned wholly by its employees.

Every effort has been made to contact the copyright holders of each of the selections. Rights holders of any selections not credited should contact W. W. Norton & Company, Inc., for a correction to be made in the next printing of our work.

Composition by Binghamton Valley Composition.
Manufacturing by the Courier Companies—Westford Division.
Production manager: Benjamin Reynolds.

Library of Congress Cataloging-in-Publication Data

Julian, of Norwich, b. 1343
    [Revelations of divine love]
    The showings of Julian of Norwich / Julian of Norwich ;
authoritative texts, contexts, criticism ; edited by Denise N. Baker.
        p. cm. — (A Norton critical edition)
    Includes bibliographical references.

    ISBN 0-393-97915-6 (pbk.)

    1. Julian, of Norwich, b. 1343. Revelations of divine love.   2.
Devotional literature, English (Middle).   I. Baker, Denise
Nowakowski, 1946–.   II. Title.   III. Series

BV4832.3.J86 2004
242—dc22   2004054774

W. W. Norton & Company, Inc., 500 Fifth Avenue, New York, N.Y.
10110-0017
www.wwnorton.com

W. W. Norton & Company Ltd., Castle House,
75 / 76 Wells Street, London W1T 3QT

2 3 4 5 6 7 8 9 0

To my sisters
Marcia and Bonnie

Contents

Introduction

In May 1373 a thirty-year-old woman lay dying in Norwich, England. On the eighth day of her illness, those caring for her summoned her curate because she seemed in danger of imminent death. As this woman looked at the crucifix the priest held before her eyes, a light radiated from the cross and the room grew dark. Suddenly her pain diminished and she saw blood running down from Jesus' head as it did at the time that the crown of thorns was pressed upon it. This vision initiated a series of revelations that lasted from early morning until the middle of the afternoon and concluded with a dream that night. She recounts her experience in the first book known to be composed by an English woman, Julian of Norwich's *Showings*. Over the next two decades or more, Julian produced two different versions of her book: the short text, probably composed a few years after the event; and the long text, six times the length of the first account and the result of almost twenty years of reflection.[1]

We know very little about the first English woman identified as an author besides what she tells us in these two texts. She is called Julian because, at least from 1394, she was an anchorite in the Church of St. Julian in Norwich.[2] The only surviving copy of the short text, MS British Library Additional 37790 (known as the Amherst manuscript after a previous owner), begins with a scribal announcement: "Here es a visionn schewed be the goodenes of god to a deuoute womann, and hir name es Julyan, that is recluse atte Norwyche and ʒitt ys onn lyfe, anno domini millesimo CCCC xiij."[3] Four wills dating from 1394 to 1416 include bequests to an anchorite of St. Julian's.[4] In 1413 Margery Kempe, a holy woman from

---

1. This text has also been titled *The Revelations of Divine Love* or *The Revelation of Love*. Most scholars believe that Julian composed the short text soon after the revelations in 1373 and the long text around 1393, but Nicholas Watson argues that the short text was written between 1382 and 1388 and the long text in the early fifteenth century. Watson, "The Composition of Julian of Norwich's *Revelation of Love*," *Speculum* 68 (1993), 637–83.

2. Julian's anchorhold was destroyed during the bombing of Norwich in World War II, but it has been rebuilt. You can see pictures of the Church of St. Julian and the reconstructed anchorhold at home.clara.net / frmartinsmith / Julian / (accessed January 2004).

3. Edmund Colledge O.S.A. and James Walsh S.J., eds., *A Book of Showings to the Anchoress Julian of Norwich,* Studies and Texts 35 (Toronto: Pontifical Institute of Mediaeval Studies, 1978), 1:201.

4. Colledge and Walsh, "Introduction," *A Book of Showings*, 1:33–35.

nearby King's Lynn and later the author of her own book, consulted Julian for spiritual guidance because "the anchoress was expert in such things and good counsel could give."[5]

Although neither the four wills nor Margery Kempe identify Julian of Norwich as an author, these references attest that by the 1390s she was an anchorite with a regional reputation for sanctity. Anchorites were recluses who voluntarily vowed to remain permanently enclosed, usually in a small room or cell within or adjacent to a monastery or church and often in an urban area. Their cells typically had one window that looked toward the altar of the church and another through which they could speak to those seeking their counsel. Candidates for enclosure, either female or male, lay or professed religious, were carefully screened by the church authorities to ensure their suitability for the solitary life and their continued financial support. Anchoritic enclosure was considered the highest religious calling. The sixth-century *Rule of St. Benedict* presented the solitary life as a more advanced ascetic vocation than the communal life of monks and nuns. By the fourteenth century, according to books of guidance composed for anchorites by Richard Rolle, Walter Hilton, and the anonymous author of the *Cloud of Unknowing*, contemplative or mystical union with God was the ultimate goal of the recluse.[6]

While she does not indicate whether she was an anchorite, nun, or lay person when she received the revelations, Julian is careful not to claim any special authority for herself in either the short or the long text. Fourteenth-century England was much more conservative in matters of spirituality than the Continent, where accounts of women's visionary experiences were quite numerous from the twelfth century on. As the first English woman identified as a writer, Julian is acutely aware that she may be criticized for violating St. Paul's prohibition in 1 Corinthians 14:34–35 against women preaching. She forestalls such criticism by presenting herself as a humble intermediary between God and humankind. In chapter 6 of the short text, for example, she proclaims her unworthiness as a woman to speak of spiritual matters.

> Botte god for bede that ȝe schulde saye or take it so that I am a techere, for I meene nouȝt soo, no I mente nevere so; for I am a womann, leued, febille and freylle. Botte I wate wele, this that I saye, I hafe it of the schewynge of hym tha(t) es souerayne techare. . . . Botte for I am a womann, schulde I therfore leve

5. Lynn Staley, ed. and trans., *The Book of Margery Kempe*, A Norton Critical Edition (New York: Norton, 2000), 32.
6. The most thorough study of this vocation in the Middle Ages is Ann K. Warren, *Anchorites and Their Patrons in Medieval England* (Berkeley: University of California Press, 1985).

> that I schulde nouȝt telle ȝowe the goodenes of god, syne that
> I sawe in that same tyme that is his wille, that it be knawenn?[7]

Even while she acknowledges the impropriety of speaking in public,
Julian insists that she speaks at God's command, and she encourages
her readers to disregard the messenger and pay heed to the message.

Although she continues to declare her unworthiness throughout
the long text, Julian's voice is more self-assured. She omits the con-
cession that as a woman she has no right to teach. Instead, she
begins the long text by introducing herself as "a symple creature
unlettyrde." Scholars debate whether this statement is the conventional protestation of humility expected of writers on spiritual matters or a literal statement about her inability to read and write.[8]
Although the meaning of *unlettered* was changing in the fourteenth
century, it probably indicates that Julian could not read and write in
Latin rather than that she was illiterate in the vernacular. Unlike
Margery Kempe, Julian does not mention a spiritual adviser who read
aloud to her or an amanuensis to whom she dictated her book. Moreover, her comprehension of the medieval theological tradition, especially in the long text, is astounding. Although it may not be possible
to identify Julian's particular method of acquiring knowledge or her
actual sources, it is important to recognize the erudition informing
her vernacular theology. Rather than being an accurate assessment
of her intellectual attainments, Julian's description of herself as "a
symple creature unlettyrde" is most likely an example of the humility
topos common to those who wrote about spirituality in the Middle
Ages.

Julian provides a significant clue to her intellectual and spiritual
formation when she subsequently reports in chapter 2 that before
May 1373 she had prayed for three gifts from God: a vision of the
Passion of Christ; a serious illness; and the three metaphoric wounds
of contrition, compassion, and longing for God. The first two—the
bodily sight and the bodily sickness—are extraordinary means of
achieving the compassion and contrition of the last request, and
Julian makes them conditional on God's will. The three emotions of
the third request, however, are the conventional stages of spiritual
progress articulated in the treatises and handbooks about contemplation that were popular in the late Middle Ages. Compassion or
empathy for the suffering Christ and contrition or remorse for sin

7. Colledge and Walsh, eds., *A Book of Showings*, 1:222. The last paragraph of Revelation I,
   chapter 8, and the first two paragraphs of chapter 9 in the long text roughly correspond
   to chapter 6 in the short text; this passage, which comes at the end of chapter 6, is
   reprinted on p. 129 herein.
8. Colledge and Walsh, for example, argue that Julian was a learned scholar and skilled
   rhetorician in "Introduction," *A Book of Showings*, 1:43–59. Brant Pelphrey regards her
   as illiterate; see *Love Was His Meaning: The Theology and Mysticism of Julian of Norwich*
   (Salzburg: Institut für Anglistik und Amerikanistik, Universität Salzburg, 1982), 18–28.

were considered the preliminary steps to contemplative, or what we might call mystical, union with God. While Julian says that she forgot her two extraordinary requests, she kept the last triad in mind. As the crucifix shone before her during her life-threatening illness, the fulfillment of her second request, Julian's renewed prayer for the three metaphoric wounds was answered with a bodily sight of Christ's bleeding head and the subsequent showings. These showings occur in three modes, "by bodyly syght, and by worde formyde in my understondyng, and by goostely syght" (Revelation I, chapter 9), that roughly correlate to the themes Julian articulates in her third request: compassion, contrition, and longing for God.

The descriptions of the "bodyly syght" of Christ's Passion that Julian offers in Revelations I, II, IV, and VIII are compellingly vivid. Her graphic language enables us to see in our mind's eye the blood running down from the crown of thorns, the face disfigured by torture, the lacerations made by the whips, and finally the body of Christ drying and dying on the cross. These striking representations of the Passion and Crucifixion manifest Julian's familiarity not only with medieval painting and sculpture but also with the common devotional practice of meditation on the life of Christ. Introduced for the professed religious, especially anchorites, in the twelfth century and popularized for the laity in the fourteenth, meditation promotes an imaginative participation in the events of Jesus' life. The meditator is encouraged to close the gap between the present time and the past time of the historical Christ by imaginatively engaging either as a participant in the events or as an eyewitness. In her *Book* Margery Kempe reports that through her meditation on the scenes of the Passion during Holy Week "she thought that she saw our Lord Christ Jesus as verily in her soul with her ghostly eye as she had seen before the crucifix with her bodily eye."[9] While Margery's meditations are theatrical, often involving her in the action, Julian's are painterly; her eye lingers on the physical details of Jesus' pain as she suffers with Christ and evokes the same compassion in her readers.

Julian's visions incite not only compassion but also contrition for the sins that caused Christ's suffering and apprehension about her inability to resist future temptations. As she confesses in Revelation VII, she vacillates between feelings of well-being and of woe, between the certainty that she will be saved and the realization that sin is unavoidable. Many of the words revealed to Julian address her anxieties about the inevitability of sin and God's response to it. In Revelation V she hears that the schemes of the fiend are overcome by Christ's Passion; in VI and in XV God promises her that she will be rewarded in heaven for her service; and in IX Jesus tells her he is

9. Staley, *Book of Margery Kempe*, 137.

very pleased to have suffered for her salvation. The various aural showings of Revelation XIII assure her that although sin is necessary, all shall be well.

Julian's preoccupation with sin indicates the challenge that it posed to her personally and to medieval Christians. The fact of evil, either as sin or as suffering, seems to contradict the belief that the universe was created by a good God who is omnipotent and omniscient. This problem of evil haunted Julian for the twenty years or more that passed between her initial vision and the final revision of the *Showings*; it acted as the irritant around which the interpretive accretions of the long text formed. Although the short text foreshadows her solution to the problem of evil, she can fully articulate its implications only after two decades of contemplation. Revelations XIII and XIV in the final version, the locus of Julian's theodicy or solution to the problem of evil, significantly expand ideas only hinted at in the short text: the secret of universal salvation (XIII.32–33), the parable of the lord and servant (XIV.51), the concept of the godly will and the essential union between the Creator and his creatures (XIV.53–57), and the representation of Jesus as Mother (XIV.58–63). In comparing the sketchiness of the short text to the intellectual sophistication of the long, we recognize that Julian developed from a visionary to a theologian as she struggled with the enigma of sin. As we shall see, her original solution to the problem of evil in the long text establishes Julian of Norwich as a brilliantly creative thinker within the constraints of medieval orthodoxy.

In Revelation III Julian confronts the dilemma of evil: " 'What is synne?' " she asks. "For I saw truly that God doth alle thyng, be it nevyr so lylyle." If the Creator is all powerful, all knowing, and all good, how does evil come to exist in creation? Responding to this problem of evil, Julian endorses the traditional contrast between the flawed judgment of humankind and the perfect judgment of God. "And I was sewer that he doth no synne. And here I saw verely that synne is no dede . . . For man beholdyth some dedys wele done and some dedys evylle, and our Lorde beholdyth them not so." From God's point of view evil does not exist because it is not an entity but a privation, an absence of good, and because it plays a role in God's inscrutable providential plan. In other words, evil is a kind of *trompe d'oeil*, a misperception due to the inadequate perspective of creatures who cannot understand the divine design of the universe.

Julian returns to the question of sin in Revelations XIII and XIV to explore its purpose in the divine design of the universe and God's response to the sinner. While the traditional view of sin emphasizes human culpability and the punishment it deserves, Julian fears that her fellow Christians will be overwhelmed by their guilt and their dread of an angry God. She receives consolation in the aural showing: "*Synne is behovely, but alle shalle be wele, and alle shalle be wele, and alle maner of thynge shalle be wele*" (XIII.27). *Behovely* means both "necessary" and "beneficial." Julian invokes both of these definitions as she explains that sin is a means of achieving self-knowledge and knowledge of God. She summarizes her conclusion near the end of Revelation XIV: "For it nedyth us to falle, and it nedyth us to see it. For yf we felle nott, we shulde nott knowe how febyll and how wrechyd we be of oure selfe, nor also we shulde not so fulsomly know the mervelous love of oure maker" (XIV.61). Just like Adam's original transgression, individual sin is a *felix culpa,* a fortunate fault, because it teaches humans about their own fallibility and the full extent of God's love.

Julian's belief that "synne is behovely" depends, of course, on her conviction that "alle shalle be wele." In Revelation XIII she explains two different means by which the punishment for sin will be rescinded. The first means, already known, is the Savior. In other words, Julian endorses the central tenet of Christianity that Jesus, as God and man, atoned for Adam's transgression with his Crucifixion and saves the elect through grace and not through any merit of their own. "Owre Lorde God shewde that a deed shalle be done and hym selfe shalle do it. . . . And this is the hyghest joy that the soule understode, that God hym selfe shall do it and I shalle do ryght nought but synne, and my synne shall nott lett his goodnes workyng" (XIII.36). Julian realizes that, despite the fact that she will inevitably sin and contrary to the church's insistence on the divine wrath incurred by sinners, God will continue to love her and ultimately transmute the wound of sin into an honor.

Julian's showing also challenges the assertion that those who do not belong to the church are eternally damned. She refers to a second, hidden understanding, God's secret or "prevy councelle," by which, she implies, even those whom the church consigns to hell will ultimately be saved.[1] After reiterating the church's condemnation of heathens and renegade Christians, Julian remarks: "And stondyng alle thys, me thought it was unpossible that alle maner of thyng shuld be wele, as oure Lorde shewde in thys tyme. And as to thys I had no other answere in shewying of oure Lorde but thys, *That that is unpossible to the is nott unpossible to me. I shalle save my worde in alle thyng, and I shalle make althyng wele*" (XIII.32). The contradiction between her revelation and the church's teaching bewilders Julian. Perplexed, she asks for a vision of hell or purgatory, but she does not receive it (XIII.33). Nonetheless, she affirms her allegiance

---

1. Nicholas Watson discusses Julian's claim in relation to the views on universal salvation expressed by other fourteenth-century writers in "Visions of Inclusion: Universal Salvation and Vernacular Theology in Pre-Reformation England," *The Journal of Medieval and Early Modern Studies* 27 (1997), 145–187.

to the church and acknowledges that she has no right to pry into God's secrets.

In Revelation XIV, however, Julian continues to struggle with the disagreement between these two authoritative sources about God's attitude toward sinners. " 'Yf I take it thus, that we be no synners nor no blame wurthy, it semyth as I shulde erre and faile of knowyng of this soth. And yf it be tru that we be synners and blame wurthy, good Lorde, how may it than be that I can nott see this truth in the, whych arte my God, my maker in whom I desyer to se alle truth?' " (XIV.50). The solution to Julian's quandary comes to her after she meditates on the enigmatic showing of the lord and servant "for twenty yere after the tyme of the shewyng save thre monthys" (XIV.51). This breakthrough enables her to resolve the apparent contradiction between the church and her revelations by developing an innovative theodicy that emphasizes the inextricable bond between humanity and the three persons of the Trinity. She begins by revising the story of the Fall in chapters 2 and 3 of Genesis that served as the justification for the traditional theodicy. In so doing, she challenges the doctrine of original sin, which asserts that evil resulted from the free choice of Adam and Eve, who bequeathed a depraved will to their descendants, and that sinners must suffer the consequences of God's wrath. Through her double reading of the tableau of the lord and servant in chapter 51, Julian rewrites the story of the Fall by identifying the servant as both the first Adam and the second Adam, Christ.[2] Not only does she refuse to blame Eve, omitting her entirely from the narrative, but she also insists that the servant Adam does not deliberately disobey his lord but rather falls to earth as he runs to do his bidding. The lord, who represents God the Father, is not angry; instead he looks with pity on the first Adam and with joy on the second Adam, whose redemption of humankind had been planned from all eternity. By linking Adam's Fall to Christ's incarnation, Julian's theodicy focuses on God's overwhelming love for sinners rather than divine wrath.

In the remaining chapters of Revelation XIV Julian continues to develop her radical theodicy through her astute explanation of the inextricable bonds linking humankind to the Creator and her astonishing comparison of Jesus to a mother. As implied in chapter 51, she believes in the preexistence of the soul before its union with the body and its fall into the material world. Julian articulates the tenets of this Christian Neoplatonism by attributing the act of creation to God the Father and Jesus the Mother. In the initial stage, God the

2. Lynn Staley reads this chapter as a revision of the parable of the Wedding Feast and compares it with similar episodes in *St. Erkenwald*, *Cleanness*, and *Piers Plowman* in "The Man in Foul Clothes and a Late Fourteenth-Century Conversation about Sin," *Studies in the Age of Chaucer* 24 (2002), 1–47.

Father creates the soul from his own substance and these two essences remain united but not identical. "And I sawe no dyfference betwen God and oure substance, but as it were all God. And yett my understandyng toke that oure substance is in God, that is to sey, that God is God and oure substance is a creature in God" (XIV.54). Her use of *substance* indicates Julian's learning, for it is a term from scholastic discourse that refers to the essence of a being, the permanent and unchanging substratum of an entity. The divine act of conferring being, she contends, situates the substance of the soul in God's being without its being God. The substance of the soul remains enclosed in the deity even after this higher part is united to the lower part or sensuality in the next stage of creation.

In this second stage, God the Father's creation of the human substance is complemented, according to Julian, by Jesus the Mother's incorporation of that substance in a material manifestation. "Oure substaunce is the hyer perty, whych we have in oure Fader God almyghty. And the Seconde Person of the Trynyte is oure Moder in kynd in oure substauncyall makyng in whom we be groundyd and rotyd" (XIV.58). Explaining the union of spirit with matter, soul with body, in humankind, Julian refers to the first of the three maternities of Jesus, his motherhood in creation. Christ unites the substance of the soul with the body, thus joining this higher part to its lower part, the sensuality. She distinguishes between the presence of the Second Person as the image of God within each soul and each soul's participation in the being of the First Person. "A hye understandyng it is inwardly to se and to know that God, whych is oure maker, dwellyth in oure soule. And a hygher understandyng it is and more inwardly to se and to know oure soule that is made dwellyth in God in substance, of whych substance by God we be that we be" (XIV.54). The two stages of creation, according to Julian, result in a reciprocal enclosure of God in the soul and the soul in God. She uses the metaphor of the soul as the city or citadel of God to refer to the first of these envelopments and the concept of God as the ground of the soul to express the second.

Julian's analysis of the two stages of creation in Revelation XIV enables her to expound her distinctive concept of the godly will of the elect. Her belief in the preexistence of the higher part of the soul in God before the creation of the body gives her confidence "that in ech a soule that shall be safe is a godly wylle that nevyr assentyd to synne ne nevyr shall" because, as she explains, its higher part is so "knytt and onyd in hym that there in were kepte a substaunce whych myght nevyr nor shulde be partyd from hym" (XIV.53). Despite lapses into sin due to the beastly will of the sensuality, this godly will ensures that the elect will never be completely separated from God and will ultimately be saved. The difference between the wills of the higher and lower parts of the soul clarifies the disparity between the divine and the human attitudes toward sinners, for the Creator judges the indefectible substance of the soul while creatures judge the fallible sensuality (XIV.45). By recognizing these two different perspectives, Julian reconciles the apparent disparity between the church's insistence on divine wrath toward sinners and the benevolent God of her revelations.

Although Julian denies God's wrath toward sinners, she maintains the necessity of humankind's redemption after the Fall of the first Adam. She therefore attributes to the Second Person of the Trinity two other forms of motherhood: re-creation and working. In addition to Christ's special role in enlivening the body in the first creation, Julian acknowledges the Second Person's unique function of assuming a body at the incarnation, the moment when God became human to atone for Adam's Fall. Because human sensuality is responsible for this rupture with the divine, Christ must take on flesh to make reparation. Through his sacrificial death, Jesus, as "Moder of mercy in oure sensualyte takyng" (XIV.58), enables the re-creation of humankind to its original integrity. The benefits of this historic act are made available to contemporary Christians through a third maternity, Christ's motherhood in working. Like a human mother, Jesus cares for his children, protecting and nourishing them through the church and its sacraments, chastising them so they can overcome their vices. Although earlier authors had pointed out similarities between Jesus and a mother, Julian develops this analogy as part of her unique and comprehensive solution to the problem of evil. "I understode thre manner of beholdynges of motherhed in God," she summarizes. "The furst is grounde of oure kynde makyng. The seconde is takyng of oure kynde, and ther begynnyth the moderhed of grace. The thurde is moderhed in werkyng, and therin is a forth spredyng by the same grace of lenght and brede, of hygh and of depnesse without ende. And alle is one love" (XIV.59). As Mother in creation, Jesus maintains the godly wills of the elect intact in his substance. As Mother in re-creation, Jesus atones for the sins of humankind. As Mother in working, Jesus bestows the grace needed for salvation.

While this introduction attempts to outline Julian's theology in a logical sequence, the *Showings* does not present her ideas in that manner. As she meditated on her experience over the course of two decades, Julian was able to comprehend both the complexity and the unity of her revelations. Although constrained by the sequential medium of language, she tries to represent in the long text her own gradual process of illumination and to balance the centrifugal impulse of analytical articulation against the centripetal force of contemplative quietude. As Julian reflects on her showings, returning again and again to the problem of evil in Revelations XIII and XIV, for example, her meditation teases out implications that were not at first obvious. At the same time, she recognizes the underlying unity of her visionary experience and uses cross-references to weave the sixteen showings into a unified text. As certain images, phrases, or themes recur, she elaborates on their significance and points out their relationship to other images, phrases, or themes. Chapter 31 of Revelation XIII provides a simple example of this technique, for she refers to three other showings to validate this revelation about the heavenly union between the Trinity and the saved. First, as she has promised, she amplifies her brief allusion to Jesus' spiritual thirst in Revelation VIII, chapter 17, by explaining it as the divine love-longing for humanity that will last until all those who are to be saved are gathered together in heaven at the end of time. Then she endorses her explication of Jesus' spiritual thirst with the proof of his dual claim to heaven as God, given in Revelation XII, and as man, given in Revelation IX. Thus Julian knits together three preceding showings to confirm a fourth and to demonstrate the fundamental integrity of her revelations. Throughout the long text she uses this intricate system of cross-references to indicate the interlocking ideas of the revelations and to create a recursive experience for the reader. She concludes the *Showings*, however, by insisting that her revelations have only one meaning.

> And fro the tyme that it was shewde, I desyerde oftyn tymes to wytt in what was oure Lord's menyng. And xv yere after and mor I was answeryd in gostly understondyng, seyeng thus, "What, woldest thou wytt thy Lordes menyng in this thyng? Wytt it wele, love was his menyng. Who shewyth it the? Love. Wherfore shewyth he it the? For love. Holde the therin, thou shalt wytt more in the same. But thou schalt nevyr witt therin other with-outyn ende" (XVI.86).

Through the interlace structure of her long text, Julian engages her audience in a meditative process that forces them to comprehend for themselves this unity in the diversity of her showings.

Although I have focused on Julian's innovative theology, her *Showings* must also be placed in a historical context.[3] Not only is Julian of Norwich the first English woman identified as an author, but she also belongs to what can legitimately be considered the first generation of writers in English. Although secular and religious texts had

---

3. Lynn Staley discusses the two texts of the *Showings* in relation to the social, political, and religious context of late-fourteenth-century England in "Julian of Norwich and the Crisis of Authority," in *The Powers of the Holy: Religion, Politics, and Gender in Late Medieval English Culture*, by David Aers and Lynn Staley (University Park: Pennsylvania State University Press, 1996), 107–78.

been composed in Middle English since the early thirteenth century, the vernacular did not begin to acquire prestige as the national language until the second half of the fourteenth century.[4] Julian of Norwich is a contemporary of Chaucer, Gower, the *Gawain* poet, and Langland. She is also one of the group known as the Middle English mystics that includes Richard Rolle (who died in 1349), Walter Hilton, the anonymous author of *The Cloud of Unknowing*, and the fifteenth-century holy woman Margery Kempe. Although there is no conclusive evidence that Julian knew the works of any of her contemporaries, she participates, as they do, in the same sociopolitical event that Nicholas Watson describes as "a huge cultural experiment involving the translation of Latin and Anglo-Norman texts, images, conceptual structures—the apparatus of *textual authority*—into what contemporary commentators termed the 'barbarous' mother tongue, English: a language whose suitability as the vehicle for complex thought of all kinds was a matter for serious doubt."[5] Julian's *Showings* undoubtedly ranks as one of the most distinctive and successful of these efforts to express subtle and sophisticated theological concepts in the vernacular. She writes in English not only because she, as an "unlettyrde" woman, does not know Latin but also because she desires to address her "evyn Cristene." By the last half of the fourteenth century, as Watson observes, the status of English "as the 'kynde langage' of the laity, whom Christ came to save, gave it a potentially radical role in constituting a body of the faithful defined not hierarchically but according to inner rectitude . . . as a community of the faithful."[6] After 1380, however, the practice of vernacular theology becomes politically dangerous as the church and then the state attempt to suppress the Lollard's project of translating the Bible into English. Julian, nonetheless, persists, composing her long text about 1393 or later. Although the small number and late date of the surviving manuscripts attest that, in the repressive atmosphere of the fifteenth century, neither of her texts circulated widely, the scholarly and popular interest in Julian of Norwich today indicates that her *Showings* is finally gaining the audience it deserves.

---

4. For a discussion of fourteenth-century attitudes toward Middle English, see Nicholas Watson, "The Politics of Middle English Writing," in *The Idea of the Vernacular: An Anthology of Middle English Literary Theory, 1280–1520*, ed. by Jocelyn Wogan-Browne, Nicholas Watson, Andrew Taylor, and Ruth Evans (University Park: Pennsylvania State University Press, 1999), 331–52.
5. Nicholas Watson, "The Middle English Mystics," in *The Cambridge History of Medieval English Literature*, ed. David Wallace (Cambridge: Cambridge University Press, 1999), 544.
6. Watson, "The Politics of Middle English Writing," 340.

The Manuscripts

There are two different versions of Julian of Norwich's *Showings:* the short text and the long text. The short text, composed sometime between 1373 and 1388, survives in one manuscript (British Library MS Additional 37790, also known as the Amherst Manuscript after a previous owner). This mid-fifteenth-century manuscript compiles texts of spiritual guidance addressed to contemplatives, including excerpts from works by Richard Rolle and Continental mystics. The headnote to the short text reveals that it was copied from a manuscript made in 1413, while Julian was still living.

The long text survives in whole or part in four important copies, the Westminster, Paris, and two Sloane manuscripts. The Westminster Cathedral Manuscript, compiled between 1450 and 1500, includes excerpts from the long text of the *Showings* and Walter Hilton's *Scale of Perfection* and his commentaries on two psalms. Neither author is identified, but Westminster establishes that the long text was composed earlier than the only surviving copies of it, the Paris and two Sloane manuscripts, which were made in the late sixteenth or early seventeenth centuries.

The Paris Manuscript (MS Bibliothèque nationale anglais 40) was copied in the Low Countries sometime between 1580 and 1650. Containing only the long text of the *Showings*, it is probably based on a Tudor manuscript readied for printing in the 1530s, just before Henry VIII broke with Rome. Julian's vocabulary has been modernized and the dialect changed to a southern one. This manuscript probably belonged to a house of English Benedictine nuns in France, from whence it was acquired by a private collector and later, the Bibliothèque du Roi; it is now in the Bibliothèque nationale de France. Because its language is closer to Modern English than that of the Sloane manuscripts, Paris was selected for this edition.

The two Sloane manuscripts (British Library MS Sloane 2499, hereafter S1, and British Library MS Sloane 3705, hereafter S2) date from the seventeenth century. S1 was once thought to be slightly earlier than S2, but the watermarks on the leaves of these manuscripts suggest that the order of composition was the reverse. Both manuscripts were copied from a different exemplar than Paris. They preserve Julian's Norfolk dialect, and their vocabularies are closer to Middle English than is Paris's modernized language. Both manuscripts belonged to English Benedictine houses in France. S1 may have been copied by Mother Clementina Cary, a daughter of Elizabeth Cary, Lady Falkland, the author of *The Tragedy of Mariam*.[7]

---

7. For analysis, transcriptions, and translations of these manuscripts, see Julian of Norwich, *Showing of Love: Extant Texts and Translation*, Biblioteche e Archivi 8, ed. Sister Anna

I am grateful to the Bibliothèque nationale de France for permission to use Manuscrits anglais 40, commonly referred to as the Paris manuscript (P), for this edition. I have silently corrected obvious scribal errors and indicated emendations made from the Sloane manuscripts in the footnotes. The Middle English character 3 has been modernized to *gh, y, or z* as has the use of *u* for *v* and *i* for *j*.

I wish to thank Derek Krueger, Stephen Stallcup, and Lynn Staley for reading this introduction and Jennie Thompson and Donna Knostman for their help with this edition. I am grateful to the University of North Carolina at Greensboro for a research assignment that enabled me to complete this project.

Maria Reynolds, C.P., and Julia Bolton Holloway (Florence: SISMEL—Edizioni del Galluzzo, 2001).

The Language of the Paris Manuscript

Copied between 1580 and 1650, the Paris Manuscript is a linguistic hybrid. It changes Julian's dialect from a northern to a southern one, similar to Chaucer's, and modernizes her Middle English vocabulary. The footnotes provide glosses of unfamiliar words or translations of difficult passages. However, students will find the language of the Paris manuscript less difficult if they remember a few simple rules:

1. The plural and possessive of nouns is usually formed by adding *-es*. I have added an apostrophe only when the possessive is formed with-*s* alone.
2. Final *-e* is often added to nouns.
3. Double negatives are allowed.
4. Spelling was not standardized; certain letters were often interchanged, such as *i/y*, *y/ie*, *ou/ow*. For example: *bodylie/*bodily; *sowle/*soul. Single letters are sometimes doubled; for example, *oone/*one; *nott/*not.
5. The suffix *-hed* is usually *-ness* in Modern English as in *fulhed/*fullness.
6. The present tense indicative plural of the verb *ben*, to be, is *be* rather than *are*.
7. Present tense indicative verbs usually follow this pattern: *I take, thow takest, he taketh* or *takyth; we, yow, they taken.* The third person singular sometimes has no ending; for example, *lettyth* or *lett* (hinders, permits). Past tense is formed by adding *-ed/-de/-id/-yd* or by a sound change within the word (*see/saw*)
8. Some verbs that are now used with personal subjects are impersonal. For example, *hym liketh*, it pleases him; or *my behovyth*, it behooves me, it is necessary for me. Other verbs used in impersonal constructions include *think, need,* and *seem.*

A Glossary of Frequently Used Words

ageane, agene, ayeen (adv.) again

anemptes, anemptis, anenst, aneynst (prep.) in regard to, in respect of

awne (pronoun) own

avisement, avysement (noun) due consideration, reflection

beclosed, beclosid, beclosyd (verb) enclosed

behovely (adj.) necessary, beneficial

behovyth me (impersonal verb) it is necessary to me, it is appropriate; **me behoveth nedes** I must of necessity

ben (verb) to be

besy (adj.) busy

bodilie, bodylie, bodely (adj.) bodily

buxom (adj.) obedient, submissive

chere, cheere (noun) facial expression, demeanor

comprehendyd (verb) understood, included

dar, druste, durst (verb) dare, dared

deerworthie, dere worthy, derwurdy (adj.) esteemed, honorable, valuable, beloved

demyth, demyd (verb) judges, judged

departeth (verb) departs, separates

desyer (noun and verb) desire, wish for

dight, dyght (verb) order, prepare, appoint, make

dyscrecion (noun) discretion, the ability to judge between divinely and diabolically inspired experiences

dysees, dysseyse (noun and verb) trouble, distress

dyspyer (noun) despair

evyn Cristen, evynn Crystyn fellow Christians

farforth, ferforth (adv.) so far, to such an extent

fayer, feyer (adj.) fair

fayleth, feylyth (verb) fails

feende, fende (noun) fiend, devil

feayth(e), feyght (noun) faith

felyng (noun) feeling

frenschyppe, frinshipe (noun) friendship

frind(es), frynd(es) (noun) friend(s)

fulhed (noun) fullness, abundance

full, fulle (adv.) very, completely

fulsomely (adv.)   abundantly, entirely
ghostly, ghostely, goostely, gostly (adj.)   spiritual
gracious (adj.)   generous, usually referring to the gift of divine grace
grett (adj.)   great, large
hey, hye (adj.)   high, great, exalted
heyly, hyly (adv.)   highly
hole (adj.)   whole, complete; (noun)   wholeness, health
homely (adj.)   familiar (as with a member of a household), intimate;
    (adv.)   intimately, familiarly, privately
inow (adj.)   enough
kynd(e) (noun)   nature, innate properties; (adj.)   natural, kind
lerneth, lernyth (verb)   teaches
let(t), lettyth (verb)   hinder, prevent, but also allow, permit
leve (verb)   believe; live; leave
lever, levyr (adj.)   more willing, rather
lyke (adj.)   alike, similar
liketh, lykyth (verb)   enjoys, pleases; (impersonal verb)   **me liketh**, it
    pleases me, I am pleased; **hym likyth**, it pleases him; he likes it
lykyng (noun)   something pleasing, delight, pleasure
marvayle, merveyle, marvailled, merveyled (noun and verb)   marvel,
    wonder; marveled
mech (adv.)   much, greatly
mede, meed (noun)   reward
medelur, medle (noun)   a mixture
medlid, medlyd, medylde (adj.)   mixed
mekyl, mekyll (adj.)   great; (adv.)   much
menyng (noun)   meaning, intention
nawght, naught, nought (noun)   nothing; (adj.)   of no value;
    (adv.)   not at all
nede (noun and verb)   need; (impersonal verb)   **my nedyth**, it is
    needed by me, I need
nedeful (adj.)   necessary
onyth, onyd, onyng (verb)   unites, makes one with; united, joined;
    uniting
or (pronoun)   before
over passing, ovyr passyng (adj.)   surpassing
parelle, perelle (noun)   peril
parte, partie, party, perty (noun)   part, side
ponysschyth (verb)   punishes
preaier (noun)   prayer
previe, prevy, prive (adj.)   private, secret
prevyte, privyties (noun)   privacy, secrets
quycken (verb)   create, enliven
right, ryght (adv.)   very, extremely; (adj.)   right, correct; **right
    nought**, nothing at all
rightfulness, ryghtfulness (noun)   righteousness, justice
rightwys, ryghtwys (adj.)   righteous, just
rode (noun)   cross
ruth (noun)   pity, compassion

ryal (adj.)   royal

schewynges, shewynges (noun)   showings, revelations

seker, siker (adj.)   sure, certain

sikernes, syckernes (noun)   certainty, security

sensualyte (noun)   physical nature; the lower part of the soul directed toward the physical and temporal existence

sethyn, sithen, sythen(e) (adv., conjunction, or prep.)   since, then, afterwards

sewer, suer (adj.)   sure

sodayly, sodenly, sodeynly (adv.)   suddenly

somdele, sumdeele (adv.)   somewhat, partly

sondry, sundry (adj.)   different, various

soth(e) (noun)   truth; (adj.)   true

sowle (noun)   soul

spede (noun and verb)   help, benefit

sped(e)fulle (adj.)   helpful, beneficial

spryte (noun)   spirit

stede (noun)   place

steryth, stirryth (verb)   stirs, moves, inspires

stynt (verb)   stop

substance, substaunce (noun)   substance; the higher part of the soul that remains united with God's substance

sufferyth (verb)   suffers, endures; permits, allows

think, thynk (impersonal verb)   **my thynkyth,** it seems to me, I think

touching, touchyng, towchyng (noun)   inspiration, influence, usually divine; (prep.)   regarding, in respect to.

travayle, travelle, traveyle (noun)   toil, hardship

unneth, unnethes, unnethis (adv.)   scarcely

vertu, vertuous, vertuse (noun)   virtue(s), power

verily, verilie (adv.)   truly; **right verily,** just as truly

wele (noun)   well-being; (adv.)   well

wene (verb)   think, expect, hope; (past tense)   **wende, went, wenyd, weenied;** (present participle)   **weenyng,** expecting, hoping

wite, witte (verb)   know, understand; (second person present)   **wiste, wyst;** (past tense)   **wot, wott** knew

worschippe, wurschyppe (noun and verb)   honor, respect

The Text of
SHOWINGS

Here begynneth the first chapter.

This is a revelacion of love that Jhesu Christ, our endles blisse, made in xvi shewynges,[1] of which the first is of his precious crownyng of thornes. And ther in was conteined and specified the blessed Trinitie with the incarnacion and the unithing betweene God and man's sowle with manie fayer schewynges and techynges[2] of endelesse wisdom and love, in which all the shewynges that foloweth be groundide and joyned.

The secunde is of the discoloring of his fayer face in tokenyng of his deerworthie passion.[3]

The third is that our Lord God, almightie, all wisdom, and all love,[4] right also verily[5] as he hath made all thinges that is, right also verilie he doeth and worketh all thinges that is done.

The iiii[th] is skorgyng[6] of his tender bodie with plenteuous sheding of his precious bloud.

The vth is that the feende[7] is overcome by the precious passion of Christ.

The vi[th] is the worschippfull[8] thangking of our Lord God, in which he rewardyth all his blessed servauntes in heaven.

The vii[th] is often tymes feeling of wele and of wooe.[9] Feeling of wele is gracious touching and lightnyng with true sekernes[1] of endlesse joy. The feeling of woo is of temptation by heavenes and werines of our fleshely livyng with ghostely[2] understanding that we be kept also verily in love, in woo as in wele, by the goodnes of God.

The viii is the last paynes of Christ and his cruel drying.

The ix[th] is of the lykyng which is in the blessed Trinitie of the hard passion of Christ after his ruwfull[3] dying, in which joy and lykyng he will that we be in solace and myrth with hym tylle that we come to the glorie in heaven.

---

1. Showings, revelations.
2. Uniting between God and man's soul with many fair showings and teachings. "Trinitie": Christian doctrine of the three persons, Father, Son, and Holy Spirit, in one Godhead; Jesus, the Second Person of the Trinity, became human to atone through his suffering and death for the original sin of Adam and Eve that consigned them and their descendants to hell.
3. Betokening Christ's valuable suffering and death.
4. These three properties are traditionally assigned, respectively, to the Father, the Son, and the Holy Spirit.
5. Just as truly.
6. Scourging or flagellation, one of the pains Jesus suffered during his Passion.
7. Fiend, devil.
8. Honorable.
9. Of weal, well-being, and of woe.
1. Benevolent and grace-giving contact and enlightenment with true sureness. Grace is the free gift of God that enables humans to recover from sin, resist temptations, perform good works, and achieve salvation.
2. Heaviness and weariness of our fleshly living with spiritual.
3. Rueful, mournful. "Lykyng": gratification, satisfaction.

The x is our Lord Jhesu shewyth by love his blessed hart evyn cloven on two.[4]

The xi is an high, ghostly shewing of his deer worthy mother.[5]

The xii is that our Lord God is all sovereyn[6] being.

The xiii[th] is that our Lord God will that we have great regarde to all the deedes which he hath done in the great noblete of all thyng makyng,[7] and of the excellence of manes[8] making, the which is above all his workes, and of the precious amendes that he hath made for man's synne,[9] turnyng all our blame in to endlesse worshippe.[1] Than meaneth he thus, *Behold and see. For by the same myght, wisdom, and goodnes that I have done all this, by the same myght, wisdom, and goodnes I shall make well all that is not well, and thou shalt see it.* And in this he will that we kepe us in the fayth and truth of holie church, not willing to wite his privyties not but as it longyth to us in this life.[2]

The xiiii is that our Lord God is grownd of our beseking.[3] Heer in was seen two fayer properties. That one is rightfull preaier, that other is verie trust, which he will both be one lyke large.[4] And thus our praier liketh[5] him, and he of his goodnes fullfillyth it.

The xv is that we shuld sodeynly[6] be takyn from all our payne and from all our woo. And of his goodnes we shall come uppe above wher we shall have our Lord Jesu to our meed[7] and for to be fulfilled with joy and blisse in heaven.

The xvi is that the blessed Trinitie, our maker, in Christ Jesu, our Saviour, endlesly dwelleth in our sowle, worschippfully rewlyng and comaunding[8] all thinges, us mightly and wisely savyng and kepyng for love. And we shall not be overcome of our enemy.

Chapter 2

This revelation was made to a symple creature unlettyrde leving in deadly flesh[9] the yer of our Lord a thousaunde and thre hundered

---

4. His blessed heart evenly broken in two.
5. Spiritual showing of his beloved mother, Mary.
6. Supreme.
7. Nobility of creating all things.
8. Man's.
9. Valuable amends or reparation for sin that Jesus made to God the Father through his suffering and death.
1. Honor.
2. To know his secrets except as it belongs to us in this life.
3. Ground or foundation of our beseeching, praying.
4. Equally abundant. "Rightfull preaier": virtuous prayer.
5. Pleases.
6. Suddenly.
7. Reward.
8. Honorably ruling and commanding.
9. A simple, unlettered creature living in a mortal body. *Unlettered* most likely means unable to read Latin; there is no evidence that Julian dictated her book to an amanuensis or scribe. Rather, such disclaimers are typical of medieval writers, especially women, on spiritual topics. Throughout her *Book,* Margery Kempe refers to herself as "this creature."

and lxxiii, the xiii daie[1] of May, which creature desyred before thre gyftes by the grace of God. The first was mynd of the passion.[2] The secund was bodilie sicknes. The thurde was to have of Godes gyfte thre woundys.

For the first me thought I had sumdeele feelyng in the passion of Christ,[3] but yet I desyred to have more by the grace of God. Me thought I woulde have ben that tyme with Magdaleyne[4] and with other that were Christus lovers that I might have seen bodilie the passion that our Lord suffered for me, that I might have suffered with him as other did that loved him. And therfore I desyred a bodely sight wher in I might have more knowledge of the bodily paynes of our Saviour and of the compassion[5] of our Lady and of all his true lovers that were lyvyng that tyme and saw his paynes. For I would have be one of them and have suffered with them. Other sight nor shewing of God desyred I never none til whan the sowle were deperted from the bodie,[6] for I beleved to be saved by the marcie[7] of God. This was my meaning, for I would after be cause of that shewyng have the more true mynd in the passion of Christ.

For the secunde came to my mynd with contricion, frely without anie sekyng,[8] a wilfull desyre to have of God's gyfte a bodily sicknes. I would that that sicknes were so hard as to the death[9] that I might in that sicknes have undertaken all my rightes of the holie church, my selfe weenyng[1] that I should have died, and that all creatures might suppose the same that saw me, for I would have no maner of comforte of fleshly ne erthely life in that sicknes. I desyred to have all maner of paynes, bodily and ghostly, that I should have if I should have died, all the dredys and temptations of fiendes, and all maner of other paynes, save the out passing of the sowle. And this ment I, for I would be purgied[2] by the mercie of God and after live more to the worshippe of God by cause of that sicknes. For I hoped that it might have ben to my a reward when I shuld have died, for I desyred to have ben soone with my God and maker.

These twey desyers of the passion and of the sicknes that I desyred of him was with a condicion, for me thought this was not the com-

1. Thirteenth day; S1 and S2 have eighth day.
2. Recollection of Christ's suffering and death.
3. I thought I had some degree of feeling for the Passion of Christ.
4. Mary Magdalene was a follower of Jesus who, together with Mary his mother and the apostle John, is often depicted at the foot of the cross in medieval art.
5. Suffering with, empathy.
6. Desired I never any until the soul had departed from the body.
7. Mercy.
8. Remorse, repentance for sin, freely without any seeking. Contrition for sin is necessary to receive the sacrament of penance.
9. Sickness were so serious as to be deadly.
1. Rites of holy church, believing myself. Extreme unction is the sacrament administered to those about to die.
2. Purged, cleansed.

mune use[3] of prayer. Therfor I sayd, "Lord, thou knowest what I would if that it be thy wille that I might have it. And if it be not thy will, good Lord, be not displesed, for I will not but as thou wilt." This sicknes I desyred in my iowth[4] that I might have it when I ware xxx[th] yeare olde.

For the third, by the grace of God and teeching of holie church, I conceived a mightie desyre to receive thre woundes[5] in my life, that is to say, the wound of verie contricion, the wound of kynd compassion, and the wound of willfull longing to God. Right as I asked the other twayne with a condicion, so asked I this third mightly with out anie condicion. These twayne desyres before sayd passid from my mynd and the third dwellid contynually.

Chapter 3

And when I was xxx[th] yere old and a halfe, God sent me a bodily sicknes, in the which I ley iii daies and iii nyghtes. And on the iiii nyght I toke all my rightes of holie church and went not to have leven tyll day.[6] And after this I lay two daies and two nightes. And on the third night I weenied often tymes to have passed,[7] and so wenyd thei that were with me. And yet in this I felt a great louthsomnes[8] to die, but for nothing that was in earth that me lyketh to leve for,[9] ne for no payne that I was afrayd of, for I trusted in God of his mercie. But it was for I would have leved to have loveved[1] God better and longer tyme that I might by the grace of that levyng have the more knowing and lovyng of God in the blisse of heaven. For my thought all that tyme that I had leved heer so litle and so shorte in regard of that endlesse blesse. I thought, "Good Lorde, may my levyng no longar be to thy worshippe?"

And I understode in my reason and by the feelyng of my paynes that I should die, and I ascentyd[2] fully with all the will of myn hart to be at God's will. Thus I indured till day, and by then was my bodie dead from the miedes[3] downward as to my feeling. Then was I holpen to be set upright, undersett with helpe,[4] for to have the more fredom of my hart to be at God's will and thinkyng on God while my life

3. Ordinary practice. "Twey desyers": two desires.
4. Youth.
5. Three wounds. A metaphor for three stages in contemplative ascent: contrition, compassion, and longing for God. In the short text, Julian compares these three metaphoric wounds to the three literal wounds from a sword that St. Cecilia received on her neck during her execution.
6. I received all my rites of holy church and believed that I would not live until day.
7. I expected often times to have passed away.
8. Loathsomeness, unwillingness.
9. That pleases me to live for.
1. Lived to have loved.
2. Assented.
3. Middle.
4. Helped to sit upright, supported with help.

laste. My curate was sent for to be at my ending, and before he cam
I had set up my eyen[5] and might not speake. He set the crosse before
my face and sayd, "I have brought the image of thy Saviour. Looke
ther upon and comfort thee ther with."

My thought I was well, for my eyen was sett upright into heaven,
where I trusted to come by the mercie of God. But nevertheles I
ascentyd to sett my eyen in the face of the crucifixe if I might, and
so I dide, for my thought I might longar dure to looke even forth
then right up.[6] After this my sight began to feyle.[7] It waxid as darke
aboute me in the chamber as if it had ben nyght, save[8] in the image
of the crosse, wher in held a comon light, and I wiste not how.[9] All
that was beseid the crosse was oglye and ferfull[1] to me as it had ben
much occupied with fiendes. After this the over part of my bodie
began to die so farforth that unneth I had anie feeling.[2] My most
payne was shortnes of breth and faielyng[3] of life. Then went I verily
to have passed.[4]

And in this sodenly all my paine was taken from me, and I was as
hole,[5] and namely, in the over parte of my bodie, as ever I was befor.
I merveiled of this sodeyn change, for my thought that it was a previe
working of God and not of kynd.[6] And yet by feeling of this ease I
trusted never the more to have lived, ne the feeling of this ease was
no full ease to me, for me thought I had lever have ben delivred of
this world,[7] for my hart was wilfully set ther to.

Then cam sodenly to my mynd that I should desyer the second
wound of our Lordes gifte and of his grace that my bodie might be
fulfilled with mynd and feeling of his blessed passion, as I had before
praied. For I would that his paynes were my paynes, with compassion
and afterward langyng[8] to God. This thought me that I might with
his grace have the woundes that I had before desyred. But in this I
desyred never no bodily sight ne no maner schewing of God, but
compassion as me thought that a kynd sowle[9] might have with our
Lord Jesu, that for love would become a deadly man. With him I
desyred to suffer, livyng in my deadly bodie, as God would give me
grace.

5. Raised up my eyes. "Curate": parish priest.
6. For I thought I might longer endure to look forward rather than upward.
7. Fail.
8. Except. "Waxid": grew.
9. Ordinary light, and I knew not how.
1. Beside the cross was ugly and fearful.
2. Upper part of my body began to die to a great extent that scarcely I had any feeling.
3. Failing.
4. Then thought I truly to have passed away.
5. Whole. "Sodenly": suddenly.
6. For I thought that it was a secret work of God and not of nature. "Merveiled": marveled.
7. I thought I would rather have been delivered out of this world.
8. Longing.
9. Except compassion that I thought a natural and empathetic soul. The adjective *kind* in
   Middle English means both "natural" and "kind."

Revelation I

Chapter 4

And in this sodenly I saw the reed bloud rynnyng downe from under the garlande, hote and freyshely, plentuously and lively, right as it was[1] in the tyme that the garland of thornes was pressed on his blessed head. Right so both God and man, the same that sufferd for me, I conceived truly and mightly that it was him selfe that shewed it me without anie meane.[2]

And in the same shewing sodeinly the Trinitie fulfilled my hart most of joy, and so I understode it shall be in heaven without end to all that shall come ther. For the Trinitie is God, God is the Trinitie. The Trinitie is our maker. The Trinitie is our keper. The Trinitie is our everlausting lover. The Trinitie is our endlesse joy and our bleisse by our Lord Jesu Christ and in our Lord Jesu Christ. And this was shewed in the first syght and in all, for wher Jhesu appireth[3] the blessed Trinitie is understand as to my sight.

And I sayd, "Benedicite, Dominus."[4] This I sayd for reverence in my menyng with a mightie voyce. And full greatly was I a stonned for wonder and marvayle that I had that he that is so reverent and so dreadfull will be so homely[5] with a synnfull creature liveing in this wretched flesh. Thus I toke it for that tyme that our Lord Jhesu of his curteys love would shewe me comfort before the tyme of my temptation, for me thought it might well be that I should by the sufferance[6] of God and with his keping be tempted of fiendes before I should die. With this sight of his blessed passion, with the Godhead that I saw in my understanding, I knew well that it was strenght inough to me, ye, and to all creaturs livyng that sould be saved against all the fiendes of hell and against all ghostely[7] enemies.

In this he brought our Ladie Sainct Mari[8] to my understanding. I saw her ghostly in bodily lykenes,[9] a simple mayden and a meeke, yong of age, a little waxen above a chylde, in the stature as she was when she conceivede.[1] Also God shewed me in part the wisdom and

---

1. Hot and fresh, plenteously and vigorously, just as it was. "Rynnyng": running.
2. Any intermediary.
3. Appears
4. "Blessed be thou, Lord."
5. So revered and awe-inspiring will be so familiar or intimate. Julian often refers to God's homely or homelike intimacy with humanity as well as his courteous, more formal relationship. "Stonned": astonished.
6. Permission. As Julian later reveals, the fiend is himself powerless, but God allows him to tempt humankind. "Curteys": courteous.
7. Spiritual.
8. St. Mary, the mother of Jesus.
9. In a spiritual manner in bodily likeness. Some of Julian's showings seem to be midway between sensory visions or auditions and incorporeal revelations.
1. Conceived Jesus.

the truth of her sowle, wher in I understode the reverent beholding
that she beheld her God that is her maker, marvayling with great
reverence that he would be borne of her that was a symple creature
of his makyng. For this was her marvayling, that he that was her
maker would be borne of her that was made. And this wisdome and
truth, knowing the greatnes of her maker and the littlehead[2] of her
selfe that is made, made her to say full meekely to Gabriell, "Loo me
here, God's handmayden."[3] In this syght I did understand verily that
she is more then all that God made beneth her in wordines and in
fullhead,[4] for above her is nothing that is made but the blessed manhood of Christ as to my sight.

Chapter 5

In this same tyme that I saw this sight of the head bleidyng, our
good Lord shewed a ghostly sight of his homely lovyng.[5] I saw that
he is to us all thing that is good and comfortable to our helpe. He is
oure clothing that for love wrappeth us and wyndeth us, halseth us
and all becloseth us,[6] hangeth about us for tender love that he may
never leeve us. And so in this sight I saw that he is all thing that is
good as to my understanding.

And in this he shewed a little thing, the quantitie of an haselnott,
lying in the palme of my hand, as me semide,[7] and it was as rounde
as a balle. I looked theran with the eye of my understanding and
thought, "What may this be?" And it was answered generaelly thus:
"It is all that is made." I marvayled how it might laste, for me thought
it might sodenly have fallen to nawght[8] for littlenes. And I was
answered in my understanding: "It lasteth and ever shall, for God
loveth it. And so hath all thing being by the love of God."

In this little thing I saw iii properties. The first is that God made
it; the secund, that God loveth it; the thirde, that God kepyth it. But
what behyld I, verely, the maker, the keper, the lover. For till I am
substantially unyted[9] to him, I may never have full reste ne verie
blisse, that is to say, that I be so fastned to him that ther be right
nought[1] that is made betweene my God and me.

This little thing that is made, me thought it might have fallen to
nought for littlenes. Of this nedeth us to have knowledge that us

2. Littleness.
3. Mary's response to the angel Gabriel's announcement that she would be the mother of
   the Son of God.
4. In worthiness and fullness.
5. A spiritual sight of his intimate love. "Bleidyng": bleeding.
6. Enfolds us, embraces us, and entirely encloses us.
7. As it seemed to me. "Haselnott": hazelnut.
8. Naught, nothing.
9. United in substance or essence. Julian explains this ontological union between God and
   humans in Revelation XIV, chapters 53–56.
1. Nothing at all.

lyketh nought all thing that is made for to love and have God that is unmade.[2] For this is the cause why we be not all in ease of hart and of sowle: for we seeke heer rest in this thing that is so little wher no reste is in. And we know not our God that is almightie, all wise, and all good, for he is verie reste.

God will be knowen, and him lyketh that we rest us in him. For all that is beneth him suffyseth not[3] to us. And this is the cause why that no sowle is in reste till it is noughted[4] of all thinges that is made. When she is wilfully noughted for loue, to have him that is all, then is she able to receive ghostly reste.

And also our good Lord shewed that it is full great plesaunce to him that a sely sowle come to him naked, pleaynly and homely.[5] For this is the kynde dwellyng of the sowle by the touchyng of the Holie Ghost,[6] as by the understandyng that I have in this schewying. "God, of thy goodnes geve me thy selfe, for thou art inough to me, and I maie aske nothing that is lesse that maie be full worshippe to thee. And if I aske anie thing that is lesse, ever me wanteth,[7] but only in thee I have all." And these wordes of the goodnes of God be full lovesum to the sowle and full neer touching the will[8] of our Lord, for his goodnes fulfillith all his creaturs and all his blessed workes without end. For he is the endlesshead[9] and he made us only to him selfe, and restored us by his precious passion, and ever kepeth us in his blessed love. And all this is of his goodnes.

Chapter 6

This shewing was geven to my understanding to lerne our soule wisely to cleve[1] to the goodnes of God. And in that same tyme the custome of our praier was brought to my mind, how that we use for unknowing of love to make menie meanes.[2] Than saw I verily that it is more worshipp to God and more verie delite that we feaithfully praie to him selfe of his goodnes and cleve ther to by his grace, with true understanding and stedfast beleve, then if we made all the meanes that hart maie thinke. For if we make all these meanes, it is to litle and not ful worshippe to God. But in his goodnes is all the hole, and ther fayleth right nought.[3]

2. Of this we need to have knowledge so that all created things do not please us except to love and have God, who is uncreated.
3. Suffices not, is not adequate
4. Stripped.
5. It is a very great pleasure to him that a blessed soul come to him stripped naked, plainly and intimately.
6. The natural dwelling of the soul by the contact or influence of the Holy Spirit.
7. Ever I am lacking, unsatisfied.
8. Are very lovely to the soul and closely conforming to the will.
9. Endlessness.
1. To teach our soul wisely to cleave, cling.
2. We use many means or intermediaries because of our ignorance of love.
3. Whole, and there nothing at all fails.

For thus as I shall say cam to my mynd in the same tyme. We praie to God for his holie flesh and for his precious bloud, his holie passion, his dere worthy death and worshipfull woundes. For all the blessed kyndnes and the endlesse life that we have of all this, it is of the goodnes of God. And we praie him for his sweete mother's love that bare him. And all the helpe that we have of her, it is of his goodnes. And we praie for his holie crosse that he died on. And all the helpe and all the vertu that we have of that crosse, it is of his goodnes. And on the same wyse, all the helpe that we have of speciall sainctes and of all the blessed companie of heaven, the dere worthie love and the holie endles frinshipe[4] that we have of them, it is of his goodnes. For the meanes that the goodnes of God hath ordeineth to helpe us be full faire and many, of which the chiefe and principall meane is the blessed kynde that he toke of the maiden[5] with all the meanes that went before and come after which be langyng to our redemption and to our endles salvation.

Wher for it pleaseth him that we seke him and worshippe him by meanes, understanding and knowing that he is the goodnes of all. For to the goodnes of God is the highest praier, and it cometh downe to us to the lowest party of our need. It quickened our sowle, and maketh it leve,[6] and make it to waxe in grace and in vertu. It is nerest in kynde and redyest in grace. For it is the same grace that the soule sekyth and evyr schalle tylle we knowe oure God verely that hath us all in hym selfe beclosyde.[7]

A man goyth uppe ryght, and the soule of his body is sparyde as a purse fulle feyer. And whan it is tyme of his nescessery, it is openyde and sparyde ayen fulle honestly.[8] And that it is he that doyth this, it is schewed ther wher he seyth he comyth downe to us to the lowest parte of oure nede. For he hath no dispite[9] of that he made. Ne he hath no disdeyne to serve us at the sympylest office that to oure body longyth in kynde,[1] for love of the soule that he made to his awne lycknesse.[2] For as the body is cladd in the cloth, and the flessch in the skynne, and the bonys in the flessch, and the harte in the bowke,[3] so ar we, soule and body, cladde and enclosydde in the goodnes of God. Yee, and more homely, for all they vanyssch and wast awey.

---

4. Friendship.
5. Blessed nature that he (Jesus) took from the maiden (his assumption of human nature at the incarnation). "Hath ordeineth": has ordained, established.
6. It (the goodness of God) enlivened our soul and made it live.
7. Enclosed.
8. A man goes upright, and the food of his body is enclosed as in a very fair purse. And when it is the time of necessity, it (the body) is opened and closed again very properly.
9. Despite, contempt.
1. Nor does he disdain to serve us in the simplest task that belongs to our body by nature.
2. Own likeness.
3. Trunk of the body.

The goodnesse of God is ever hole[4] and more nere to us withoute any comparison.

For truly oure lovyr desyereth that the soule cleve to hym with all the myghtes and that we be ever more clevyng to hys goodnes. For of alle thyng that hart may thynke, it plesyth most God and soneste spedyth.[5] For oure soule is so presciously lovyd of hym that is hyghest that it over passyth the knowyng of alle creatures. That is to say, ther is no creature that is made that may witt how much, and how swetely, and how tenderly that oure maker lovyth us. And therfore we may with hys grace and his helpe stande in gostly beholdyng with ever-lastyng marveylyng in this hygh, overpassyng, unmesurable love that oure Lorde hath to us of his goodnes.

And therfore we may aske of oure lover with reverence all that we wille. For oure kyndely wille is to have God, and the good wylle of God is to have us, and we may never sesse of wyllyng ne of lovyng tylle we have hym in fulhede[6] of joy. And than we may no more wylle. For he wylle that we be occupyed in knowyng and lovyng tylle the tyme comyth that we shalbe fulfyllede in hevyn.

And here fore was this lesson of love schewyd with alle that folow-yth, as ye schall see. For the strenght and the grounde of alle was schewed in the furst syght. For of alle thyng the beholdyng and the lovyng of the maker makyth the soule to seme lest in his awne syght and most fyllyth hit with reverent drede and trew meknesse and with plente of charyte to his evyn Crysten.[7]

Chapter 7

And to lerne[8] us thys, as to my understandyng, our good Lorde shewyd our Lady Sent Mary in the same tyme, that is to meane the hyghe wysdom and truth that she had in beholdyng of her maker. This wysdom and truth made her to beholde hyr God so gret, so hygh, so myghty, and so good. This gretnesse and this nobylnesse of her beholdyng of God fulfyllyd her of reverend drede. And with this she sawe hyr selfe so lytylle and so lowe, so symple and so poer in regard of[9] hyr God that thys reverent drede fulfyllyd her of meknes. And thus by thys grounde sche was fulfyllyd of grace and of alle maner of vertuous[1] and passyth alle creatours.

And in alle that tyme that he schewd thys that I have now seyde

---

4. Whole.
5. Soonest helps.
6. Fullness. "Sesse": cease.
7. Seem least in his own sight and most fills it with revered awe and true meekness and with plenty of charity to his fellow Christians.
8. To teach us. While she is seeing Christ's bleeding head and receiving the spiritual reve-lation of God's goodness, Julian has a second incorporeal showing of Mary.
9. Poor in comparison to.
1. Virtues.

in gostely syght, I saw the bodely syght lastyng of the plentuous ble-dyng of the hede. The grett droppes of blode felle downe fro under the garlonde lyke pelottes semyng as it had comynn oute of the veynes.[2] And in the comyng oute they were browne rede, for the blode was full thycke. And in the spredyng abrode they were bryght rede. And whan it camme at the browes,[3] ther they vanysschyd. And not wythstonding, the bledyng contynued tylle many thynges were sene and understondyd. Nevertheles, the feyerhede and the lyvely-hede continued in the same bewty and lyvelynes.[4]

The plentuoushede is lyke to the droppes of water that falle of the evesyng of an howse[5] after a grete shower of reyne that falle so thycke that no man may nomber them with no bodely wyt. And for the roundnesse they were lyke to the scale of heryng[6] in the spredyng of the forhede. Thes thre thynges cam to my mynde in the tyme: pelet-tes for the roundhede in the comyng oute of the blode, the scale of heryng for the roundhede in the spredyng, the droppes of the evesyng of a howse for the plentuoushede unnumerable.

Thys shewyng was quyck and lyvely and hydows[7] and dredfulle and swete and lovely. And of all the syght that I saw, this was most comfort to me, that oure good Lorde, that is so reverent and dred-fulle, is so homely and so curteyse. And this most fulfyllyd me with lykyng and syckernes in soule.[8]

And to the understondyng of thys he shewde thys open example. It is the most wurschypp that a solempne kyng or a gret lorde may do to a pore servante yf he wylle be homely with hym and, namely, yf he shew it hym selfe of a fulle true menyng and with a glad chere boyth in prevyte and opynly.[9] Than thyngkyth thys pore creature thus: "Loo, what myght thys noble lorde do more wurschyppe and joy to me than to shew to me that am so lytylle thys marvelous home-lynesse? Verely, it is more joy and lykyng to me than if he gave me grett geftes and wer hym selfe strange[1] in maner." This bodely exsam-ple was shewde so hygh that thys mannes hart myght be ravyssched[2] and almost foryet hym selfe for joy of thys grette homelynesse.

Thus it faryth by oure Lorde Jhesu and by us, for verely it is the most joy that may be, as to my syght, that he that is hyghest and myghtyest, noblyest and wurthyest, is lowest and mekest, homlyest

2. Pellets seeming to have come out of the veins.
3. Came to the eyebrows.
4. Fairness and liveliness continued in the same beauty and liveliness.
5. Eaves of a house.
6. Herring.
7. Hideous.
8. With pleasure and certainty in the soul.
9. A glad expression in private and in public. Julian presents her comprehensive interpreta-tion of this example of the lord and servant in Revelation XIV, chapter 51.
1. Aloof.
2. Ravished or carried away in spirit. This term is often used in Middle English texts to describe the state of mystical or contemplative union with God.

and curtysest. And truly and verely this marvelous joy shalle be shew us all when we shall see hym. And thys wille oure good Lorde that we beleve and trust, joy and lyke, comfort us and make solace as we may with his grace and with his helpe in to the tyme that we see it verely. For the most fulhede of joy that we shalle have, as to my syght, ys thys marvelous curtesy and homelynesse of oure Fader, that is oure maker, in oure Lorde Jhesu Crist, that is oure Broder and oure Savior.

But this marvelous homelynesse may no man know in this lyfe, but yf he have it by specialle schewyng of oure Lorde or of gret plenty of grace inwardly yeven[3] of the Holy Gost. But feyth and beleve with charyte deserve the mede,[4] and so it is had by grace. For in feyght with hope and cheryte[5] oure lyfe is groundyd. The shewyng, made to whom that God wylle, pleynely techyth the same, openyd and declaryd with many prevy poyntes[6] be longyng to our feyth and beleve, which be wurshipfull to be knowen. And whan the shewyng which is yeven for a tyme is passyde and hydde, than fayth kepyth it by grace of the Holy Goste in to our lyvys ende.[7] And thus by the shewyng it is none other than the feyth, ne lesse ne more, as it may be seene by oure Lordes menyng in the same matter by than it come to the last ende.

Chapter 8

And as longe as I saw thys syght of the plentuousnesse of bledyng of the heed, I myght never stynte of these wordes, "Benedicite, Dominus."[8] In which shewyng I understodd vi thynges:

The furst is the tokyns[9] of the blessydfulle passion and the plentuous shedyng of his precious blode.

The seconde is the mayden that is his deer wurthy mother.

The thurde is the blessydefulle Godhede that ever was and is and schalle be, alle myghty, alle wysdom, and all love.

The iiii is all thynge that he hath made. For wele I wot[1] that hevyn and erth and alle that is made is great, large, and feyer, and good, but the cause why it shewyth so lytylle to my syght was for I saw it in the presence of hym that is the maker. For a soul that seth the maker of all thyng, all that is made semyth fulle lytylle.

---

3. Given.
4. Reward.
5. For in faith with hope and charity. These three theological virtues are instilled by grace freely given by the Holy Spirit.
6. Secret points.
7. Lives' end.
8. Never stop saying these words, "Blessed be thou, Lord."
9. Signs.
1. Well I know.

The vth is that he[2] made all thyng that is made for love, and by the same love it is kepte and schall be withoute ende, as it is before sayde.

The vi[th] is that God is alle thyng that is good as to my sight; and the goodnesse that alle thyng hath, it is he.

And alle thys our Lorde shewde in the furst syght and yave[3] me space and tyme to beholde it. And the bodely syght styntyd and the goostely syghte dwellth in my understondyng.[4] And I aboode with reverent dreed,[5] joyeng in that I saw and desyeryng as I durste[6] to see more, if it were hys wylle, or lengar tyme the same syght.

In alle this I was much steryde in cheryte to myne evyn Christen[7] that they myght alle see and know the same that I sawe. For I wolde that it were comfort to them, for alle this syght was shewde in gener-alle. Than sayde I to them that were with me, "It is this daye domys day[8] with me." And this I seyde for I went[9] to have dyed. For that day that man or woman dyeth is he demyde particulerly as he schalbe withoute ende[1] as to my understandyng. This I sayde for I wolde they schulde love God the better, for to make them to have mynde that this lyfe is short, as they myght se in exsample. For in alle thys tyme I wenyd to have dyed, and that was marveyle to me and wonder in perty, for my thought this avysion[2] was schewde for them that shuld lyve.

Alle that I say of me I mene in person of alle my evyn Cristen,[3] for I am lernyd in the gostely shewyng of our Lord God that he meneth so. And therfore I pray yow alle for God's sake and counceyle yow for yowre awne profyght, that ye leve the beholdyng of a wrech[4] that it was schewde to and myghtely, wysely, and mekely behold in God, that of his curteyse love and endlesse goodnesse wolld shew it generally in comfort of us alle. For it is Goddes wylle that ye take it with a grete joy and lykyng as Jhesu hath shewde it to yow.

---

2. P has "The vth is that he that it made," with "it" added in the margin. "Seth": sees. "Semyth fulle lytylle": seems very little.
3. Gave.
4. The bodily sight (of Christ's bleeding head) stopped and the spiritual sight (of God's good-ness and of Mary) remained in my understanding.
5. Waited with revered awe.
6. I dared.
7. Stirred in charity to my fellow Christians.
8. Doomsday, judgment day.
9. Expected.
1. Judged individually as he shall be without end (whether saved or damned).
2. Vision. "Wenyd": expected. "Perty": part.
3. I mean as a representative of all my fellow Christians.
4. Counsel you for your own profit that you believe or leave the beholding of a wretch. Either translation of *leve* is possible. Either Julian is advising her reader to believe the showings despite the fact that she, a wretch, received them or she is counseling the reader to leave or forget her revelations and attempt to behold God personally.

Chapter 9

For the shewyng I am nott good, but if I love God the better. And in as much as ye love God the better, it is more to yow than to me. I say nott thys to them that be wyse, for they wytt it wele. But I sey it to yow that be symple, for ease and comfort, for we be alle one in love. For verely it was nott shewde to me that God lovyth me better than the lest soule that is in grace. For I am suer ther be meny that never hath shewyng ne syght but of the comyn techyng of holy chyrch that love God better than I. For yf I looke syngulery to my selfe, I am ryght nought.[5] But in generall I am, I hope, in onehede of cheryte with alle my evyn Cristen.[6] For in thys oned stondyth the lyfe of alle mankynd that shalle be savyd.[7]

For God is alle that is goode as to my syght. And God hath made alle that is made. And God lovyth alle that he hath made. And he that generally lovyth all hys evyn Cristen for God, he lovyth alle that is. For in mankynd that shall be savyd is comprehendyd[8] alle, that is to sey, alle that is made and the maker of alle. For in man is God and in God is alle. And he that lovyth thus, he lovyth alle. And I hope by the grace of God he that behold it thus shalle be truly taught and myghtly comfortyd, yf hym nedyth comfort.[9] I speke of them that shalle be savyd, for in this tyme God shewde me no nother.

But in all thing I beleve as holy chyrch prechyth and techyth. For the feyth of holy chyrch, which I had before hand understondyng and as I hope by the grace of God wylle fully kepe it in use and in custome, stode contynually in my syghte, wyllyng and meanyng never to receyve ony thyng that myght be contrary ther to. And with this intent and with this meanyng I beheld the shewyng with all my dyligence. For in all thys blessed shewyng I behelde it as in God's menyng.

All this was shewde by thre partes, that is to sey, by bodyly syght, and by worde formyde in my understondyng, and by goostely syght. But the goostely syght I can nott ne may shew it as openly ne as fully as I would, but I trust in our Lord God almyghtie that he shall of his godnes and for iour love make yow to take it more ghostely and more sweetly then I can or may tell it.

---

5. For if I look individually to my self, I am nothing whatever.
6. Oneness of charity with my fellow Christians.
7. For in this union stands the life of all humankind that shall be saved.
8. Understood and included.
9. If comfort is needed by him.

Revelation II

Chapter 10

And after this I saw with bodely sight in the face of the crucifixe that hyng[1] before me, in the which I beheld contynually a parte of his passion: dyspyte, spyttyng, solewyng, and buffetyng, and manie languryng paynes mo[2] than I can tell, and offten chaungyng of colour. And one tyme I saw how halfe the face, begynnyng at the ere, overrede with drye bloud tyll it closyd in to the myd face.[3] And after that, the other halfe beclosyd[4] on the same wyse. And the whiles it vanyssched in this party evyn as it cam.[5]

This saw I bodely, swemly and darkely,[6] and I desyred mor bodely light to have seen more clerly. And I was answeryde in my reason, "If God will shew thee more, he shalbe thy light. Thou nedyth none but him." For I saw him and sought him, for we be now so blynde and so unwyse that we can never seke God till what tyme that he of his goodnes shewyth hym to us. And whan we see owght of hym graciously,[7] then are we steryd by the same grace to seke with great desyer to see hym more blessedfully. And thus I saw him and sought him, and I had hym and wantyd hym. And this is and should be our comyn workyng in this life as to my syght.

One tyme my understandyng was lett downe in to the sea grounde, and ther saw I hilles and dales grene, semyng as it were mosse begrowyng with wrake and gravell.[8] Then I understode thus, that if a man or woman wher there unther the brode water[9] and he myght have syght of God, so as God is with a man contynually, he shoulde be safe in sowle and body and take no harme. And ovyr passyng, he should have mor solace and comforte then all this wordle[1] may or can tell. For he will that we beleve that we see hym contynually, thow that us thynke that it be but litle. And in the beleve he maketh us evyr more to gett grace. For he will be seen, and he will be sought, and he will be abyden,[2] and he will be trustyd.

This secounde shewyng was so lowe, and so little, and so symple

---

1. Hung.
2. Despite or contempt, spitting, soiling, buffeting or beating, and many more languishing pains.
3. Overspread with dry blood until it closed in upon the middle of the face.
4. Was covered up.
5. In the meantime it vanished in this part even as it came (on the other side).
6. Sorrowfully and darkly.
7. Aught or anything of him by means of the benevolent gift of grace. Julian believes that grace freely given by God initiates and sustains the search for God.
8. One time my understanding extended down to the bottom of the sea, and there I saw hills and green valleys, seeming as if moss were growing with wreckage and gravel.
9. Under the broad water.
1. World.
2. Awaited.

that my spirytes were in great traveyle[3] in the beholdyng, mornyng dredfull and longyng. For I was some tyme in a feer wheder it was a shewyng or none. And then dyverse tymes our Lord gafe me more syght, wherby that I understonde truly that it was a shewyng.

It was a fygur and a lyknes of our fowle, blacke dede[4] which that our feyre, bryght, blessed Lord bare for our synne. It made me to thynke of the holie vernacle of Rome,[5] which he portrude with his one blessed face when he was in his hard passion, wilfully goyng to his death, and often chaungyng of coloure, of the brownhead and the blackhead, rewly head and leenhead.[6] Of this ymage many marveyled how that myght be, standyng that he portrude it with his blessed face,[7] which is the feyerest of heavyn, flower of earth, and the frute of the mayden's wombe. Then how myght this ymage be so dyscolouryde and so farre from feyerhead? I desyred to see as I have understonde by the grace of God.

We knowe in our feayth and in our beleve by the teachyng and the prechyng of holy church that the blessyd fulle Trinitie made mankynd to his ymage and to his lykenes.[8] In the same maner wyse we know that when man fell so depe and so wretchedly by synne, ther was no nother helpe to restore man but thorow hym that made man. And he that made man for love, by the same love he woulde restore man to the same blysse and ovyr passyng. And ryght as we were made lyke to the Trynyte in oure furst makyng, our maker would that we should be lyke to Jhesu Cryst our Saviour in hevyn without ende by the vertu of oure geynmakyng.[9] Then betwene thes two he would for love and for worshipe of man make hym selfe as lyke to man in this deadly lyfe, in our fowlhede and in our wretchednes, as man myght be without gylt. Wherof it menyth, as is before sayd, it was the ymage and the lyknes of our fowle, blacke dede where in oure feyer, bryght, blessyd Lorde hyd his Godhede.

But verely I dare say and we ought to beleve that so feyer a man was never none but he tylle what tyme that his feyer coloure was changyd with traveyle[1] and sorow, passion and dyeng. Of this it spe-

---

3. Toil, hardship.
4. It (Christ's face disfigured by his suffering) was an image and likeness of our foul, black deed (sin).
5. Holy vernicle of Rome. The picture or representation of Christ's face said to be impressed upon the handkerchief that Veronica offered him as he carried the cross to Calvary. This handkerchief was preserved as a relic at St. Peter's in Rome.
6. The brownness and the blackness, painfulness and leanness.
7. In spite of the fact that he portrayed it with his blessed face.
8. The entire blessed Trinity made mankind in his image and to his likeness. Julian is referring to Genesis 1:26–27: "And God said, Let us make man in our image, after our likeness. . . . So God created man in his own image, in the image of God created he him; male and female created he them."
9. Remaking (reforming of the image of God deformed through sin). Corrected from S1. P has *awne making*, own making.
1. Toil, hardship.

kyth in the **viii revelation in the xvi chapter,**[2] wher it spekyth more
of the same lyknesse. And ther it seyeth of the vernacle of Rome, it
menyth by dyverse chaungyng of colour and chere, somtyme more
comfortable and lyvely, and some tyme more rewfull[3] and deadly, as
it may be seen here after.

And this vision was a lernyng[4] to my understandyng that the contynually sekyng of the soule plesyth God moch. For it may do no
more than seke, suffer, and trust. And this is wrought[5] in everie soule
that hath it by the Holy Gost. And the clernesse of fyndyng, it is of
his speciall grace when it is his will. The sekyng with feyth, hope,
and charitie plesyth oure Lord, and the fyndyng plesyth the sowle
and fulfyllyth it with joy. And thus was I lernyd to my understandyng
that sekyng is as good as beholdyng for the tyme that he wille suffer
the sowle to be in traveyle. It is God's will that we seke in to the
beholdyng of hym, for by that shall he shew us hym self of his speciall
grace when he will.

And how a sowle shall have her in his beholding he shall teach
hym selfe, and that is most worshippe to hym, and most profyght to
the sowle, and most receyved of mekenesse and vertuse[6] with the
grace and ledyng of the Holy Gost. For a sowle that only resynyth
hym[7] to God with very truste, eyther in sekyng or beholdyng, it is the
most worshippe that he may do as to my syght. Theyse be two
workynges that may be seen in this vision: that one is sekyng, the
other is beholdyng. The sekyng is comyn; that ech sowle may have
with his grace and owyth to have dyscrecion[8] and techyng of holy
church.

It is God's will that we have iii thynges in our sekyng of his gefte.[9]
The furst is that we seke wyllfully and besyly withoute slowth, as it
may be with his grace, gladly and merely, without unresonable
hevynesse and veyne[1] sorow. The seconde, that we abyde hym sted-
fastely for his love withoute gronyng and stryvyng agaynst hym in to
our lyvys ende,[2] for it shall last but a whyle. The iii is that we truste
in hym myghtely, of fulle and tru feyth. For it is his wille that we
know that he shall aper sodenly[3] and blyssydefully to all his lovers.
For his workyng is prevy, and he wille be perceyved, and his aperyng

---

2. Revelation number corrected from S1, and chapter number corrected to correspond to
   appropriate chapter in Revelation VIII; P has *the secounde revelation in the xviii chapter.*
3. Rueful, sorrowful. "Chere": facial expression.
4. Lesson.
5. Created.
6. Virtues.
7. Resigns himself.
8. The seeking is common; that (seeking) each soul may have with his grace and ought to
   have discretion, the ability to distinguish between divinely and diabolically inspired visions.
9. Gift.
1. Vain, worthless. "Besyly withoute slowth": busily without sloth, laziness.
2. Lives' end.
3. Appear suddenly.

shalle be swete sodeyn.[4] And he wylle be trustyd, for he is fulle
homely curteyse, blessyd mott he be.[5]

Revelation III

Chapter 11

And after this I saw God in a poynte,[6] that is to say, in my understandyng, by which syght I saw that he is in althyng. I beheld with
avysement,[7] seeyng and knowyng in that syght that he doth alle that
is done. I merveyled in that syght with a softe drede[8] and thought,
"What is synne?" For I saw truly that God doth alle thyng, be it nevyr
so lylyle.[9]

And I saw veryly that nothyn is done by happe ne by aventure, but
alle by the foreseing[1] wysdom of God. Yf it be happ or aventure in
the syght of man, our blyndhede and unforsyght[2] is the cause. For
tho thynges that be in the foreseing wysdom of God bene fro without
begynnyng, which, ryghtfully and worshippfully, contynually he ledyth to the best ende, as it comyth aboughte, fallyng to us sodeynly,
our selfe unwetyng.[3] And thus by our blyndnes and our unforsyghte
we say these thynges be by happes and aventure.

Thus I understonde in this shewyng of love, for wele I wott[4] in the
syght of our Lord God is no happe ne aventure. Wherfore me
behovyd nedes[5] to graunt that alle thynges that is done is welle done,
for our Lord God doth all. For in this tyme the workyng of creatures
was nott shewde, but of our Lord God in the creatures. For he is in
the myd poynt of all thynges, and all he doth.

And I was sewer[6] that he doth no synne. And here I saw verely
that synne is no dede,[7] for in alle thys synne was nott shewde. And
I would no longer marveyle in this, but behelde our Lorde, what he
would shew. And thus as it myghte be for the tyme, the ryghtfulnes[8]

4. Very sudden.
5. Very intimate courtesy, blessed may he be. Julian insists that God treats humanity with
   the familiar intimacy of a family member (homely) and the dignified graciousness (courtesy) of a prince.
6. Point of the soul, the apex at which the substance of the soul is joined to the Godhead.
7. Due consideration.
8. Calm awe.
9. Little.
1. By luck nor by chance, but all by the foreseeing. Corrected from S1 here and throughout
   this paragraph; P has *forsayde*, foresaid.
2. Lack of foresight.
3. Unwitting, unaware. "Rightfully and worshippfully": righteously and honorably.
   "Aboughte": about.
4. Well I know.
5. It is necessary to me, I must.
6. Surer.
7. Sin is no deed. I.e., evil is not an entity but a defect, the privation or absence of good.
8. Righteousness.

of God's workyng was shewyd to the sowle. Ryghtfulnes hath to feyer properteys: it is ryght and it is fulle. And so be all the workes of our Lorde. And therto nedyth neyther workyng of mercy ne grace, for they be alle ryghtfulle, wher in feylyth ryght nought.[9] And in a other tyme he shewde for beholdyng of synne nakedly, as I shall say after,[1] when he usyth workyng of mercy and of grace.

This vision was shewyd to my understandyng, for our Lord wylle have the sowle turned truly in to the beholdyng of hym and generally of all his workes. For they be fulle good. And alle his domys be esy and swete and to grett ees bryngyng the sowle that is turned fro the beholdyng of the blynd demyng[2] of man in to the feyer, swette demyng of our Lorde God. For man beholdyth some dedys wele done and some dedys evylle, and our Lorde beholdyth them not so. For as alle that hath beyng in kynde is of God's makyng, so is alle thyng that is done in properte of God's doyng.[3] For it is esy to understand that the beste dede is wele done. And so wele as the best dede that is done and the hyghest, so wele is the leest dede done, and all in the properte and in the order that our Lord hath it ordeynyd to for withoute begynnyng, for ther is no doer but he.

I saw fulle truly that he chaungyd nevyr hys purpose in no manner of thyng, ne nevyr shalle without end. For ther was nothyng un-knowyn to hym in hys ryghtfulle ordenaunce[4] fro without begynnyng. And therfore all thynges wer sett in ordyr or[5] any thyng was made as it should stand without ende. And no manner thyng shalle feyle of that poynt, for he hath made alle thyng in fulheed of goodnes.

And therfore the blessed Trynyte is evyr fulle plesyd in alle his workes. And all this shewyd he full blessedly, meanyng thus: *See, I am God. See, I am in all thyngs. See, I do all thyng. See, I nevyr lefte my handes of*[6] *my workes, ne never shalle without ende. See, I lede all thyng to the end that I ordeyne it to for without begynnyng by the same myght, wysdom, and love that I made it with. How shoulde any thyng be a mysse?*[7] Thus myghtly, wysely, and lovyngly was the sowle exam-ynyd in this vision. Than saw I verely that my behovyth nedys to assent[8] with great reverence and joy in God.

---

9. And in those matters (the works of the Lord) neither the working of mercy nor of grace are needed, for they are all righteous, wherein nothing whatever fails.
1. Revelation XIII.
2. Judging. "Domys": judgments.
3. For as all that have being in nature are of God's making, so all things that are done are characteristic of God's doing.
4. Righteous arrangement.
5. Before.
6. Lift my hands off.
7. Amiss.
8. It is necessary that I assent, I must assent.

Revelation IV

Chapter 12

And after this I saw, beholdyng the body, plentuous bledyng in semyng of the scoregyng[9] as thus. The feyer skynne was broken full depe in to the tendyr flessch with sharpe smytynges[1] all a bout the sweete body. The hote blode ranne out so plentuously that ther was neyther seen skynne ne wounde, but as it were all blode. And when it cam wher it shulde have falle downe, ther it vanysschyd. Not with standyng, the bledyng contynued a whyle tyll it myght be seen with avysement.[2] And this was so plentuous to my syght that me thought if it had ben so in kynde and in substance[3] for that tyme, it shulde have made the bedde all on bloude and have passyde over all about.

Than cam to my mynde that God hath made waters plentuous in erth to our servys and to our bodely eese for tendyr love that he hath to us. But yet lykyth hym better that we take full holsomly hys blessyd blode to wassch us of synne.[4] For ther is no lycour that is made that lykyth hym so wele to yeve us.[5] For it is most plentuous as it is most precious, and that by the vertu of the blessyd Godhead. And it is our owne kynde and blessydfully ovyr flowyth us by the vertu of his precious love. The dere worthy bloude of our Lorde Jhesu Crist, also verely as it is most precious, as verely it is most plentuous. Beholde and see the vertu of this precious plenty of hys dere worthy blode. It descendyd downe in to helle and brak her bondes and delyverd them all that were there which belongh to the courte of hevyn.[6] The precious plenty of his dere worthy blode ovyrflowyth all erth and is redy to wash all creatuers of synne which be of good wyll, have been, and shall be. The precious plenty of his dere worthy blode ascendyth up into hevyn in the blessed body of our Lorde Jesu Crist[7] and ther is in hym bledyng, preyeng for us to the Father, and is and shalbe as long as us nedyth. And ovyr more it flowyth in all heaven, enjoying the salvacion of all mankynd that be ther and shall be, fulfylling the number that faylyth.[8]

---

9. In appearance like the scourging, whipping.
1. Smitings, striking with heavy blows.
2. Due consideration.
3. I thought that if it had actually been so in nature and substance (rather than in a vision).
4. But it pleases him better that we take very wholesomely, healthfully his blessed blood to wash ourselves of sin.
5. No liquid that is made that pleases him so well to give us.
6. The harrowing or spoiling of hell, believed to have occurred when Jesus descended to hell between his death and resurrection to rescue the souls of the Old Testament patriarchs and prophets who were held in bondage by the devil until Christ could make reparation for Adam's and Eve's original sin.
7. The ascension of Christ's body into heaven forty days after his resurrection.
8. Taking the place of the number that failed. I.e., the rebellious angels who were driven out of heaven.

Revelation V

Chapter 13

And after, or that God shewed any wordes, he sufferde me to beholde hym a conveniable tyme,[9] and all that I had seen, and all the understandyng that was ther in, as the sympylnes of the sowle myght take it. Then he without voys and openyng of lyppes formyd in my sowle these wordes: *Here with is the feende ovyr come.* This worde sayde our Lorde menyng his blessyd passyon, as he shewed before.

In this our Lord shewed a parte of the feendes malyce and fully hys unmyght,[1] for he shewed that the passion of hym is the ovyr-comyng of the feende. God shewed that the feend hath nowe the same malyce that he had before the incarnacion.[2] And also sore he traveyleth, and as contynually he seeth[3] that all sowles of salvacion eskape hym worshyppfully by the vertue of his[4] precious passion. And that is his sorow and full evyl is he ashamyd.[5] For all that God suf-feryth hym to do turnyth us to joy and hym to shame and payne. And he hath as mech sorow when God gevyth hym leve to werke[6] as when he workyth nott. And that is for he may nevyr do as ylle as he wolde, for hys myght is alle lokked in God's hande.[7]

But in God may be no wrath as to my syght. For our good Lorde endelessly havyng regard to his awne worshyppe and to the profyghte of all them that shalbe savyd, with myght and ryght he withstondyth the reprovyd, the which of malyce and of shrewdnes besye them to contrary and do against Goddes wyll.[8]

Also I saw oure Lorde scornyng hys malys and nowghtyng hys unmyght,[9] and he wille that we do so. For this syght, I laght[1] myght-ely. And that made them to lagh that were abowte me, and ther lawchyng was a lykyng[2] to me. I thought that I wolde that alle my evyn Crysten had seen as I saw, then shoulde all they a lawchyd with me. But I saw not Cryst laghyng, but wele I wott that syght that he

9. Permitted me to behold him an appropriate time. "Or": before.
1. His lack of might, powerlessness.
2. Incarnation, when Jesus, the Second Person of the Trinity, became human to atone through his suffering and death for the original sin of Adam and Eve that consigned their descendants to hell.
3. As forcefully as he toils, so also continually he sees.
4. Christ's.
5. His (the fiend's) sorrow and he is very wretchedly ashamed.
6. As much sorrow when God gives him leave, permission to work.
7. He may never do as much evil as he would like to, for his might is all locked in God's hand.
8. The reproved or condemned, who, out of malice and wickedness, occupy themselves by being contrary and acting against God's will.
9. Scorning his malice and depreciating his powerlessness.
1. Laughed.
2. Laughing was a pleasure.

shewed me made me to laugh. For I understode that we may laugh in comfortyng of oure selfe and joyeng in God, for the feend is overcome. And ther I sawe hym scorne his malis, it was be holdyng to my understandyng in to oure Lorde, that is to say, an inwarde shewyng of sothfastnesse without chaungyng of chere.[3] For as to my syght it is a wurschyppfull propyrte that is in God, which is durable.

And after this I felle in to a sadnes and sayde, "I see thre thynges: game,[4] scorne, and ernest. I see game that the feend is ovyrcome. And I se scorne that God scorneth hym and he shalle be scornyd. And I se ernest that he is overcome by the blessydfulle passion and deth of oure Lorde Jhesu Crist that was done in fulle grette ernest and with sad traveyle." And ther I seyde he is scornyd, I ment that God scornyth hym, that is to sey, for he seeth hym now as he shall do withought ende. For in this God shewde that the feende is dampnyd. And this ment I ther I seide he schulde be scornyd, for I saw he schalle be scornyde at domys day generally of all that schalbe savyd, to whos salvacion he hath had grett envye. For then he shall see that all the woo and tribulacion that he hath done them shalle be turned in to encrese of ther joy without ende. And all the payne and the sorow that he wolde have brought them to shalle for evyr goo with hym to helle.

Revelation VI

Chapter 14

After this oure Lorde seyde, *I thangke the of thy servys and of thy travelle of thy yowyth.*[5] And in thys my understondyng was lyftyd uppe in to hevyn wher I saw our Lorde God as a lorde in his owne howse, whych lorde hayth callyd alle hys derewurthy frendes to a solempne fest. Than I saw the lorde takyng no place in hys awne howse, but I saw hym ryally[6] reigne in hys howse and all fulfyllyth it with joy and myrth hym selfe, endelesly to glad and solace hys derewurthy frendes, fulle homely and fulle curtesly, with mervelous melody in endelesse love in hys awne feyer, blessydfulle chere, which glorious chere of the Godhede fulfyllyth alle hevyn of joy and blysse.

God shewde thre degrees of blysse that ech soule shalle have in hevyn that wyllyngfully hayth servyd God in any degree in erth. The furst is the wurshyppe thangke of our Lorde God that he shall receyve when he is delyverde of payne. This thangke is so hygh and

---

3. An inward showing of compassion without changing of facial expression.
4. Amusement.
5. I thank thee for thy service and for the toil of thy youth.
6. Royally.

so wurshyppfulle that hym thyngkyth that it fyllyth hym though ther were no more.[7] For my thought alle the payne and traveyle that myght be suffrede of all lyvyng men myght nott have deservyde the wurschypfull thank that one man shalle have that wylfully hath servyd God.

For the secunde, that alle the blessyd creatures that be in hevyn shalle se the wurschypfulle thangkyng. And he makyth hys servys knowyn to alle that be in hevyn. And in thys tyme thys exsample was schewd: A kyng, yf he thanke hys subjettes, it is a grett wurschyppe to them. And yf he make it knowen to all the realme, then ther wurschypp is mech incresyd.

And for the thurde, that as new and as lykyng as it is undertaken that tyme, ryght so schalle it laste without ende.[8] And I saw that homely and swetly was thys shewd, that the age of every man shalbe knowen in hevyn and be rewardyd for hys wyllfulle servys and for hys tyme. And namly, the age of them that wylfully and frely offer ther yowth to God passynly[9] is rewarded and wonderfully thangkyd. For I saw that when or what tyme that a man or woman be truly turned to God, for one day servys and for hys endelesse wylle, he shall have alle these thre degrees of blesse. And the more that the lovyng soule seeth this curtesy of God, the levyr she ys to serve hym all her lyfe.

Revelation VII

Chapter 15

An after thys he shewde a sovereyne gostely lykynge[1] in my soule. In thys lykyng I was fulfyllyde of the evyrlastyng suernesse, myghtely fastnyd[2] without any paynefulle drede. This felyng was so glad and so goostely that I was all in peese, in eese, and in reste that ther was nothyng in erth that shulde have grevyd[3] me. This lastyd but a whyle, and I was turned and left to my selfe in hevynes and werynes of my life and irkenes of my selfe that unneth[4] I could have pacience to lyve. Ther was no comfort ne none eese to my felyng but feyth, hope, and cheryte. And these I had in truth, but fulle lytylle in felyng.

And anon after thys oure blessyd Lorde gave me a geane the comfort and the rest in soule, lykyng and suernesse so blyssydfully and so myghtely that no drede, ne sorow, ne no peyne bodely ne gostely

7. It seems to him that it fills him as though there were no more left.
8. That as new and as pleasing as it is at the time it is received, just so shall it last without end.
9. Surpassingly.
1. Supreme, spiritual pleasure.
2. Strongly fastened or secured.
3. Grieved.
4. Weariness of myself that scarcely.

that myght be sufferde shulde have dyssesyde[5] me. And than the payne sheweth ayeeun[6] to my felyng and than the joy and the lykyng, and now that ooun and now that other dyverse tymes, I suppose about twenty tymes. And in the tyme of joy I myght have seyde with Seynt Paule, "Nothyng schalle departe me fro the charyte of Crist."[7] And in the payne I myght have seyd with Seynt Peter, "Lorde, save me. I peryssch."[8]

This vision was shewde to lerne me att my understandyng that it is spedfulle[9] to some soules to feele on thys wyse, some tyme to be in comfort and some tyme for to fayle and to be lefte to them selfe. God wylle that we know that he kepyth us evyr in lyke suer,[1] in wo and in wele. And for profyghte of man's soule, a man is somtyme left to hym selfe, all thogh hys synne is nott evyr the cause. For in this tyme I synned nott were for[2] I shulde be left to my selfe, for it was so sodeyne. Also I deservyd nott to have this blyssydfulle felyng, but frely our Lorde gaveth it whan he wylle and sufferyth us in wo some tyme, and both is one love.

For it is Goddes wylle that we holde us in comfort with alle oure myght. For blysse is lastyng without ende and payne is passyng and shall be brought to nowght to them that shall be savyd. Therfore it is nott Goddes wylle that we folow the felyng of paynes in sorow and mownyng for them, but sodayly[3] passe ovyr and holde us in the end-lesse lykyng that is God.

Revelation VIII

Chapter 16

After thys Crist shewde a parte of hys passyon nere his dyeng. I saw the swete face as it were drye and blodeles with pale dyeng, and deede, pale langhuryng, and than turned more deede in to blew and after in browne blew as the flessch turned more depe dede.[4] For his passion shewde to me most propyrly in his blessyd face and, namely,

5. Dis-eased, troubled. "A geane": again.
6. Again.
7. St. Paul was an early Christian missionary and the author of several epistles of the New Testament. Julian paraphrases Romans 8:35: "Who shall separate us from the love of Christ? shall tribulation, or distress, or persecution, or famine, or nakedness, or peril, or sword?"
8. St. Peter was one of the twelve apostles. Two stories involve the disciples calling for Jesus' help with similar words: when they are in danger at sea in Matthew 8:25 and when Peter walks on water in Matthew 14:30.
9. Helpful.
1. Alike sure.
2. Wherefore.
3. Suddenly. "Mownyng": moaning.
4. Dry and bloodless with pale dying, and dead, with pale languishing, and then turned more dead into blue and after into brownish blue as the flesh became more fully dead.

in hys lyppes. Ther in saw I these iiii colours, tho that were be fore fressch and rody,[5] lyvely and lykyng to my syght.

This was a petufulle chaungyng to se, this depe dying and also hys nose clange to geder[6] and dryed to my syght. And the swete body waxid browne and blacke, alle chaungyd and turned oute of the feyer, fressch, and lyvely coloure of hym selfe in to drye dyeng. For that same tyme that oure blessyd Savyour dyed uppon the rode it was a dry, sharp wynd, wonder[7] colde as to my syght. And what tyme that the precyous blode was bled out of the swete body that myght passe ther fro, yet ther was a moyster[8] in the swete flessch of Crist as it was shewde. Blodlessehed and payne dryed with in and blowyng of the wynde and colde comyng from with out mett to geder in the swete body of Christ, and thesse iiii dryed the flessch of Crist by prosses of tyme.[9] And thowe[1] this peyne was bitter and sharp, yet it was fulle longe lastyng as to my syght. And the payne dryede uppe alle the lyvely spyrites of Cristes flessh.

Thus I saw the swete flessch dry in my syght, parte after perte dryeng with mervelous payne. And as long as any spryte[2] had lyffe in Cristes flessch, so longe sufferde he. This long peyne semyde to me as if he had be sennyght[3] deede, dyeng, at the poynt of out passyng, alwey sufferyng the gret peyne. And ther I say it semyd as he had bene sennyght deed, it specyfyeth that the swet body was so dyscolouryd, so drye, so clongyn, so dedly, and so pytuous[4] as he had bene sennyght deed, contynually dyeng. And me thought the dryeng of Cristes flessch was the most peyne and the last of his passion.

Chapter 17

And in this dryeng was brought to my mynde this worde that Crist seyd, "I thurst."[5] For I sawe in Crist a dowbylle thurst, oon bodely and a nother gostly. This worde was shewyd for the bodyly thurste, and for the gostely thurst was shewyd as I shalle sey after. And I understode by the bodyly thurste that the body had feylyng of moyster,[6] for the blessyde flessch and bonys was lefte alle aloone without blode and moyster. The blessyd body dryed alle a loon long tyme with

5. Ruddy.
6. Shriveled together. Corrected from S1; P has *cloeggeran*, a word that appears in no other Middle English text. "Petufulle": pitiful.
7. Wondrously. "Rode": cross.
8. Moisture.
9. In the course of time.
1. Though.
2. Spirit.
3. Seven nights.
4. Piteous. "Clongyn": shriveled.
5. The fifth of the seven words or phrases that Jesus spoke from the cross according to John 19:28. The double thirst was both physical and spiritual; the spiritual thirst is explained in Revelation XIII, chapter 31, as Christ's longing to be united with the elect in heaven.
6. Failing of moisture.

wryngyng of the nayles and weyght of the body.[7] For I understode
that for tendyrnes of the swete handes and the swete feet by the
grete hardnes and grevous of the naylys the woundys waxid wyde and
the body satylde for weyght, by long tyme hangyng and persyng and
rausyng of the heed and byndyng of the crowne alle bakyn with drye
blode, with the swet here[8] clyngyng the drye flessch to the thornys
and the thornys to the flessch dryeng.

And in the begynnyng, whyle the flessch was fressch and bledyng,
the contynualle syttyng[9] of the thornes made the woundes wyde. And
ferthermore I saw that the swet skynne and the tendyr flessch with
the here and with the blode was alle rasyd and losyde above with the
thornes and brokyn in many pecis and were hangyng as they wolde
hastely have fallen downe whyle it had kynde moyster.[1] How it was
doone I saw nott, but I understode that it was with the sharpe
thornes and the boystours, grevous syttyng on[2] of the garlonde, not
sparyng and without pytte, that alle tho brake the swet skynne with
the flessch and the here losyd it from the boone. Wher thorow it was
broken on pecys as a cloth and saggyng downwarde,[3] semyng as it
wolde hastely have fallen for hevynes and for lowsenes.[4] And that
was grete sorow and drede to me, for me thought that I wolde nott
for my life have seene it fall.

This contynued a whyle and after it began to chaunge, and I
behelde and marveylyd how it myght be. And than I saw it was, for
it beganne to dry and stynt a parte of the weyght[5] that was rownd
about the garland. And so it was envyroned[6] all about as it were
garland upon garland. The garlonde of thornes was deyde with the
blode; and that other garlond and the hede, all was one colowre as
cloteryd blode[7] when it was dryed. The skynne and the flesshe that
semyd of the face and of the body was smalle rympylde with a tawny
coloure, lyke a drye bord when it is agyd,[8] and the face more browne
than the body.

I saw iiii maner of dryeng. The furst was blodlesse; the secunde,
payne folowyng after; the thurde is that he was hangyng uppe in the
eyer as men hang a cloth for to drye; the fowyrth, that the bodely

---

7. Twisting of the nails and weight of the body.
8. Hair. "Satylde": settled. "Persyng and rausyng": piercing and raising. "Bakyn": baked.
9. Continual sitting, constant pressure.
1. (The skin was) broken in many pieces that were hanging as if they would quickly have
   fallen down while it had natural moisture. "Alle rasyed and losyde": all raised and loosened.
2. Crude, grievous setting on.
3. Through this it was broken in pieces like a cloth and sagging downward.
4. Looseness.
5. Stop or reduce a part of the weight or pressure.
6. It (Jesus' head) was encircled.
7. That other garland (the ring of blood caused by the crown of thorns) and the head, all
   were the same color as clotted blood. "Deyde": dyed.
8. Slightly wrinkled with a tawny color, like a dry board when it is aged.

kynde askyd lycoure,[9] and ther was no maner of comfort mynystryd to hym. A, hard and grevous was that payne, but moch more harder and grevous it was when the moystur fayled and all began to drye, thus clyngyng. Theyse were ii paynes that shewde in the blyssed hed. The furst wrought to the dryeng whyle it was moyst;[1] and that other, slow, with clyngyng and dryeng, with blowyng of wynde fro without that dryed hym more and payned with colde than my hart[2] can thingke, and all other peynes, for which paynes I saw that alle is to lytylle that I can sey, for it may nott be tolde. The shewyng of Cristes paynes fylled me fulle of peynes, for I wyste welle he suffyryde but onys,[3] but as he wolde shewe it me and fylle me with mynde as I had before desyerde.

And in alle thys tyme of Cristes presens, I felte no peyne but for Cristes paynes. Than thought me I knew fulle lytylle what payne it was that I askyd,[4] and as a wrech I repentyd me, thyngkyng if I had wyste what it had be, loth me had been to have preyde it. For me thought my paynes passyd ony bodely deth. I thought, "Is ony payne in helle lyk thys?" And I was answeryd in my reson: "Helle is a nother peyne, for ther is dyspyer.[5] But of alle peyne that leed to salvacion, thys is the most, to se the lover to suffer." How myght ony peyne be more then to see hym that is alle my lyfe, alle my blysse, and all my joy suffer? Here felt I stedfastly that I lovyd Crist so much above my selfe that ther was no peyne that myght be sufferyd lyke to that sorow that I had to see hym in payne.

Chapter 18

Here I saw in parte the compassion of our blessed Lady Sainct Mary, for Crist and she was so onyd[6] in love that the grettnes of her love was cause of the grettnes of her peyne. For in this I saw a substance of kynde love contynued by grace[7] that his creatures have to hym, which kynde love was most fulsomly[8] shewde in his swete mother and ovyrpassyng, for so much as she lovyd hym more then alle other, her peyne passyd alle other. For ever the hygher, the myghtyer, the swetter that the love is, the more sorow it is to the lover to se that body in payne that he lovyd. And so alle hys dyscyples and alle his tru lovers sufferyd more payne than ther awne bodely

9. Drink. "Eyer": air.
1. Was wrought or made by the drying while it (the head) was moist.
2. Dried and pained him with cold more than my heart.
3. I knew well he suffered only once.
4. I knew very little what pain I asked for (when Julian requested a vision of Christ's Passion as one of the three gifts from God; see chapter 2).
5. Despair.
6. United.
7. A substance of natural love continued, preserved by grace.
8. Fully.

dyeng, for I am suer by my awne felyng that the lest of them lovyd
hym so farre abovyn them selfe that it passyth alle that I can sey.

Here saw I a grett onyng[9] betwene Crist and us to my understondyng. For when he was in payne, we ware in payne. And alle
creatures that myght suffer payne sufferyd with hym, that is to say,
alle creatures that God hath made to oure servys. The fyrmantente
and erth feylyd for sorow in ther kynd[1] in the tyme of Cristes dyeng,
for it longyth kyndly to ther properte[2] to know hym for ther Lorde,
in whom alle ther vertuse[3] stondyth. And whan he feylyd, then
behovyd nedys to them for kyndnes to feyle[4] with hym, in as moch
as they myght, for sorow of hys paynes. And thus tho that were hys
fryndes[5] suffered payne for love. And generally alle, that is to sey,
they that knew hym nott, sufferde for feylynge of all maner comfort,
save the myghty, pryve kepyng of God.[6]

I mene of ii maner of people that knew hym nott, as it may be
understond by ii persons. That oone was Pylate;[7] that other person
was Seynt Dyonisi of France whych was that tyme a paynym.[8] For
whan he saw wonders and merveyles, sorowse and dredys that befelle
in that tyme, he seyde, "Eyther the worlde is now at an ende, or elles
he that is maker of kyndes sufferyth." Wherfore he dyd wryte on an
awter:[9] "Thys is an awter of the unknowyn God." God of hys goodnes,
that makyth planettes and the elementes to worke in ther kynde to
the blessyd man and to the cursyde, in that tyme it was withdraw fro
both. Wher for it was that they that knew hym nott were in sorow
that tyme.

Thus was oure Lord Jhesu payned for us, and we stonde alle in
this maner of payne with hym and shalle do tylle that we come to
his blysse, as I shalle sey after.

Chapter 19

In this tyme I wolde have lokyde fro the crosse and I durst nott,
for I wyst wele[1] whyle that I behelde the crosse I was suer and safe.

---

9. Oneness, unity.
1. Nature. "Fyrmantente": firmament, sky.
2. For it belongs naturally to their attributes.
3. Powers.
4. It was necessary to them because of their nature to fail.
5. Friends.
6. Except the mighty, secret keeping or guardianship of God.
7. Pontius Pilate was the Roman procurator of Judea who allowed Jesus to be crucified.
8. St. Denis of France was at that time a pagan. Like her contemporaries, Julian conflates
the patron saint of France with pseudo-Dionysius the Areopagite, the fifth-century mystical theologian mistakenly identified in the Middle Ages with the man whose conversion
by St. Paul on the Areopagus in Athens is described in Acts 17:34.
9. Altar.
1. I would have looked (away) from the cross and I dared not, for I well knew.

Ther fore, I wolde nott assent to put my soule in perelle, for besyde[2] the crosse was no surenesse fro drede of fendes.

Than had I a profyr[3] in my reason, as it had ben frendely seyde to me, "Loke uppe to hevyn to hys Father." And than sawe I wele with the feyth that I felt that ther was nothyng betwene the crosse and hevyn that myght have dyssesyde[4] me. Here my behovyd[5] to loke uppe or elles to answere. I answeryd inwardly with alle the myght of my soule and sayd, "Nay, I may nott, for thou art my hevyn." Thys I seyde for I wolde nott. For I had levyr a bene[6] in that payne tylle domys day than have come to hevyn other wyse than by hym. For I wyst wele that he that bounde me so sore, he shuld unbynd me whan he wolde.[7]

Thus was I lernyd to chese Jhesu for my hevyn,[8] whom I saw only in payne at that tyme. Me lykyd no nother hevyn than Jhesu,[9] whych shalle be my blysse when I come ther. And this hath evyr be a comfort to me, that I chose Jhesu to be my hevyn by his grace in alle this tyme of passion and sorow. And that hath ben a lernyng to me that I shulde evyr more do so, to chese Jhesu only to my hevyn in wele and in woe. And though I as a wrech hath repentyd me, as I seyde before, yff I had wyst what payne it had be, I had be loth to have prayde it,[1] heer I saw werely that it was grugyng and fraelte[2] of the flessch without assent of the soule, in whych God assignyth no blame.

Repentyng and wylfulle choyse be two contrarytes, whych I felt both at that tyme. And tho be two partes, that oon outward, that other inwarde. The outwarde party is our dedely flessh, whych is now in payne and now in woo and shalle be in this lyfe, where of I felte moch in thys tyme. And that party was that I repentyd. The inward party is a hygh and a blessydfulle lyfe, whych is alle in peece and in love, and this is more pryvely felte. And this party is in whych myghtly, wysely, and wyllfully I chose Jhesu to my hevyn. And in this I saw truly that the inward party is master and sovereyne to the outward, nought chargyng nor takyng hede of the wylles of that,[3] but alle the intent and the wylle is sett endlesly to be onyd to our Lorde Jhesu. That the outward party sholde drawe the inward to assent was

2. Aside from. "Perelle": peril.
3. Proposal.
4. Dis-eased, troubled.
5. It was necessary for me, I must.
6. Rather have been.
7. For I knew well that he that bound me so closely, he should unbind me when he would.
8. Taught to choose Jesus for my heaven. By refusing to take her eyes from the cross, Julian affirms that her salvation comes through Jesus.
9. No other heaven but Jesus pleased me.
1. Julian expresses regret for requesting a vision of Christ's Passion and death in chapter 17.
2. Truly that it was grouching and frailty.
3. Not giving charge or authority nor taking heed of the desires of that (the outward part, the mortal body).

not shewde to me. But that the inwarde party drawyth the outward party by grace, and both shalle be onyd in blysse without ende by the vertu of Christ, this was shewde.

Chapter 20

And thus saw I oure Lorde Jhesu languryng long tyme, for the unyng of the Godhed gave strenght to the manhed[4] for love to suffer more than alle man myght. I meene nott oonly more payne than alle man myght suffer, but also that he sufferd more payne than all man of salvacion that evyr was from the furst begynnyng in to the last day myght telle or fully thynke, havyng regard to the worthynes of the hyghest worshypfful kyng and the shamfulle and dyspyteous,[5] peynfull deth. For he that is hyghest and worthyest was foulest comdempnyd and utterly dyspysed. For the hyest poynt that may be seen in his passion is to thynke and to know that he is God that sufferyd, seeyng after these other two poyntes whych be lower. That one is what he sufferyd, and that other for whom that he sufferyd.

And in thys he brought to mynd in parte the hygh and the nobylyte[6] of the glorious Godhede, and ther with the precioushede and the tendyrnesse of the blessydfulle body whych be to gether onyd, and also the lothfullnesse that in our kynde is to suffer peyne. For as moch as he was most tendyr and clene,[7] ryght so he was most strong and myghty to suffer. And for every mannys synne that shalbe savyd he sufferyd. And every mannes sorow, desolacion, and angwysshe[8] he sawe and sorowd for kyndnes and love. For in as mech as our Lady sorowde for his paynes, as mech sufferde he sorow for her sorowse. And, more over, in as mech as the swete manhed of hym was wurthyer in kynde, for as long as he was passyble[9] he sufferde for us and sorowde for us. And now he is uppe resyn and no more passibylle, yett he sufferyth with us, as I shalle sey after.

And I, beholdyng alle this by hys grace, saw that the love in hym was so strong whych he hath to oure soule that wyllyngfully he chose it with grett desyer and myldely he sufferyd it with grett joy. For the soule that beholdyth thus whan it is touchyd by grace, he shalle verely see that tho paynes of Cristes passion passe all payne, that is to sey, whych paynes shalbe turned in to everlastyng joy by the vertu of Cristes passion.

It is God's wylle, as to my understandyng, that we have iii maner of beholdyng of his blessyd passion. The furst is the harde payne that

4. Uniting with the Godhead gave strength to the manhood. Jesus combined divine and human natures.
5. Cruel.
6. The eminence and the nobility.
7. Pure.
8. Anguish.
9. Capable of suffering.

he sufferyd with a contricion and compassion.[1] And that shewde oure Lorde in this tyme and gave me myght and grace to see it. And I lokyd after the departying with alle my myghtes and wende[2] to have seen the body alle deed, but I saw him nott so. And right in the same tyme that me thought, by semyng, that the lyfe myght no lenger last and the shewyng of the ende behovyd nydes to be nye,[3]

Chapter 21

sodenly, I beholdyng in the same crosse, he chaungyd in blessydfulle chere.[4] The chaungyng of hys blessyd chere chaungyd myne, and I was as glad and mery as it was possible. Then brought oure Lorde meryly to my mynd, *Wher is now any poynt of thy payne or of thy anguysse?*[5] And I was fulle mery. I understode that we be now, in our Lordes menyng, in his crosse, with hym in our paynes and in our passion dyeng, and we willfully abydyng in the same crosse with his helpe and his grace in to the last poynt. Sodeynly he shalle chaunge hys chere to us, and we shalbe with hym in hevyn. Betwene that one and that other shalle alle be one tyme, and than shall alle be brought in to joy. And so ment he in thys shewyng, *Wher is now any poynt of thy payne or of thy agreffe?*[6] And we shalle be fulle of blysse.

And here saw I verely that if he shewde now to us his blyssedfulle chere, there is no payne in erth ne in no nother place that shuld trobylle[7] us, but alle thyng shulde be to us joy and blysse. But for he shewyth us chere of passion as he bare in this lyfe hys crosse, therfore we be in dysees[8] and traveyle with hym as our kynd askyth. And the cause why that he sufferyth is for he wylle of hys goodnes make us the eyers[9] with hym in hys blysse. And for this lytylle payne that we suffer heer we shalle have an high, endlesse knowyng in God, whych we myght nevyr have without that. And the harder oure paynes have ben with hym in hys crosse, the more shalle our worschippe be with hym in his kyngdom.

---

1. Contrition and compassion are the first two metaphoric "wounds" that Julian requests of God (see chapter 2). Julian identifies the second manner of beholding Christ's Passion in chapter 22 and the third in chapter 23.
2. Expected. "Departying": departing (of soul from body), death.
3. Must be near. P continues this sentence in a new chapter, thus emphasizing the suddenness of the change; S1 begins chapter 21 with the last paragraph of P's chapter 20. "By semyng": by appearance.
4. Facial expression.
5. Anguish.
6. Aggravation.
7. Trouble.
8. Unease, distress.
9. Heirs.

Revelation IX

Chapter 22

Then seide oure good Lorde, askyng, *Arte thou well apayd*[1] *that I sufferyd for thee?* I seyde, "Ye, good Lorde, gramercy.[2] Ye, good Lorde, blessyd moet[3] yow be." Then seyde Jhesu, our good Lord, *If thou arte apayde, I am apayde. It is a joy, a blysse, an endlesse lykyng to me that evyr I sufferd passion for the. And yf I myght have sufferyd more, I wolde a sufferyd more.* In thys felyng my understandyng was leftyd uppe in to hevyn. And ther I saw thre hevyns, of whych syght I was gretly merveyled and thought, "I see iii hevyns and alle of the blyssedfulle manhed of Criste. And noone is more, noone is lesse, noone is hygher, noone is lower, but evyn lyke[4] in blysse."

For the furst hevyn Crist shewyd me his Father in no bodely lycknesse, but in hys properte and in hys wurkyng.[5] That is to sey, I saw in Crist that the Father is. The werkyng of the Father is this: that he geavyth mede[6] to hys Sonne Jhesu Crist. This gyft and this mede is so blyssydfulle to Jhesu that his Father myght have geavyn hym no mede that myght have ben lykeyd to hym better. For the furst hevyn, that is the plesyng of the Father, shewyd to me as an hevyn, and it was fulle blyssydfulle. For he is wele plesyde with alle the dedes that Jhesu hath done about our salvacion, where for we be nott only hys by his byeng, but also by the curteyse gyfte of hys Father. We be his blysse, we be his mede, we be hys wurshype, we be his crowne. And this was a syngular marveyle and a full delectable beholdyng, that we be hys crowne.

Thys that I sey is so grete blysse to Jhesu that he settyth at naught hys traveyle,[7] and his passion, and his cruelle and shamfulle deth. And in these wordes, *If I myght suffer more, I wolde suffer more*, I saw truly that as often as he myght dye, as often he wolde, and love shulde nevyr lett hym have rest tille he hath done it. And I behelde with grete dyligence for to wet[8] how often he wolde dye yf he myght. And truly the nomber passyd my understandyng and my wittes so ferre that my reson myght nott nor cold nott comprehende it[9] ne take it. And whan he had thus oft dyed or shuld die, yet he wolde sett it at nought for love. For alle thynkyth hym but lytylle in regard of his love. For though the swete manhode of Crist myght suffer but

---

1. Pleased.
2. Thank you.
3. May.
4. Equally alike.
5. In his attributes and in his works.
6. Gives reward.
7. Sets at naught, is untroubled by his toil.
8. Know.
9. Could not comprehend, understand it. "So ferre": so far, to such an extent.

oonse, the goodnes of hym may nevyr seese of profer.[1] Every day he is redy to the same, yf it myght be. For yf he seyde he wolde for my love make new hevyns and new erthys, it ware but lytylle in regarde, for this myght he do ech day, yf that he wolde, without any traveyle. But for to dye for my love so often that the nomber passyth creatures' reason, thys is the hyghest profer that our Lorde God myght make to mannes soule as to my syght.

Than menyth he thus, *How shulde it than be that I shulde nott for thy love do alle that I myght? Whych deed grevyth me nought sethyn[2] that I wolde for thy love dye so oftyn, havyng no regard to my harde paynes.* And heer saw I, for the seconde beholding in his blessyde passion,[3] the love that made hym to suffer it passith as far alle his paynes as hevyn is above erth. For the payne was a noble, precious, and wurschypfulle dede done in a tyme by the workyng of love. And love was without begynnyng, is and shall be without ende. For whych love he seyde fulle swetely thys worde, *If I myght suffer more, I wolde suffer more.* He seyde nott, Yf it were nedfulle to suffer more, but if I myght suffer more. For though it were nott nedfulle and he myght suffer more, he wolde.

This dede and thys werke abowt oure salvation was ordeyned as wele as God myght ordeyne it. It was don as wurshypfully as Crist myght do it. And heer in I saw a fulle blysse in Crist, for his blysse shuld nott have ben fulle yf it myght ony better have ben done than it was done.

Chapter 23

And in these thre wordes, *It is a joy, a blysse, and endlesse lykyng to me,* were shewyd thre hevyns, as thus. For the joy, I understode the plesaunce of the Father; and for the blysse, the wurshyppe of the Sonne; and for the endlesse lykyng, the Holy Gost. The Father is plesyd, the Sonne is wurschyppyd, the Holy Gost lykyth. And heer saw I for the thyrde beholdyng in hys blessydfulle passion,[4] that is to sey, the joy and the blysse that makyth hym to lyke it.

For oure curteyse Lorde shewyd his passyon to me in fyve manneres, of whych the furst is the bledyng of the hede; the seconde, dyscolowryng of his blessyd face; the thyrde is the plentuous bledyng of the body in semyng of scorgyng; the iiii[th] is the depe drying.[5] Theyse iiii as it is before seyde for the paynes of the passion. And

---

1. Cease offering.
2. Does not grieve me since.
3. The first manner of beholding Christ's Passion is identified in the last paragraph of chapter 20 and the third manner in chapter 23.
4. The first is identified in chapter 20 and the second in chapter 22.
5. Revelations I, II, IV, and VIII, respectively.

the fyfte is thys that was shewyth for the joy and the blysse of the passion.[6]

For it is Goddes wylle that we have true lykyng with hym in oure salvacion, and ther in he wylle that we be myghtly comfortyd and strengthyd, and thus wylle he meryly with hys grace that oure soule be occupyed. For we be his blysse, for in us he lykyth without end and so schall we in him with hys grace. Alle that he doyth for us and hath done and evyr shalle was nevyr cost ne charge to hym ne myght be, but only that he dyed in our manhede, begynnyng at the swete incarnation and lastyng to the blessyd uprysyng on Ester morow.[7] So long duryd the cost and the charge abowt our redempcion in deed,[8] of whych dede he evyr joyeth endlesly, as it is befor seyd.

A, Jhesu, wylle we take hede to thys blysse that is in the blessyd-fulle Trinytie of our salvacion, and that we desyre to have as much gostly lykyng with his grace, as it is before seyde? That is to say, that the lykyng of our salvacion be lyke to the joy that Crist hath of oure salvation, as it may be whylle we be here. Alle the Trinyte wrought in the passion of Crist, mynystryn habboundance of vertuse and plente of grace[9] to us by hym. But only the maydyn's sonne sufferyd, werof[1] alle the blessed Trynyte enjoyeth. And thys was shewyd in thys worde, *Arte thou welle apayde?* By that other worde Crist seyd, *Yf thou arte welle apayd, I am welle apayde,* as yf he had sayde, *It is joy and lykyng enough to me, and I aske not elles of the of my travayle but that I myght apaye the.*

And in this he brought to my mynd the propyrte of a gladde geaver.[2] Evyr a glade geaver takyth but lytylle hede at the thyng that he geavyth, but alle hys desyr and alle hys intent is to plese hym and solace hym to whome he geavyth it. And yf the receyver take the gyft gladly and thankefully, than the curtesse gevyr settyth at nought alle hys cost and alle hys traveyle for joy and deleyght that he hath, for he hath plesyd and solacyd hym that he lovyth. Plentuously and fully was thys shewyd.

Thynk as wysely of the gretnesse of thys worde, *evyr*. For in that was shewyth an hygh knowyng of love that he hath in our salvation, with manyfolde joyes that folowen of the passion of Crist. One is that he joyeth that he hath done it in dede, and he shalle no more suffer. That other is that he hath therwith bought us from endlesse paynes of helle. A nother is that he brought us up in to hevyn and made us for to be hys crowne and hys endlesse blysse.

---

6. Revelation IX.
7. Resurrection on Easter morning.
8. So long lasted the cost and the responsibility for our redemption in dying or in deed (*deed* can mean either).
9. Worked in the Passion of Christ, administering abundance of virtues and plenty of grace.
1. Wherefore, on account of which.
2. Glad giver.

Revelation X

Chapter 24

Wyth a good chere oure good Lorde lokyd in to hys syde and behelde with joy, and with his swete lokyng he led forth the understandyng of hys creature by the same wound in to hys syd with in.[3] And ther he shewyd a feyer and delectable place and large inow[4] for alle mankynde that shalle be savyd and rest in pees and in love. And ther with he brought to mynde hys dere worthy blode and hys precious water whych he lett poure out for love. And with the swete beholdyng he shewyd hys blessyd hart clovyn on two.[5] And with hys enjoyeng he shewyd to my understandyng in part the blyssydfulle Godhede as farforth[6] as he wolde that tyme, strengthyng the pour soule for to understande, as it may be sayde, that is to mene the endlesse love that was without begynnyng and is and shalbe evyr.

And with this oure good Lorde seyde well blessydfully, *Lo, how I love the*, as yf he had seyde, *My darlyng, behold and see thy Lorde, thy God, that is thy maker and thy endlesse joy. See thyn owne Brother, thy Savyoure. My chylde, behold and see what lykyng and blysse I have in thy salvacion, and for my love enjoye with me.* And also to more understandyng thys blessyd worde was sayde, *Lo, how I love thee*, as yf he had sayde, *Behold and see that I lovyd thee so much or that I dyed for thee that I wolde dye for the. And now I have dyed for the and suffred wyllyngfully that I may. And now is all my bitter payne and alle my harde traveyle turnyd to evyrlastyng joy and blysse to me and to the. How schulde it now be that thou shuldest any thyng pray me that lykyd me, but yf I shulde fulle gladly graunte it the? For my lykyng is thyne holynesse and thy endlesse joy and blysse with me.* This is the understandyng symply as I can sey of this blessyd worde, *Lo, how I lovyd the*. This shewyd oure good Lorde to make us glade and mery.

Revelation XI

Chapter 25

And with thys chere of myrth and joy our good Lord lokyd downe on the ryght syde and brought to my mynde where our Lady stode in the tyme of hys passion and seyd, *Willt thou see her?* And in this

---

3. The wound in Jesus' side leading to his heart made by Longinus' lance to ensure he was dead on the cross.
4. Enough.
5. Broken in two.
6. To as great an extent.

swete word, as yf he had seyd, *I wott welle that thou wilt se my blessyd mother, for after my selfe she is the hyghest joy that I myght shewe the, and most lykyng and worschyppe to me, and most she is desyred to be seen of alle my blessyd creatures.* And for the marvelous hygh and syngular love that he hath to thys swete mayden, his blessyd mother our Layde Sainct Mary, he shewyth her blysse and joy as by the menyng of thys swete word, as if he seyde, *Wylte thou se how that I love her, that thou myght joy with me in the love that I have in her and she in me?*

And also to more understandyng thys swete word oure good Lorde spekyth in love to all mankynd that shall be savyd as it were alle to one person, as yf he sayde, *Wylt thou se in her how thou art lovyd? For thy love I have made her so hygh, so noble, so worthy. And thys lykyth me, and so wille I that it do the.* For after hym selfe she is the most blessydfulle syght. But here of am I nott lernyd[7] to long to see her bodely presens whyle I am here, but the vertuse of her blyssydfulle soule, her truth, her wysdom, her cheryte, wher by I am leern to know my self and reverently drede my God.

And whan oure good Lorde had shewyd thys and seyde thys worde, *Wylte thou see her?* I answeryd and seyde, "Ye, good Lorde, graunt mercy. Ye, good Lorde, yf it be thy wylle." Often tymes I preyde this and I went[8] to have seen her in bodely lykyng, but I saw her nott so. And Jhesu in that worde shewyd me a gostly syght of her. Ryght as I had seen her before,[9] lytylle and symple, ryght so he shewyd her than hygh and noble and glorious and plesyng to hym above all creatures. And so he wylle that it be knowen that all tho that lycke in hym[1] shuld lyke in her.

And to mor understandyng he shewyd thys exsample, as yf a man love a creature syngulary a bove alle creatures, he wylle make alle other creatures to love and to lycke that creature that he lovyth so much. And in thys worde that Jesu seyde, *Wylte thou see her?* me thought it was the most lykyn[2] worde that he myght geve me of her with the gostely shewyng that he gave me of her. For oure Lorde shewyd me nothyng in specialle but oure Lady Sent Mary, and her he shewyd thre tymes. The furst was as she conceyvyd; the secunde, as she was in her sorowes under the crosse;[3] and the thurde was as she is now in lykynge, worschyppe, and joy.

---

7. Taught.
8. Hoped.
9. Revelation I, chapters 4 and 7.
1. Take pleasure in him.
2. Pleasing.
3. Revelation I, chapters 4 and 7, and Revelation VIII, chapter 18, respectively.

Revelation XII

Chapter 26

And after thys our Lorde shweyd hym more gloryfyed as to my syght than I saw hym before, wher in I was lerned that oure soule shalle nevyr have reste tylle it come into hym, knowyng that he is full of joye, homely and curteys and blessydffulle and very lyfe.

Often tymes oure Lorde Jhesu seyde, *I it am, I it am. I it am that is hyghest. I it am that thou lovyst. I it am that thou lykyst. I it am that thou servyst. I it am that thou longest. I it am that thou desyryst. I it am that thou menyste.*[4] *I it am that is alle. I it am that holy church prechyth the and techeyth thee. I it am that shewde me before to the.* The nomber of the words passyth my wyttes and my understandyng and alle my myghtes. For they were in the hyghest as to my syght, for ther in is comprehendyd I can nott telle what. But the joy that I saw in the shewyng of them passyth alle that hart can thynk or soule may desyre. And therfore theyse wordes be nott declaryd here, but evyry man, aftyr the grace that God gevyth hym in under standyng and lovyng, receyve them in our Lordes menyng.

Revelation XIII

Chapter 27

And after thys oure Lorde brought to my mynde the longyng that I had to hym before. And I saw nothyng lettyd my but synne,[5] and so I behelde generally in us alle. And me thought yf synne had nott be, we shulde alle have be clene and lyke to oure Lorde as he made us. And thus in my foly before thys tyme often I wondryd why, by the grete forseyng[6] wysdom of God, the begynnyng of synne was nott lettyd. For then thought me that alle shulde have be wele.

Thys steryng[7] was moch to be forsaken. And, nevyrthelesse, mornyg and sorow I made therfore withoute reson and dyscrecion.[8] But Jhesu, that in this vysyon enformyd me of alle that me nedyd, answeryd by thys worde and seyde, *Synne is behovely,*[9] *but alle shalle be wele, and alle shalle be wele, and alle maner of thynge shalle be wele.* In this nakyd worde, *synne,* oure Lorde broughte to my mynde

---

4. Mean, intend.
5. Hindered me except sin.
6. Foreseeing. Corrected from S1; P has *forseyde,* foresaid.
7. Stirring, prompting.
8. Discretion, judgment of good and evil promptings.
9. Necessary, beneficial.

generally alle that is nott good, and the shamfull despyte[1] and the uttermost trybulation that he bare for us in thys lyfe, and hys dyeng and alle hys paynes, and passion of alle hys creatures gostly and bodely. For we be alle in part trobelyd and we schal be trobelyd, folowyng our master Jhesu, tylle we be fulle purgyd of oure dedely flessch and of alle oure inwarde affections whych be nott very good. And with the beholdyng of thys, with alle the paynes that evyr were or evyr shalle be, I understode the passion of Criste for the most payne and ovyr passyng.[2] And alle thys was shewde in a touch and redely passyd ovyr in to comfort, for oure good Lorde wolde nott that the soule were aferde of this oygly syghte.[3]

But I saw nott synne, for I beleve it had no maner of substaunce, ne no part of beyng,[4] ne it myght not be knowen but by the payne that is caused therof. And thys payne is somthyng as to my syghte for a tyme, for it purgyth and makyth us to know oure selfe and aske mercy. For the passion of oure Lorde is comfort to us agenst alle thys, and so is his blessyd wylle. And for the tender love that oure good Lorde hath to alle that shalle be savyd, he comfortyth redely and swetly, menyng thus, *It is tru that synne is cause of alle thys payne, but alle shalle be wele, and alle maner of thyng shalle be wele.*

Theyse wordes were shewde fulle tendyrly, shewyng no maner of blame to me ne to none that shalle be safe. Than were it grett unkyndnesse of me to blame or wonder on God of my synne, sythen[5] he blamyth nott me for synne. And in theyse same wordes I saw an hygh, mervelous prevyte[6] hyd in God, whych pryvyte he shalle opynly make and shalle be knowen to us in hevyn. In whych knowyng we shalle verely se the cause why he sufferde synne to come, in whych syght we shalle endlessely have joye.

Chapter 28

Thus I saw how Crist hath compassyon on us for the cause of synne. And ryght as I was before in the passion of Crist fulfyllyd with payne and compassion, lyke in thys I was in party fulfylled with compassion of alle my evyn Cristen. For fulle wele he lovyth pepylle[7] that shalle be savyd, that is to seye, Goddes servauntes. Holy chyrch

---

1. Contempt.
2. Sentence emended. P has *And the beholdyng of thys with alle the paynes that evyr were or evyr shalle be. And with alle thys I understode the passion of Criste for the most payne and ovyr passyng.*
3. Afraid of this ugly sight.
4. It had no manner of substance nor any part of being. As Julian says in Revelation III, chapter 11, evil is a defect, a privation or absence of the good, rather than an entity or power.
5. Since.
6. Secret.
7. People.

shalle be shakyd in sorow and anguyssch[8] and trybulacion in this worlde as men shakyth a cloth in the wynde. And, as to thys, oure Lorde answeryd, shewyng on this maner, *A, a grett thyng shalle I make herof in hevyn of endlesse wurshyppe and of evyrlastyng joye.* Ye, so farforth I saw oure Lord enjoyeth of the tribulacions of hys sarvauntes with pyte and compassion. And to ech person that he lovyth to his blysse for to bryng, he leyth on him somthyng that is no lacke in his syght, wherby they be lowhyd and dyspysed[9] in thys worlde, scornyd and mokyd and cast out. And thys he doth for to lett[1] the harm that they shulde take of the pompe and of the pryde and the veyne glorye of thys wrechyd lyffe and make ther wey redy to come to hevyn in blysse without ende evyrlastyng. For he seyth, *I shal alle to breke yow from yowre veyne affeccions and yowre vyscious pryde, and aftyr that I shalle gader yow and make yow meke and mylde, clene and holy by onyng to me.* And than saw I that ech kynde compassion that man hath on hys evyn Cristen with charyte, it is Crist in hym.

That ych maner noughtyng[2] that he shewde in hys passion, it was shewde agene here in thys compassion, wher in were two maner of understondynges in oure Lordes menyng. That one was the blysse that we be brought to, wher in he wille that we enjoye. That other is for comfort in oure payne, for he wille that we wytt that alle shalle turn us to wurschyp and to profyghte by the vertu of hys passyon, and that we wytte that we sufferyd ryght nought aloone, but with hym, and see hym oure grownde, and that we see his paynes and hys trybulacoun passe so ferre alle that we may suffer that it may nott be full thought. And the well beholdyng of thys wylle save us from grugyng and despeyer[3] in the felyng of our paynes. And yf we see verely that oure synne deserve it, yett hys love excusyth us. And of hys gret curtesy he doth away alle oure blame and beholdeth us with ruth and pytte as chyldren innocens and unlothfulle.[4]

Chapter 29

But in this I stode beholdyng generally, swemly and mornyngly[5] seyyng thus to oure Lorde in my menyng with fulle gret drede: "A, good Lorde, how myght alle be wele for the gret harme that is come by synne to thy creatures?" And here I desyeryd as I druste[6] to have some more opyn declaryng wher with that I myght be esyd in thys. And to thys oure blessyd Lorde answeryd, fulle mekely and with fulle

---

8. Anguish.
9. Lowered, humiliated, and despised.
1. Prevent.
2. Each kind of humiliation, effacement.
3. Grouching and despair.
4. Not loathsome, not inciting disgust.
5. Sorrowfully and mournfully.
6. Dared.

lovely chere, and shewd Adam's synne was the most harme that evyr was done or evyr shalle in to the worldes end. And also he shewde that thys is opynly knowyn in alle holy church in erth.

Ferthermore, he lernyd that I shulde beholde the glorious asseeth,[7] for thys asseeth makyng is more plesyng to the blessyd Godhed and more wurschypfulle for mannys salvacion with oute comparyson than evyr was the synne of Adam harmfulle. Then menyth oure blessyd Lorde thus, and in thys techyng that we shulde take hede to thys: *For sythen[8] that I have made welle the most harm, than it is my wylle that thou know ther by that I shalle make wele alle that is lesse.*

Chapter 30

He gave understondyng of ii partyes.[9] That one party is oure Saviour and oure salvacyon. Thys blessyd parte is opyn, clere, feyer, and lyght and plentuouse, for alle mankynde that is of good wylle and that shalle be is comprehendyd[1] in this part. Here to we be bounde of God and drawyn and counceylyd and lernyd inwardly by the Holy Gost and outward by holy chyrch in the same grace. In this wylle oure Lorde that we be occupyed and joyeng in hym, for he enjoyth in us. And the more plentuously that we take of thys with reverence and mekenesse, the more thanke we deserve of hym and the more spede[2] to oure selfe. And thus may we see and enjoye oure parte is oure Lorde.

That other is hyd and sparryd fro us, that is to sey, alle that is besyde oure salvacion. For that is oure Lordes prevy councelle.[3] And it longyth to the ryalle[4] lordschyppe of God to have hys pryvy counceyles in pees, and it longyth to his sarvauntes for obedyence and reverence nott wylle to know hys counceyles.

Oure Lorde hath pitte and compassion on us for that some creatures make them so besy therin. And I am suer yf we wyst[5] how gretly that we shuld plese hym and ese oure selfe to leve it, we wolde. The seyntes in hevyn, they wylle nothyng wytt but that oure Lorde wylle shew them, and also ther charyte and ther desyer is rulyd after the

---

7. Reparation, payment of debt. According to the late-medieval conception of the redemption, Christ had to assume human form to make amends for Adam's and Eve's offense to God.
8. Since.
9. In the subsequent chapters, Julian refers to two deeds that God shall perform to make all things well. The open deed or part, "oure Saviour and oure salvacyon," is discussed in chapters 31 and 34 through 40. The secret or great deed, God's "prevy councelle," is considered in chapters 32 and 33.
1. Included and understood.
2. Help.
3. Private counsel, plan.
4. Royal.
5. Knew.

wylle of oure Lorde. And thus oght we that oure wylle be lyke to them. Than shalle we nothyng wylle ne desyer but the wylle of oure Lorde lyke as they do, for we be alle one in Goddes menyng.[6] And here was I lernyd that we shulde onely enjoye in oure blessyd Savioure Jhesu and trust in hym for alle thyng.

Chapter 31

And thus oure good Lorde answeryd to alle the questyons and dowtys[7] that I myght make, sayeng full comfortabely, *I may make alle thyng wele. And I can make alle thyng welle. And I shalle make alle thyng wele. And I wylle make alle thyng welle. And thou shalt se thy selfe that alle maner of thyng shall be welle.* There he seyth, *I may,* I understonde for the Father. And there he seyth, *I can,* I understond for the Sonne. And there he seyth, *I wylle,* I understonde for the Holy Gost. And there he seyth, *I shalle,* I understonde for the unyte of the blessyd Trinite, thre persons and oon truth. And there he seyth, *Thou shalt se thy selfe,* I understond the comyng of alle man kynde that shalle be savyd in to the blyssedfulle Trynite. And in theyse v wordes God wyll that we be enclosyd in rest and in pees.

And thus shalle the goostly thyrst[8] of Crist have an end. For thys is the gostly thyrst of Cryst, the love longyng that lastyth and evyr shall tylle we se that syght at domys day. For we that shalle be safe and shalle be Crystes joy and hys blysse ben yet here, and some be to come, and so shalle some be in to that day. Therfore, this is his thurste and love longyng of us all to geder here in hym to oure endlesse blysse as to my syght. For we be nott now fully as hole in hym as we shalle be than.

For we know in oure feyth, and also it was shewde in alle, that Crist Jhesu is both God and man. And aneynst the Godhed, he is hym selfe hyghest blysse, and was fro without begynnyng, and shalle be without end, whych very endlesse blesse may nevyr be hyghed nor lowyde in the selfe.[9] And thys was plentuously sene in every shewyng, and namely in the **xii**, wher he seyth, *I it am that is hyghest.* And as aneynst Cristes manhode, it is knowyn in our feyth and also shewde that he, with the vertu of the Godhede, for love to bryng us to hys blysse, sufferyd paynes and passion and dyed.

And theyse be the workes of Cristes manhed wher in he enjoyeth, and that shewde he in the **ix**th where he sayth, *It is a joy, a blysse, an endlesse lykyng to me that evyr I sufferd passion for the.* And this is the blysse of Cristes werkes, and thus he menyth ther he seyth in the same shewyng, we be his blysse, we be hys meed, we be hys

6. Understanding or, possibly, fellowship.
7. Doubts.
8. Spiritual thirst, first mentioned in Revelation VIII, chapter 17.
9. Heightened nor lowered in the self. "Aneynst": as regards.

worship, we be his crowne. For as aneynst that Crist is oure hede, he is glorifyed and unpassable.[1] And as anenst his body, in whych alle his membris be knytt, he is nott yett fulle glorifyed ne all unpassable. For the same thurst and longyng that he had uppe on the rode tre,[2] which desyre, longyng, and thyrste, as to my syght, was in hym from without begynnyng, the same hath he yett and shalle in to the tyme that the last soule that shalle be savyd is come uppe to hys blysse.

For as truly as ther is a propyrte in God of ruth and pyte, as verely ther is a properte in God of thurst and longyng. And of the vertu of this longyng in Crist, we have to long agene[3] to hym, without whych no soule comyth to hevyn. And this properte of longyng and thyrst comyth of the endlesse goodnes of God, ryght as the propyrte of pytte comyth of his endlesse goodnesse. And thowgh he have longyng and pytte, they ben sondry[4] propyrtees as to my syght. And in thys standyth the poynte of gostly thyrst, whych is lastyng in hym as long as we be in need, us drawyng uppe to his blysse. And alle this was seen in shewyng of compassion, for that shalle ceacyn at domyes day.[5] Thus he hath ruthe and compassion on us, and he hath longyng to have us, but hys wysdom and hys love suffer nott the ende to come tyll the best tyme.

Chapter 32

Oone tyme oure good Lorde seyde, *Alle maner a thyng shalle be wele*. And another tyme he seyde, *Thou shalt se thy selfe that alle maner of thyng shalle be wele*. And in theyse two the soule toke sundry maner of understondyng. Oon was this: that he wylle we wytte that nott oonly he takyth heed to nobylle thynges and to grett, but also to lytylle and to small, to lowe and to symple, to oone and to other. And so menyth he in that he seyth, *Alle maner thyng shall be welle*. For he wylle that we wytt that the lest thyng shall nott be forgeten.

Another understandyng is this: that ther be many dedys evyll done in oure syght and so gret harmes take that it semyth to us that it were unpossible that evyr it shuld come to a good end. And up on thys we loke, sorrow, and morne therfore, so that we can nott rest us in the blyssedfulle beholding of God as we shuld do. And the cause

1. For in the respect that Christ is our head, he is glorified and incapable of suffering. And as regards his body, in which all his members are knit, he is not yet completely glorified or entirely incapable of suffering. Julian is alluding to the concept of the Mystical Body of Christ that referred to Christ and Christians as a figurative body; the idea derived from 1 Corinthians 12:27 where St. Paul writes: "Now ye are the body of Christ, and members in particular."
2. Cross.
3. In response.
4. Different.
5. Cease at judgment day.

is this: that the use of oure reson is now so blynde, so lowe, and so symple that we can nott know the high, marvelous wysdom, the might, and the goodnes of the blyssedfull Trynyte. And thus menyth he where he seyth, *Thou shalt se thy selfe that alle manner thyng shall be wele*; as yf he seyde, *Take now feythfully and trustely and at the last end thou shallt se verely in fulhede of joye.*

And thus in the same v wordes before seyde, *I may make all thyng wele*, I understonde a myghty comfort of alle workes of oure Lorde God that are for to come. There is a deed the whych the blessydfulle Trynyte shalle do in the last day as to my syght, and what the deed shall be and how it shall be done, it is unknowen of alle creaturys whych are beneth Crist and shall be tylle whan it shalle be done. The goodnesse and the love of our Lorde God wylle that we wytte that it shall be. And the myght and the wysdom of hym by the same love wylle heyle[6] it and hyde it fro us, what it shalle be and how it shalle be done. And the cause why he wylle we wytte it thus is for he wylle we be the more esyd in oure soule and peesable in love, levyng the beholdying of alle tempestes that myght lett[7] us of true enjoyeng in hym.

This is the grett deed ordeyned of oure Lorde God fro without begynnyng, tresured and hyd in hys blessyd brest, only knowyn to hym selfe, by whych deed he shalle make all thyng wele. For ryght as the blessyd Trinite made alle thyng of nought, ryght so the same blessyd Trynyte shalle make wele alle that is nott welle. And in this syght I marveyled gretly and be held oure feyth, menyng thus: oure feyth is groundyd in Goddes worde, and it longyth to oure feyth that we beleve that Goddys worde shalle be savyd in alle thyng.[8] And one poynt of oure feyth is that many creatures shall be dampnyd, as angelis that felle out of hevyn for pride whych be now fendys, and meny in erth that dyeth out of the feyth of holy chyrch, that is to sey, tho that be hethyn,[9] and also many that hath receyvyd Criston-dom and lyvyth uncristen lyfe and so dyeth oute of cheryte. All theyse shalle be dampnyd to helle without ende, as holy chyrch techyth me to beleve.

And stondyng alle thys, me thought it ~~was~~ unpossible that alle maner of thyng shuld be wele, as oure Lorde shewde in thys tyme. And as to thys I had no other answere in shewyng of oure Lorde but thys, *That that is unpossible to the is nott unpossible to me. I shalle save my worde in alle thyng, and I shalle make althyng wele.* And in thys I was taught by the grace of God that I shuld stedfastly holde me in the feyth as I had before understond, and ther with that I

---

6. Heal.
7. Prevent. "Peesable": peaceable, peaceful.
8. God's word shall be confirmed. Julian is attempting to reconcile the revelation that all shall be well with the church's teaching that many are damned to hell.
9. Heathen.

shulde stonde and sadly[1] beleve that alle maner thyng shall be welle, as oure Lorde shewde in that same tyme. For thys is the grete dede that oure Lorde God shalle do, in whych dede he shalle save his worde in alle thyng. And he shalle make wele all that is nott welle. But what the dede schal be and how it shall be done, there is no creature beneth Crist that wot[2] it, ne shalle wytt it tyll it is done, as to the understandyng that I toke of oure Lordys menyng in this tyme.

Chapter 33

And yitt in this I desyeryd as I durste[3] that I myght have had som syght of hel and of purgatory. But it was nott my menyng to take prefe[4] of ony thyng that longyth to oure feyth, for I beleved sothfastly that hel and purgatory is for the same ende that holy chyrch techyth for. But my menyng was that I myght have seen for lernyng in alle thyng that longyth to my feyth, wher by I myght lyve the more to Goddes wurschyppe and to my profyghte. And for ought that I culde desyer, I ne culde se of thys ryght nought[5] but as it is before seyde in the **fyfte** shewyng, wher that I saw the devylle is reprovyd of God and endlessly dampned. In whych syght I understond that alle the creatures that be of the devylles condiscion in thys lyfe and ther in endyng, ther is no more mencyon made of them before God and alle his holyn[6] then of the devylle, notwythstondyng that they be of man-kynde, wheder they have be cristend or nought.

For though the revelation was shewde of goodnes, in whych was made lytylle mencion of evylle, yett I was nott drawen ther by from ony poynt of the feyth that holy chyrch techyth me to beleve. For I had syght of the passion of Crist in dyverse shewyng: in the **furst**, in the **secunde**, in the **iiii**th, in the **viii**th as it is before seyde, wher in I had in part felyng of the sorow of oure Lady and of hys tru frendys that saw hys paynes. But I saw nott so properly specyfyed the Jewes that dyd hym to deth,[7] but nott withstondyng I knew in my feyth that they ware a cursyd and dampnyd without ende, savyng tho that were convertyd by grace. And I was strenghed and lernyd generally to kepe me in the feyth in evyry poynt and in all as I had before understonde, hopyng that I was ther in with mercy and the grace of God, desyryng

1. Firmly.
2. Knows.
3. Dared.
4. To test. Julian continues to attempt to reconcile the revelation that all shall be well with the church's teaching about purgatory and hell.
5. Nothing at all.
6. Saints.
7. But I saw not so particularly specified the Jews who put him to death. In many medieval narratives of the Passion, the Jews are held responsible for Christ's death. Julian's state-ment that the Jews were not specified is another discrepancy between her revelations and the church's teaching to which she is calling attention.

and preyeng in my menyng that I myght contenue ther in unto my lyvys ende.

It is Goddes wylle that we have grete regarde to alle the dedys that he hath done, for he wille ther by we know, trust, and beleve alle that he shalle do. But evrymore us nedyth leve the beholdyng what the dede shalle be and desyer we to be lyke to our bretherne, whych be the seyntes in hevyn, that wille ryght nought but Goddes wylle. Than shalle we only enjoye in God and be welle apayde[8] both with hydyng and shewyng. For I saw verely in our Lordes menyng the more we besy us to know hys prevytes in that or in any other thyng, the ferthermore shalle we be from the knowyng.

Chapter 34

Oure Lord shewyd two maner of prevytes.[9] One is thys grett pre-vyte with all the prevy poyntes therto belongyng. And theyse prevytes he wylle we know thus hyd in to the tyme that he wylle clerly shew them to us. That other are the prevytes whych hym selfe shewyd openly in thys revelation, for tho are prevytes whych he wylle make open and knowyn to us for he wylle that we wytt that it is hys wylle we knowe them. They are prevytes to us, but nott only for that he wylle they be prevytes to us, but they are prevytes to us for oure blyndhed and oure unknowyng. And therfore hath he grett ruth. And therfore he wylle make them opyn to us hym selfe, wher by we may knowe hym and love hym and cleve[1] to hym. For alle that is spedfulle[2] to us to wytt and for to knowe, fulle curtesly oure good Lorde wylle shew us what it is with alle the prechyng and techyng of holy chyrch.

God shewde fulle grett plesaunce that he hath in alle men and women that myghtly and wysely take the prechyng and the techyng of holy chyrch, for he it is, holy chyrch. He is the grounde. He is the substaunce. He is the techyng. He is the techer. He is the ende and he is the mede wherfore every kynde soule travelyth. And thys is knowen and shall be knowen to ech soule to whych the Holy Gost declaryth it. And I hope truly alle tho[3] that seke thus, they shalle spede, for they seke God.

Alle thys that I have now seyde and more as I shalle sey aftyr is comfortyng ageynst synne. For in the **thyrde** shewyng whan I saw that God doyth all that is done, I saw nott synn, and than saw I that alle is welle. But whan God shewyde me for synne, than sayde he, *Alle schalle be wele.*

8. Pleased.
9. Two types of secrets. These secrets correspond to the open and hidden understandings mentioned at the beginning of chapter 30 and developed in subsequent chapters.
1. Cleave, cling to.
2. Beneficial.
3. Those.

Chapter 35

And whan God alymyghty had shewyd so plentuosly and so fully of hys goodnesse, I desyred to wytt of a serteyn[4] creature that I lovyd yf it shulde contynue in good levyng, whych I hopyd by the grace of God was begonne. And in this syngular desyer it semyd that I lettyd my selfe,[5] for I was nott taught in thys tyme. And then was I answeryd in my reson, as it were by a frendfulle mene,[6] "Take it generally and beholde the curtesy of thy Lorde God as he shewyd to the, for it is more worshype to God to beholde hym in alle than in any specyalle thyng." I assentyd and ther with I lernyd that it is more wurschyppe to God to know althyng in generalle than to lyke in[7] ony thyng in specialle. And if I shuld do wysely after thys techyng, I shuld nott by glad for any thyng in specialle, ne gretly dyssesyd for any manner thyng, for alle shalle be wele.

For the fulhed of joy is to beholde God in alle. For by the same blyssyd myght, wysdom, and love that he made alle thyng, to the same end oure good Lorde ledyth it contynually and ther to hym selfe shalle bryng it. And when it is tyme, we shalle see it. And the ground of thys was shewyd in the **furst** and more openly in the **thyrde**, wher it seyth, "I saw God in a poynt." Alle that oure Lorde doyth is right fully, and alle that he sufferyth[8] is wurschypfulle. And in theyse two is comprehendyd good and evylle. For alle that is good oure Lorde doyth, and that is evyll oure Lord sufferyth. I say nott that evylle is wurschypfulle, but I sey the sufferaunce of oure Lorde God is wurschypfulle, wher by hys goodnes shalle be know without ende and hys mervelous mekenesse and myldhed by thys werkyng of mercy and grace.

Ryghtfulhed[9] is that thyng that is so good that may nott be better than it is. For God hym selfe is very ryghtfulhed, and all hys werkes be done ryghtfully as they be ordeyned fro without begynnyng by hys hygh myght, hys hygh wysdom, hys hygh goodnesse. And ryght as he hath ordeyned it to the best, ryght so he werkyth contynually and ledyth it to the same ende. And he is evyr fulle plesyd with hym selfe and with alle hys workes. And the beholdyng of thys blessyd acord is full swete to the soule that seeth it by grace. Alle the soules that shalle be savyd in hevyn without ende be made ryghtfulle in the syght of God and by hys awne goodnesse, in whych ryghtfullnes we be endlessly kepte and marvelously above all creatures.

And marcy is a werkyng that comyth of the goodnes of God, and

---

4. Certain.
5. And in this personal, selfish desire it seemed that I hindered myself.
6. Friendly intermediary.
7. To delight in.
8. Allows and endures.
9. Righteousness.

repetition throughout the book:
'all shall be well'

it shalle last wurkynge as long as synne is sufferyd to pursew ryghtfulle soules.[1] And whan synne hath no lenger leve to pursew, than
shalle the werkyng of mercy cees.[2] And than shalle alle be brought
into ryghtfulnes and ther in stonde withoute ende. By hys syffer-
aunce we falle, and in hys blessyd love with his myght and hys wysdom we are kept, and by mercy and grace we be reysyd to manyfolde
more joy. And thus in ryghtfulnes and in mercy he wyll be know and
lovyd now and without ende. And the soule that wysely beholdeth in
grace is wele payde with both and endlessely enjoyeth.

Chapter 36

Owre Lorde God shewde that a deed shalle be done and hym selfe
shalle do it.[3] And it shall be wurschypfulle and mervelous and plentuous. And by hym it shall be done and hym selfe shalle do it. And
this is the hyghest joy that the soule understode, that God hym selfe
shall do it and I shalle do ryght nought but synne, and my synne
shall nott lett his goodnes workyng.

And I saw that the beholdyng of this is a hevynly joy in a dredfulle
soule whych evyr more kyndly by grace desyeryth Goddes wylle. This
dede shalle be begon here, and it shalle be wurschypfulle to God and
plentuously profetable to alle hys lovers in erth. And evyr as we come
to hevyn we shalle se it in marvelous joy, and it shalle last thus in
werkyng to the last day. And the worschyppe and the blysse of that
shalle last in hevyn before God and alle hys holy seyntes without
ende. Thus was this dede seen and understonde in oure Lordes
meynyng. And the cause why he shewyde it is to make us to enjoy
in hym and in alle his werkys.

When I saw the shewyng contynued, I understode it was shewyde
for a grett thyng that was than for to come, whych thyng God shewde
that hym selfe shuld do it, whych dede hath the propertes before
sayde. And thys shewde he full blessydfully, menyng that I shuld
take it wysely, feytfully,[4] and trustely. But what the dede shuld be,
it was kepte pryvy to me. And in thys I saw that he wylle nott we
drede to know tho thynges that he shewth. He shewyth them for he
wylle we know them, by whych knowyng he wylle we love hym and
lyke in hym, and endlesly enjoy in hym. And for the grett love that
he hath to us, he shewyth us alle that is wurshypfulle and profitable
for the tyme. And tho thynges that he wylle now have prevy, yett of
hys grett goodnesse he shewyth them cloose.[5] In whych shewyng he

1. Allowed to pursue righteous souls.
2. Cease.
3. A deed shall be done and (he) himself shall do it. Julian is referring to the open understanding of chapter 30 involving "oure Saviour and oure salvacyon." She emphasizes that
   salvation is achieved through Christ and grace, not through human effort.
4. Faithfully.
5. Closed. Although God does not reveal the precise nature of this deed, Julian is assured it

wylle we beleve and understande that we shuld se it verely in hys endlesse blysse. Than oughte we to enjoy in hym for alle that he shewyth and for all that he hydyth. And yf we wylfully and mekely do thus, we shalle fynde ther in grett ees, and endlesse thankyng we shalle have of hym therfore.

And thys is the understondyng of this worde, that it shalle be done by me,[6] that is, the generalle man, that is to sey, alle that shalle be safe. It shalle be wurschypful, mervelous, and plentuous. And by me it shalle be done, and God hym selfe shalle do it. And thys shalle be hyghest joy that may be beholdyn of the dede, that God hym selfe shalle do it, and man shall do ryght nought but synne.

Than menyth oure good Lorde thus, as yf he seyde, *Beholde and se. Here hast thou mattyr of mekenesse. Here hast thou mattyr of love. Here hast thou matter of knowyng thy selfe. Here hast thou mattyr of enjoyyng in me. And for my love enjoy in me, for of alle thyng, therwith myght thou most plese me.* And as long as we be in this lyfe, what tyme that we by oure foly turne us to the beholdyng of the reprovyd,[7] tendyrly oure Lorde towchyth us and blysydfully callyth us, seyeng in oure soule, *Lett me aloone, my derwurdy chylde. Intende to me.*[8] *I am inogh to the, and enjoy in thy Saviour and in thy salvation.* And that this is oure Lordys werkyng in us, I am suer. The soule that is perced therwith by grace shalle se it and fele it. And though it be so that thys dede be truly take for the generall man, yett it excludyth nott the specyalle. For what oure good Lorde wylle do by his poure creatures, it is now unknowyn to me.

But this dede and that other before seyde, it is nott both one, but two sondry.[9] But thys dede shalle be knowen soner and that shalle be as we come to hevyn. And to whom oure Lorde geveth it, it may be knowen here in party. But the grett dede afore seyde shalle neyther be knowen in hevyn nor in erth tylle that it be done.

And farthermore he gave speciall understandyng and techyng of workyng and shewyng of myracles, as thus: *It is knowyn that I have done myracles here before, many and full hygh and mervelous, wurschypfulle and grett. And so as I have done, I do now contynually and shall in comyng of tyme.* It is knowyn that before myracles, come sorows and angwyssch and trobyll.[1] And that is that we shuld know oure owne febylnesse and mysschef[2] that we be fallen in by synne,

---

will lead to salvation for those who cannot avoid sin. At the end of this chapter, she distinguishes this deed from the other secret deed by which God will make all things well.

6. That it shall be done in respect to me. Julian is emphasizing the preeminence of grace rather than works in salvation.

7. As Julian did in chapter 33.

8. Leave me alone, my precious child. Pay attention to me.

9. These two deeds, the open and the hidden, correspond to the two understandings of chapter 30.

1. Anguish and trouble.

2. Feebleness and mischief.

to meke us[3] and make us to cry to God for helpe and grace. And grett myracles come after, and that of the hygh myght and wysdom and goodnesse of God, shewyng hys vertu and the joyes of hevyn, so as it may be in thys passyng lyfe, and that for the strenghyng of our feyth and encrese oure hope in charyte. Wherfore it plesyth hym to be knowyn and worschyppyd in myracles. Then menyth he thus: he wylle that we be nott borne ovyr lowe[4] for sorows and tempestys that falle to us, for it hayth evyr so been before myracles comyng.

Chapter 37

God brought to mynde that I shuld synne. And for lykyng that I had in beholdyng of hym, I entendyd nott redely to that shewyng.[5] And oure Lorde fulle marcifully abode[6] and gave me grace for to entende, and this shewyng I toke syngulary to my selfe. But by alle the gracious comfort that folowyth, as ye shalle see, I was lernyd to take it to alle myn evyn Cristen, alle in generalle and nothyng in specialle.

Though oure Lorde shewyd me that I shuld synne, by me aloone is understonde alle. And in thys I conceyvyd a softe drede,[7] and to this oure Lorde answeryd, *I kepe the fulle suerly*. Thys worde was seyde with more love and suernes of gostly kepyng than I can or may telle. For as it was afore shewde to me that I shuld synne, ryght so was the comfort shewyde, suernesse of kepyng for alle myn evyn Cristen.

What may make me more to love myn evyn Cristen than to see in God that he lovyth alle that shalle be savyd as it were alle one soule? For in every soule that shalle be savyd is a godly wylle[8] that nevyr assentyth to synne nor nevyr shalle. Ryght as there is a bestely wylle in the lower party that may wylle no good, ryght so there is a godly wylle in the hygher party,[9] whych wylle is so good that it may nevyr wylle evylle, but evyr good. And therfore we be that he lovyth, and endlesly we do that he lykyth. And thys shewyde oure good Lorde in the hoolhed[1] of love that we stande in in hys syght—yeea, that he lovyth us now as welle, whyle that we be here, as he shalle do when we be there before hys blessyd face. But for feylyng of love in oure party, therfore is alle oure traveyle.

3. To humble us.
4. Oppressed.
5. I did not readily pay attention.
6. Awaited.
7. Conceived a mild dread.
8. Godly will. Julian develops her concept of the godly will in Revelation XIV, chapters 53 and 58, where she explains the substantial union between the Second Person of the Trinity and those who will be saved.
9. The lower and higher parts of the soul, sensuality and substance, which Julian explains in Revelation XIV.
1. Wholeness.

Chapter 38

And God shewed that synne shalle be no shame, but wurshype to man. For ryght as to every synne is answeryng a payne by truth, ryght so for every synne to the same soule is gevyn a blysse by love.[2] Ryght as dyverse synnes be ponysschyd with dyvers paynes after that it be grevous,[3] ryght so shalle they be rewardyd with dyvers joyes in hevyn for theyr victories after as the synne have ben paynfulle and sorowfulle to the soule in erth. For the soule that shalle come to hevyn is so precyous to God and the place so wurshypfulle that the goodnes of God sufferyth nevyr that soule to synne fynally that shalle come ther.[4] But what synners they are that so shalbe rewarded is made knowen in holy church in erth and also in heaven by over passyng worshypes.

For in thys syght my understandyng was lyftyd up in to hevyn. And then God brought merely to my mynde David[5] and other in the olde lawe with hym without nomber. And in the new lawe he brought to my mynde furst Magdaleyne, Peter and Paule, Thomas of Inde,[6] Sent John of Beverly,[7] and other also without nomber: how they be knowen in the chyrch on erth with ther synnes. And it is to them no chame,[8] but alle is turned them to worshyppe. And, therfore, oure curtesse Lorde showyth for them here in party lyke as it is ther in fulheed, for there the tokyn of synne is turnyd to worshyppe.[9]

And Seynt Johnn of Beverley, oure Lorde shewed hym full hyly[1] in comfort of us for homelynesse and brought to my mynde how he

2. For just as a pain responds to every sin by justice, just so to the same soul is given a bliss for every sin by love.
3. Just as different sins are punished with different pains commensurate with their seriousness.
4. Never allows that soul to sin decisively at the end. The church distinguishes between two kinds of sin, mortal and venial. Mortal sin involves a serious transgression committed with the sinner's full knowledge and consent; venial sin is less serious and less deliberate. Dying in a state of mortal or deadly sin leads to damnation; dying in a state of venial sin requires appropriate punishment in purgatory before one can enter heaven. Both kinds of sin can be absolved by the sacrament of penance.
5. Second king of Israel and Judah (c. 1000–960 B.C.E.), who committed adultery with Bathsheba. *Merely* added in margin.
6. Disciple who doubted Jesus' resurrection and who, according to legend, brought Christianity to India. Corrected from S2. P has *Thomas and Jude.* Jude is another discipline, but there is no evidence of his transgression. Magdaleyne was a follower of Christ who was mistakenly identified in the Middle Ages with the repentant woman who washed Jesus' feet and wiped them with her hair in Luke 7:36–50. The apostle Peter denied knowing Jesus after he was arrested. Before he was converted, Paul persecuted Christians.
7. An Anglo-Saxon bishop of Hexham and York associated with Hilda of Whitby and Bede. In 720 he retired from the bishopric of York to a monastery at Beverley and soon died. Bede recounts his miracles of healing the sick in Book 5 of *Ecclesiastical History of the English People.* In 1037 his remains were transported from Beverley to York, and his shrine became a popular pilgrimage site. There is no record of a sin he committed. His feast day is May 7. According to S1, Julian's illness began on May 8, the day following the feast of St. John of Beverley.
8. Shame.
9. Shows them here in part just as it is there in fullness, for there the sign of sin is turned to honor.
1. Highly.

is a kynd neyghbur and of oure knowyng. And God callyd hym Seynt Johnn of Beverley pleynly as we do, and that with a fulle glade and swet chere, shewyng that he is a full hygh seynt in hys syght and a blessydfulle. And with thys he made mencyon that in hys yowth[2] and in hys tendyr age he was a dereworthy sarvaunt to God, full gretly God lovyng and dredyng. And, nevyrthelesse, God sufferyd hym to falle, hym mercifully kepyng that he perysschyd[3] nott ne lost no tyme. And afterward God reysed hym to manyfolde more grace. And by the contrycion and the mekenesse that he had in hys lyvyng, God hath gevyn hym in hevyn manyfolde joyes, ovyr passyng that he shuld have had yf he had nott synnyd or fallen. And that this is tru God shewyth in erth with plentuous meraclys doyng[4] about his body contynually, and alle was thys to make us glad and mery in love.

Chapter 39

Synne is the sharpest scorge that ony chosyn soule may be smyttyn with, whych scorge alle to betyth man or woman and alle to brekyth hym and purgyth hym in hys owne syght so ferforth that othyr whyle he thynkyth hym selfe he is nott wurthy but, as it were, to synke in to helle tylle whan contriscion takyth hym by touchyng of the Holy Gost and turnyth the bytternesse in to hope of Goddes mercy.[5] And than begynn his woundys to heele and the soule to quycken,[6] turned in to the lyfe of holy chyrch. The Holy Gost ledyth hym to confession, wylfully to shew hys synnes nakydly and truly with grett sorow and with grett shame that he hath so defowlyd the feyer ymage of God.[7] Than undertakyth he penaunce for every synne enjoyned by his domys man[8] that is groundyd in holy chyrch by the techyng of the Holy Gost—and this is one mekenesse that gretly plesyth God—and also meekely takyth bodely sycknesse of Goddes sendyng, also sorow and shame outwardly with reprefe and despyte[9] of the worlde with alle maner of grevance and temptations that we be cast in, gostly and bodely.

Fulle preciously oure good Lorde kepyth us whan it semyth to us that we be neer forsaken and cast away for oure synne and for we se

2. Mention that in his youth.
3. Perished.
4. Doing many miracles.
5. Sin is the sharpest whip that any chosen soul may be struck with, which whip thoroughly beats down a man or a woman and thoroughly breaks him and purges him in his own sight to such a great extent that sometimes he thinks himself not worthy except, as it were, to sink into hell until contrition overtakes him by the influence of the Holy Spirit and turns the bitterness into hope of God's mercy.
6. Enliven.
7. Disfigured the fair image of God (in the soul).
8. Judge, confessor. Julian outlines the steps in the sacrament of penance: contrition or repentance for sin, confession or the telling of sins to the priest, and satisfaction or performing the penance the priest assigns.
9. Reproof and contempt.

that we have deservyd it. And because of the meekenes that we gett here by, we be reysyd fulle hygh in Goddes syght by his grace. And also whom oure Lord wylle he vysytyth of hys specialle grace with so grett contricion and also with compassion and tru longyng to God[1] that they be sodeynly delyverde of synne and of payne and taken up to blysse and made evyn with seyntes. By contryscion we be made clene, by compassion we be made redy, and by tru longyng to God we be made wurthy. Theyse be thre menys,[2] as I understode, wher by that alle soules com to hevyn, that is to sey, that have ben synners in erth and shalle be savyd.

For by theyse medycins behovyth[3] that every synnfulle soule be helyd. Though that he be helyd, hys woundys be sene before God nott as woundes, but as wurshyppes. And so on the contrary wyse, as we be ponysschyd here with sorow and with penaunce, we shall be rewardyd in hevyn by the curtesse love of oure God almyghty that wylle that none that come ther leese hys travelye[4] in any degre. For he beholdyth synne as sorow and paynes to his lovers, in whom he assignyth no blame for love.

The mede[5] that we undertake shall nott be lytylle, but it shalle be hygh, glorious, and wurshyppfulle. And so shalle alle shame turne to worschyppe and to joy. For oure curtesse Lorde wylle nott that hys servantys despeyer for ofte fallyng ne for grevous fallyng, for oure fallyng lettyth nott hym to love us. Pees and love is evyr in us, beyng and workyng, but we be nott evyr in pees and in love. But he wylle we take hede thus that he is ground of alle oure hoole lyfe in love and, ferthermore, that he is oure evyrlastyng keper and myghtely defendyth us agenst alle oure enmys that be full felle and full fers upon us.[6] And so much oure nede is the more, for we geve them occasion by oure fallyng.

Chapter 40

And this is a sovereyne frenschypp of oure curtesse Lorde, that he kepyth us so tenderly whyle we be in oure synne. And, ferthermore, he touchyth us fulle prevely and shewyth us oure synne by the swet lyght of mercy and grace. But when we se oure selfe so fowle, then we wene that God were wroth[7] with us for oure synne. Than be we steryd of the Holy Gost by contriscion in to prayer and desyer amendyng of oure selfe with alle oure myght to slake the wrath of God

1. The three metaphoric "wounds" Julian requests in chapter 2.
2. Means.
3. Medicines it is necessary.
4. Lose his toil.
5. Reward.
6. Against all our enemies that be very cruel and very fierce against us.
7. We believe that God were angry.

unto the tyme we fynde a rest in soule and softnes in consciens.[8]
And than hope we that God hath forgevyn us oure synne. And it is
true. And than shewyth oure curtesse Lorde hym selfe to the soule
merely and of fulle glad chere, with frendfully wellcomyng as if it
had ben in payne and in preson, seyeng thus, *My dere darlyng, I am
glad thou arte come to me in alle thy woe. I have evyr ben with the,
and now seest thou me lovyng, and we be onyd[9] in blysse.* Thus are
synnes forgevyn by grace and mercy and oure soule worschypfully
receyvyd in joy, lyke as it shalle be whan it comyth in to hevyn, as
ofte tymes as it comyth by the gracious werkyng of the Holy Gost
and the vertu of Cristes passion.

Here understode I verely that alle maner of thyng is made redy to
us by the grett goodnes of God so ferforth that what tyme we be oure
selfe in pees and in charyte we be verely safe. But for we mey nott
have thys in fulhed whyle we be here, therefore it befallyth us evyr
to lyve in swete prayeng and in lovely longyng with oure Lorde Jhesu.
For he longyth evyr for to bryng us to the fulhed of joy, as it is before
seyde wher he shewyth the gostly thryste.[1]

But now because of alle thys gostly comfort that is before seyde,
if any man or woman be steryd by foly to sey or to thynke, if this be
tru, than were it good for to synne to have the more mede or elles
to charge the lesse to synne, beware of this steryng. For truly, if it
come, it is untrue and of the enemy. For the same tru love that
touchyth us alle by hys blessyd comfort, the same blessyd love techyth us that we shalle hate syn only for love. And I am suer by my
awne felyng the more that ech kynde soule seeth this in the curtesse
love of our Lorde God, the lother is hym to synne[2] and the more he
is asschamyd. For if it were leyde before us, alle the payne that is in
hell and in purgatory and in erth, deed and other than synne, we
shulde rather chese[3] alle that payne than synne. For syn is so vyle
and so mekylle for to hate that it may be lycounyd[4] to no payne whych
payne is nott synne. And to me was shewed none harder helle than
synne, for a kynd soule hatyth no payne but synne. For alle is good
but syn, and nought is yvell but synne.

And whan we geve oure intent to love and meknesse by the
werkyng of mercy and grace, we be made alle feyer and clene. And
as myghty and as wyse as God is to save man, as wyllyng he is. For
Crist hym selfe is ground of alle the lawes of Cristen men, and he
taught us to do good agenst evylle. Here we may se that he is hym
selfe thys charite and doyth to us as he techyth us to do, for he wylle

8. Calmness in conscience. "Slake": diminish.
9. United, made one.
1. Spiritual thirst (see chapter 31).
2. The more hateful is sin to him.
3. Choose. "Deed": death.
4. Likened. "So mekylle": so much.

that we be lyke hym in hoolhed[5] of endlesse love to oure selfe and
to oure evyn Cristene. No more than hys love is brokyn[6] to us for
oure synne, no more wylle he that oure love be broken to oure selfe
nor to our evyn Cristen, but nakydly hate synne and endlesly love
the soule as God lovyth it. Than shulde we hate synne lyke as God
hateth it and love the soule as God loveth it. For these wordes that
God seyd is an endlesse comfort, *I kepe the fulle truly.*

Revelation XIV

Chapter 41

Affter thys oure Lorde shewed for prayer, in whych shewyng I saw
two condicions in our Lordes menyng. One is ryghtfulle prayer. A
nother is seker[7] trust. But yett oftymes oure trust is not fulle, for we
be nott suer that God heryth[8] us, as we thyngke, for oure unwurthy-
nesse and for we fele ryght nought. For we be as bareyne[9] and as
drye ofte tymes after oure prayers as we were before. And thus in
oure felyng oure foly is cause of oure wekenesse, for thus have I felt
by my selfe.

And all this broughte our Lorde sodenly to my mynde and shewed
theyse wordes and seyde, *I am grounde of thy besekyng. Furst it is my
wylle that thou have it. And sythen*[1] *I make the to wylle it. And sythen
I make the to beseke it, and thou sekyst it.*[2] *How schoulde it than be
that thou shuldyst nott have thy sekyng?* And thus in the furst reson
with the thre that folowe oure good Lorde shewyth a myghty comfort,
as it may be sene in the same wordes.

And in the furst reson there he seyeth, *And thou beseke it,* ther he
shewyth full grett plesaunce and endlesse mede that he wylle geve
us for oure besekyng. And in the vi[te] reson there he seyth, *How schuld
it than be,* this was seyde for an unpossible thyng. For it is the most
unpossible that may be that we shulde seke mercy and grace and
nott have it. For of alle thyng that oure good Lord makyth us to
beseke, hym selfe he hath ordeyned it to us from without begynnyng.
Here may we than see that oure besechyng is nott cause of the goodnesse and grace that he doyth to us, but his propyr goodnesse.[3] And
that shewed he verely in alle theyse swete wordes ther he seyeth, *I*

5. Wholeness.
6. Removed from.
7. Secure, certain.
8. Hears.
9. Barren, unproductive.
1. Then.
2. I make thee beg earnestly for it, and you seek it.
3. Julian asserts that God's freely given grace initiates prayer rather than that prayer earns
   grace.

am ground. And our good Lorde wylle that thys be knowen of his lovers in erth. And the more that we know, the more shalle we besech, if it be wysely take, and so is our Lordes menyng.

Besechyng is a trew and gracious lestyng wylle of the soule, onyd[4] and fastenyd in to the wylle of oure Lorde by the swet prevy werkyng of the Holy Gost. Oure Lorde hym selfe, he is the furst receyvoure[5] of our prayer as to my syght, and he takyth it full thankefully. And hyghly enjoyeng, he sendeth it uppe above and setteth it in tresure wher it shall nevyr peryssch. It is ther before God with all hys holy seyntes, contynually receyvyd, evyr spedyng oure nedys.[6] And whan we shalle undertak oure blysse, it shall be gevyn us for a degre of joy with endlesse wurschyppfulle thankyng of hym.

Ful glad and mery is oure Lord of oure prayer, and he lokyth ther after, and he wyll have it. For with his grace it makyth us lyke to hym selfe in condescion as we be in kynde,[7] and so is his blessyd wylle. For he seyth thus, *Pray interly*[8] *inwardly. Thoughe the thyngke it savour the nott, yett it is profytable inowgh, though thou fele it nowght. Pray interly inwardly, though thou fele nought, though thou se nought, yea, though thou thynk thou myght nott. For in dryenesse and barnesse, in sicknesse and in febelnes, than is thy prayer fulle plesaunt to me, though thou thynk it saver the nott but lytylle. And so is all thy lyvyng prayer in my syght.*

For the mede and the endelesse thanke that he wylle geve us, ther for he is covetous[9] to have us prayeng contynually in his syght. God acceptyth the good wylle and the traveyl of his servuantes, how so ever we felle. Wherfore it plesyth hym that we werke in prayer and in good lyvyng by his helpe and his grace, resonable with discrecion kepyng oure myghtys to hym[1] tyll whan we have hym that we seke in fulhede of joy that is Jhesu. And that shewed he in the **xv** revelation wher he seyth, *Thou shalt have me to thy mede.*

Also to prayer longyth thankyng. Thankyng is a true inward knowyng, with grett reverence and lovely drede turnyng oure selfe with alle oure myghtes in to the werkyng that oure Lorde steryd us to, enjoyeng and thankyng inwardly. And some tyme for plenteuousnes it brekyth out with voyce and sey, "Good Lorde, graunt mercy, blessyd mott thou be." And some tyme whan the harte is dry and felyth

---

4. United, made one. "Lestyng": lasting.
5. Receiver.
6. Ever satisfying our needs or desires.
7. For with his grace it (prayer) makes us like him (our Lord) in condition or state of being as we are in nature. The image of God resides in the higher reason or substance of the soul and renders humans like God by nature, but this image is deformed by sin. Grace and prayer restore the soul to its original condition of likeness to God.
8. Devoutly.
9. Ardently desirous.
1. Reasonable with good judgment, keeping our faculties, powers to him.

nought, or ellys by temptacion of oure enemy, than it is drevyn[2] by reson and by grace to cry up on oure Lorde with voyce rehersyng his blessyd passion and his grett goodnes. And so the vertu of oure Lordes worde turnyth in to the soule, and quyckynnyth the hart, and entryth[3] by hys grace in to tru werkyng, and makyth it to pray fulle blessydfully and truly to enjoy in oure Lorde. It is a fulle lovely thangkyng in his syght.

Chapter 42

Owre Lorde wylle that we have tru understondyng, and namely, in thre thynges that longyth to oure prayer. The furst is by whom and howe that oure prayer spryngyth. By whom he shewyth whan he seyth, *I am grounde*; and how, by hys goodnesse, for he seyth, *Furst it is my wylle*. For the seconde, in what maner and how that we shulde use oure prayers. And that is that oure wylle be turned in to the wylle of oure Lorde enjoyeng. And so menyth he whan he seyeth, *I make the to wylle it*. For the thurde, that we know the fruyt and the ende of oure prayer, that is, to be onyd and lyke to oure Lorde in althyng. And to this menyng and for thys ende was alle thys lovely lesson shewed. And he wylle helpe us, and he shalle make it so, as he seyth hym selfe, blessyd mot he be.

For this is oure Lordes wylle, that oure prayer and oure trust be both a lyke large.[4] For if we trust nott, as mekyll[5] as we praye, we do nott fulle worshyppe to oure Lorde in oure prayer. And also we tary[6] and payne oure selfe. And the cause is, as I beleve, for we know not truly that oure Lorde is grounde in whom that oure prayer spryngyth, and also that we know nott that it is gevyn us by grace of hys love. For yf we knew thys, it wolde make us to truste to have of oure Lordes gefte alle that we desyer. For I am suer that no man askyth mercy and grace with tru menyng but yf mercy and grace be furst gevyn to hym. But somtyme it comyth to oure mynde that we have prayde long tyme and yett it thyngkyth us that we have nott oure askyng. But here fore shulde we nott be hevy, for I am suer by oure Lordes menyng that eyther we a byde a better tyme or more grace or a beter gyfte.

He wylle that we have true knowyng in hym selfe that he is beyng.[7] And in thys knowyng he wylle that oure understandyng be groundyd with alle oure myghtes and alle oure intent and alle our menyng. And in this grounde he wylle that we take oure stede[8] and oure dwel-

2. Drawn.
3. Enters. "Quyckynnyth": enlivens.
4. Alike great.
5. Much.
6. Worry.
7. Being.
8. Place.

lyng. And by the gracious lyght of hym selfe he wylle that we have understandyng of thre thynges that folow. The furst is our noble and excelent makyng; the seconde, oure precious and derwurthy agayne beyng;[9] the thyrde, althyng that he hath made beneth us to serve us and for oure love kepyth it. Than menyth he thus, as if he seyde, *Beholde and se that I have done alle thys before thy prayer, and now thou arte and prayest me.* And thus he menyth that it longyth to us to wytt that the grettest dedys be done as holy chyrch techyth.

And in the beholdyng of thys with thankyng we ow to pray fore the dede that is now in doyng, and that is, that he ruwle us and gyde us[1] to his wurshyppe in this lyfe and bryng us to hys blysse. And therefore he hath done alle. Than menyth he thus, that we se that he doth it, and we pray therfore. For that one is nott inow. For yf we pray and se nott that he doitt, it makyth us hevy and doughtfulle,[2] and that is nott his wurschyppe. And yf we se that he doth it, and we pray nott, we do nott oure dewty.[3] And so may it nott be, that is to sey, so is it nott in his beholdyng. But to se that he doyth it and to pray forthwithalle, so is he worschyppyd and we sped.[4] Althyng that oure Lorde hath ordeyned to do, it is his wylle that we pray therfore eyther in specialle or in generalle. And the joy and the blysse that is to hym, and the thanke and the wurschyppe that we shalle have therfore, it passyth the understandyng of all creatures in this life as to my syght.

For prayer is a ryghtwys[5] understandyng of that fulhed of joy that is for to come with tru longyng and very trust. Saworyng or seyng oure blysse that we be ordeyned to kyndely makyth us to longe. Trew understondyng and love with swete menyng in[6] oure Savyoure graciously makyth us to trust. And thus have we of kynde to long and of grace to trust. And in these two werkynges oure Lord beholdyth us contynually. For it is our dewty, and hys goodnes may no lesse assyne in us that longyth to us to do oure diligence there to.[7] And when we do it, yett shall us thynke that it is nought. And true it is. But do we as we may and mekly aske mercy and grace, and alle that us feylyth[8] we shalle it fynde in hym. And thus menyth he there he seyth, *I am the grounde of thy besechyng.* And thus in theyse blessydfulle wordes with the shewyng I saw a fulle ovyrcomyng agaynst alle oure wyckydnesse and alle oure doutfull dredys.

9. Honorable redemption.
1. Rule us and guide us. "Ow": ought.
2. Doubtful, uncertain.
3. Duty.
4. Pray immediately, so is he honored and we benefited.
5. Righteous.
6. Savoring or seeing our bliss that we are naturally ordained for makes us long. True understanding and love with sweet remembrance of.
7. May assign to us no less than what belongs to us to do with constant and earnest effort.
8. All that fails us.

Chapter 43

Prayer onyth the soule to God. For though the soule be evyr lyke to God in kynde and in substaunce restoryd by grace, it is ofte unlike in condescion by synne of mannes perty.[9] Than is prayer a wytnesse that the soule wylle as God wyll, and comfortyth the conscience, and ablyth man to grace.[1] And thus he techyth us to pray and myghtyly to trust that we shalle have it. For he beholdyth us in love and wylle make us perteyner[2] of his good wylle and dede. And therfore he steryth us to pray that that lykyth hym to do, for whych prayer and good wylle that we have of hys gyfte he wylle rewarde us and geve us endlesse mede. And thys was shewyd in this worde, *And thou besekyst it.*

In this worde God shewyd so grett plesaunce and so grett lykyng as he were much beholdyng to us for ech good dede that we do, and yet it is he that doth it. And for that we besech hym myghtly to do that thyng that hym lykyth, as yf he seyd, *What myght thou plese me more then to besech myghtly, wysely, and wylfully to do that thyng that I wyll have doen?* And thus the soule by prayer is acordyd with God.

But whan oure curtesse Lorde of his speciall grace shewyth hym selfe to oure soule, we have that we desyer. And then we se nott for the tyme what we shulde more pray,[3] but all oure entent with alle oure myghtys is sett hoole in to the beholdyng of hym. And this is an high, unperceyvable[4] prayer as to my syghte. For alle the cause wherfore we pray is to be onyd in to the syght and the beholdyng of him to whom we pray, mervelously enjoyeng with reverent drede and so grett swettnesse and delyghte in hym that we can pray ryght nought but as he steryth us for the tyme.

And welle I wott the more the soule seeth of God, the more she desyeryth hym by grace. But whan we se hym nott so, than fele we nede and cause to praye for feylyng and for unablynes[5] of oure selfe to Jhesu. For whan a soule is temptyd, troblyde, and lefte to her selfe by her unrest, then is it tyme to praye to make her selfe suppull and buxom[6] to God. But she by no manner of prayer makyth God suppell to hym, for he is evyr oon lyke in love.[7] And thus I saw that what tyme we se nede wherfore we praye, then our Lord God folowyth us,

---

9. For although the soul is always like God in nature and in substance restored by grace, it is often unlike him in condition because of sin on man's part.
1. Enables, makes man fit for grace.
2. Partner.
3. What more we should pray for.
4. Imperceptible, not known by the senses.
5. Inability.
6. Compliant and obedient.
7. But she (the soul) by no manner of prayer makes God compliant to him (the supplicant), for he (God) is ever one and the same in love. Although Julian uses the feminine pronoun *she* for the soul to agree with the Latin *anima,* she follows the convention of using the masculine pronoun for the individual.

helpyng our desyre. And whan we of his speciall grace pleynly beholde hym, seyeng none other nedys,[8] then we folowe hym, and he drawyth us to hym by love. For I saw and felt that his mervelous and his fulsom[9] goodnesse fulfyllyth all oure myghtys.

And ther with I saw that hys contynuall werkyng in alle maner thynges is done so godly, so wysely, and so myghtely that it ovyrpassyth alle oure ymagynyng and alle that we can mene or thynke. And than we can do no more but beholde hym, and enjoye with an high, myghty desyer to be alle onyd in to hym, and entende to his motion, and enjoy in his lovyng, and delyghte in his goodnesse.

And thus shalle we with his swete grace in our owne meke continuall prayer come in to hym now in this lyfe by many prevy touchynges of swete, gostly syghtes and felynges mesuryd to us as oure sympylhed may bere it.[1] And this is wrought and shall be by the grace of the Holy Gost so long tyll we shall dye in longyng for love. And than shall we alle come in to oure Lorde, oure selfe clerely knowyng and God fulsomly having. And we endlesly be alle hyd in God, verely seyeng and fulsomly felyng, and hym gostely heryng, and hym delectably smellyng, and hym swetly swelwyng.[2] And ther shall we se God face to face, homely and fulsomly. The creature that is made shall see and endlesly beholde God whych is the maker. For thus may no man se God and leve aftyr, that is to sey, in this dedely lyffe.[3] But whan he of his speciall grace wyll shewe hym here, he strengthyth the creature a bovyn the selfe, and he mesuryth the shewyng aftyr his awne wylle, and it is profytable for the tym.

Chapter 44

God shewed in all the revelations ofte tymes that man werkyth evyr more his wylle and his wurschyppe duryngly without styntyng.[4] And what thys werkyng is was shewed in the **furst**, and that in a mervelous grounde. For it was shewed in the werkyng of the blessydfull soule of our Lady Sent Mary by truth and wysedom, and how, I hope by the grace of the Holy Gost, I shall sey as I saw.

Truth seeth God and wisdom beholdyth God. And of theyse two comyth the thurde, and that is a mervelous delyght in God whych is love. Where truth and wysdom is verely, there is love verely, comyng of them both and alle of Goddes makyng. For God is endlesse sovereyne truth, endelesse sovereyne wysdom, endelesse sovereyne love

8. Seeing no other needs.
9. Abundant.
1. Secret contacts of sweet, spiritual sights and feelings measured to us as our simpleness may bear it.
2. Truly seeing and fully feeling, and spiritually hearing him, and delightfully smelling him, and sweetly tasting him. These are the five spiritual senses.
3. Mortal life.
4. Continuously without stopping.

unmade. And a man's soule is a creature in God whych hath the same propertes made. And evyr more it doyth that it was made for: it seeth God, and it beholdyth God, and it lovyth God. Wherfore God enjoyeth in the creature and the creature in God, endelesly merve-lyng. In whych mervelyng he seeth his God, hys Lorde, hys maker, so hye, so grett, and so good in regarde of hym that is made that unnethys the creature semyth ought to the selfe.[5] But the bryghtnes and clernesse of truth and wysedome makyth hym to see and to know that he is made for love, in whych love God endlesly kepyth hym.

Chapter 45

God demyth us upon oure kyndely substance, whych is evyr kepte one in hym,[6] hole and safe without ende. And this dome is of his ryghtfulhede. And man demyth uppon oure chaungeable sensu-alyte,[7] whych semyth now oone and now a nother, after that it takyth of the partyes and shewed outward. And this dome is medelyd,[8] for som tyme it is good and esy, and somtyme it is hard and grevous. And in as moch as it is good and esy, it longyth to the ryghtfulnes. And in as moch as it is hard and grevous, oure good Lorde Jhesu reformyth it by mercy and grace thorow vertu of his blessyd passion and so bringyth in to the ryghtfulnesse. And though thyse two be thus acordyd and oonyd, yytt it shall be knowen both in hevyn with-out ende.

The furst dome, whych is of Goddes ryghtfulnes, and that is of his owne hygh, endlesse love, and that is that feyer, swete dome that was shewed in alle the feyer revelation in whych I saw hym assignys to us no maner of blame. And though theyse were swete and delec-table, yytt only in the beholdyng of this I culde nott be fulle esyd. And that was for the dome of holy chyrch, whych I had before under-stondyng and was contynually in my syght. And therfore by this dome me thought that me behovyth nedys to[9] know my selfe a synner. And by the same dome I understode that synners be sometyme wurthy blame and wrath, and theyse two culde I nott see in God. And ther-fore my advyce[1] and desyer was more than I can or may telle. For the hygher dome God shewed hym selfe in the same tyme, and ther-fore we behovyd nedys to take it. And the lower dome was lernyd me before tyme in holy chyrche, and therfore I myght nott by no weye leve the lower dome.

---

5. Scarcely the creature seems aught or anything to the self.
6. God judges us according to our natural substance (the higher part of the soul), which is ever kept one in him. In Revelation XIV, chapters 53–56, Julian explains the ontological union between God and humankind.
7. Changeable sensuality (the lower part of the soul).
8. Mixed.
9. It is necessary to me, I must.
1. Deliberation.

Then was this my desyer, that I myght se in God in what manner that the dome of holy chyrch here in erth is tru in his syght, and howe it longyth to me verely to know it, where by they myght both be savyd,[2] so as it ware wurschypfulle to God and ryght wey to me. And to alle this I nee had no nother answere but a mervelous example of a lorde and of a servaunt, as I shall sey after, and that full mystely shewed.[3] And yytt I stode in desyer and wylle in to my lyvys ende that I myght by grace know theyse ii domys as it longyth to me. For alle hevynly thynges and alle erthely thynges that long to hevyn be comprehendyd in theyse ii domys. And the more knowyng and understondyng by the gracious ledyng of the Holy Gost that we have of these ii domes, the more we shalle see and know oure felynges. And evyr the more that we see them, the more kyndly by grace we shall long to be fulfyllyd of endlesse joy and blysse, for we be made ther to. And oure kyndely substaunce is now blessydfulle in God, and hath bene sythen it was made, and shalle be withoute ende.

Chapter 46

But oure passyng lyvyng that we have here in oure sensualyte[4] knowyth nott what oure selfe is but in our feyth. And whan we know and see verely and clerely what oure selfe is, than shalle we verely and clerly see and know oure Lorde God in fulhed of joye. And therfore it behovyth nedys to be that the nerer we be oure blysse, the more we shall long, and that both by kynde and by grace. We may have knowyng of oure selfe in this lyfe by contynuant helpe and vertu of oure hygh kynd, in which knowyng we may encrese and wax by fortheryng and spedyng[5] of mercy and grace. But we may nevyr fulle know oure selfe in to the last poynt, in which poynte thys passyng life and alle manner of woo and payne shalle have an ende. And therfore it longyth properly to us both by kynde and by grace to long and desyer with alle oure myghtes to know oure selfe, in whych full knowyng we shall verely and clerely know oure God in fulhede of endlesse joy.

And yytt in alle this tyme, fro the begynnyng to the ende, I had ii manner of beholdinges. That one was endlesse, countynuant love with suernesse of kepyng and blysful salvacion, for of this was all the shewyng. That othyr was the comyn techyng of holy chyrch, of whych I was befor enformyd and groundyd and wylfully havyng in use and

2. Confirmed.
3. I had no other answer except a marvelous example of a lord and of a servant, as I shall say afterwards, and that very obscurely and figuratively showed. Julian recounts this showing and the understanding of it she achieved after nearly twenty years of reflection in chapter 51.
4. Sensuality. Julian's term for the lower part of the soul concerned with the body and temporal matters.
5. Furthering and helping. "Contynuant": continuing.

in understondyng. And the beholdyng of thys cam nott from me, for by the shewyng I was nott steryd nor led ther fro in no manner poynt. But I had ther in techyng to love it and lyke it, wher by I myght with the helpe of oure Lorde and his grace encrese and ryse to more hevynly knowyng and hyer lovyng.

And thus in alle this beholdyng me thought it behovyd nedys to se and to know that we be synners and do many evylles that we oughte to leve, and leve many good dedys undone that we oughte to do, wherfore we deserve payne, blame, and wrath. And nott withstondyng alle this, I saw verely that oure Lorde was nevyr wroth nor nevyr shall. For he is God, he is good, he is truth, he is love, he is pees; and hys myght, hys wysdom, hys charyte, and his unyte sufferyth hym nott to be wroth. For I saw truly that it is agaynst the propyrte of hys myght to be wroth, and agaynst the properte of hys wysdom, and agaynst the propyrte of hys goodnes. God is that goodnesse that may nott be wroth, for God is nott but goodnes. Oure soule is onyd to hym, unchaungeable goodnesse. And betwen God and oure soule is neyther wrath nor forgevenesse in hys syght. For oure soule is so fulsomly onyd to God of hys owne goodnesse that betwene God and oure soule may be ryght nought.

And to this understondyng was the soule led by love and drawyn by myght in every shewyng. That it is thus, oure good Lorde shewed; and how it is thus, verely of his grett goodnesse; and that he wylle we desyer to wytt, that is to sey, as it longyth to his creature to wytte it. For all thyng that the symple soule understode, God wyll that it be shewed and knowyn. For those thynges that he wylle have prevy, myghtely and wysely hym selfe hydyth them for love. For I saw in the same shewyng that moch pryvete is hyd whych may nevyr be knowen in to the tyme that God of hys goodnes hath made us wurthy to se it. And ther with I am well apayde, abydyng oure Lord's wylle in this hye marveyle. And now I yelde me to my modyr holy chyrch as a sympyll chylde owyth.[6]

Chapter 47

Two poyntes longyn to our soule by dett.[7] One is that we reverently marveyle. That othyr is that we meekly suffer, evyr enjoyeng in God.[8] For he wyll that we know that we shalle in short tyme se clerely in hym selfe all that we desyer. And not withstondyng all thys, I behelde and merveylyd gretly what is the mercy and forgevenesse of God. For by the techyng that I had before, I understode that the mercy of God shalle be forgevenesse of hys wrath after the tyme that we have

6. I yield myself to my mother holy church as a simple child ought. The metaphor of the church as a mother is a commonplace.
7. Debt or obligation.
8. Ever rejoicing in God.

synned. For me thought that to a soule whose menyng and desyer is to love, that the wrath of God were harder than ony other payne. And therefore I toke that the forgevenesse of his wrath shulde be one of the pryncypall poyntes of his mercy. But for oughte[9] that I myght beholde and desyer, I culde nott see this poynt in all the shewyng. But how I saw and understode of the workyng of mercy I shall sey som dele[1] as God wyll gyve me grace.

I understode thus: Man is chaungeabyll in this lyfe, and by sympyl-nesse and uncunnyng[2] fallyth in to synne. He is unmyghty and unwyse of hym selfe, and also his wyll is ovyr leyde[3] in thys tyme he is in tempest and in sorow and woe. And the cause is blynnes,[4] for he seeth not God. For yf he saw God contynually, he shulde have no myschevous felyng ne no maner steryng, no sorowyng that servyth to synne.

Thus saw I and felt in the same tyme, and me thowght that the syght and the felyng was hye and plentyuous and gracious in regarde that oure commun felyng is in this lyfe. But yett me thought it was but lowe and smalle in regard of the grett desyer that the soule hath to se God. For I felt in me fyve maner of werkynges, whych be theyse: enjoyeng, mornyng, desyer, drede, and trew hope. Enjoyeng, for God gave me knowyng and understondyng that it was hym selfe that I sawe. Mornyng, and that was for felyng. Desyer, that was that I myght se hym evyr more and more, understondyng and knowyng that we shalle nevyr have fulle rest tylle we se hym clerly and verely in hevyn. Drede was for it semyd to me in alle that tyme that syght shulde feyle, and I to be lefte to my selfe. Trew hope was in the endlesse love that I saw, that I shulde be kepte by hys mercy and brought to the blysse.

And the joyng in hys syght with this trew hope of hys mercyfull kepyng made me to have felyng and comfort, so that mornyng and drede were nott grettly paynfull. And yet in all thys I behelde in the shewyng of God that this maner syght of hym may not be contynuant in this life, and that for his owne wurschyppe and for encrese of oure endlesse joy. And therfore we fayle oftymes of the syght of hym, and anon[5] we falle in to oure selfe. And than fynde we felyng of ryght nowght but the contraryous that is in oure selfe, and that of the olde rote of oure furst synne with all that folowyth of oure owne con-tynuance.[6] And in this we be traveyled and temptyd with felyng of

9. Aught, anything.
1. To some extent.
2. Ignorance.
3. Overcome.
4. Blindness.
5. At once.
6. Contrariness that is in our self and that of the old root of our first sin (original sin) with all that follows of our own continuance (in personal sin).

synne and of payne in many dyverse maner, gostely and bodely, as it is knowyn to us in this lyfe.

Chapter 48

But oure good Lorde the Holy Gost, whych is endlesse lyfe dwellyng in oure soule, full truly kepyth us, and werketh ther in a pees, and bryngyth it to ees by grace, and makyth it buxom,[7] and accordyth it to God. And this is the mercy and the wey that oure good Lord contynually ledyth us in as longe as we be in this lyfe whych is chaungeable. For I saw no wrath but on mannes perty, and that forgevyth he in us. For wrath is nott elles but a frowerdnes and a contraryousnes[8] to pees and to love. And eyther it comyth of feylyng of might, or of feylyng of wysdom, or of feylyng of goodnesse, whych feylyng is nott in God, but it is in oure party. For we by synne and wrechydnesse have in us a wrath and a contynuant contraryousnes to pees and to love. And that shewed he full ofte in his lovely chere of ruth and pytte.

For the ground of mercy is in love, and the werkyng of mercy is oure kepyng in love. And this was shewed in such a manner that I culde not perceyve of the properte of mercy other wyse but as it were all love in love. That is to sey, as to my syght mercy is a swete gracious werkyng in love medlyd[9] with plentuous pytte. For mercy werkyth us kepyng, and mercy werkyth turnyng to us all thyng to good. Mercy for love sufferyth us to feyle by mesure.[1] And in as moch as we fayle, in so moch we falle. And in as much as we falle, in so moch we dye. For us behovyth nedys to dye in as moch as we fayle syghte and felyng of God that is oure lyfe. Oure faylyng is dredfulle, oure fallyng is shamfull, and oure dyeng is sorowfull.

But yet in all this the swet eye of pytte and of love departeth nevyr from us, ne the werkyng of mercy cesyth[2] nott. For I behelde the properte of mercy, and I behelde the properte of grace, whych have ii maner of workyng in one love. Mercy is a pyttefull properte whych longyth to moderhode in tender love. And grace is a wurshypfull properte whych longyth to ryall lordschyppe in the same love. Mercy werkyth kypyng, sufferyng, quyckyng, and helyng; and alle is of tendyrnesse of love. And grace werkyth with mercy, reysyng, rewarding, endlesly ovyr passyng that oure lovyng and our traveyle deservyth, spredyng abrode and shewyng the hye plentuousnesse, largesse of Goddes ryall lordschyppe in his mervelouse curtesy.[3] And this is

7. Obedient.
8. Obstinacy and contrariness.
9. Combined, mixed.
1. To a limited extent, in moderation.
2. Ceases.
3. The high plentitude, generosity of God's royal lordship in his marvelous courtesy. "Reysyng": raising.

of the habundaunce[4] of love, for grace werkyth oure dredfull faylyng in to plentuouse and endlesse solace. And grace werkyth oure shamefull fallyng in to hye, wurschyppefull rysyng. And grace werkyth oure sorowfull dyeng in to holy, blyssyd lyffe.

For I saw full truly that evyr as oure contraryousnes werkyth to us here in erth payne, shame, and sorow, ryght so, on the contrary wyse, grace werkyth to us in hevyn solace, wurschyp, and blysse, ovyr passyng so ferforth[5] that when we come uppe and receyve that swete reward whych grace hath wrought to us there, we shall thanke and blysse oure Lorde, endlessly enjoyeng that evyr we sufferyd woo. And that shalle be for a properte of blessyd love that we shalle know in God, whych we myght nevyr have knowen withoute wo goyng before. And whan I saw all thys, me behovevyd nedys to graunt that the mercy of God and the forgyvenesse slaketh and wastyth[6] oure wrath.

Chapter 49

For it was an hye marveyle to the soule, whych was contynuantly shewed in alle and with grett diligence beholdyng, that oure Lorde God as a neynst[7] hym selfe may not forgeve, for he may not be wroth. It were unpossible. For this was shewed: that oure lyfe is alle grounded and rotyd[8] in love, and without love we may nott lyve. And therfor to the soule that of his speciall grace seeth so ferforth of the hye,[9] marvelous goodnesse of God that we be endlesly onyd to hym in love, it is the most unpossible that may be that God shulde be wrath.

For wrath and frenschyppe[1] be two contrarioese. For he that wastyth and dystroyeth oure wrath and makyth us meke and mylde, it behovyth us nedys to beleve that he be evyr in one love, meke and mylde, whych is contrary to wrath. For I saw full truly that where oure Lorde aperyth, pees is takyn and wrath hath no stede.[2] For I saw no manner of wrath in God, neyther for shorte tyme nor for long. For truly, as to my syght, yf God myght be wroth a whyle, we shuld neyther have lyfe ne stede ne beyng. For as verely as we have oure beyng of the endlesse myght of God, and of the endlesse wysdom, and of the endlesse goodnesse, also verely we have oure kepyng in the endles myght of God, in the endlesse wysdom, and in the endlesse goodnesse. For thowe we fele in us wrath, debate, and

---

4. Abundance.
5. To such an extent.
6. Diminishes and consumes.
7. With respect to.
8. Rooted.
9. To the extent of the high.
1. Friendship.
2. Place.

stryfe, yett we be all mercyfully beclosyd in the myldehed of God, and in his mekehed, in his benyngnite, and in his buxsomnesse.[3]

For I saw full truly that alle oure endlesse frenschypp, oure stede, our lyfe, and oure beyng is in God. For that same endlesse goodnesse that kepyth us whan we synne that we peryssch nott, that same endlesse goodnesse contynually tretyth[4] in us a pees agaynst oure wrath and our contraryouse fallyng and makyth us to see oure nede with a true drede myghtely to seke unto God to have forgyvenesse with a gracious desyer of oure salvacyon. For we may nott be blesfully savyd tyll we be verely in pees and in love, for that is oure salvation.

And though we be wrath and the contraryousnes that is in us be nowe in tribulacion, deseses, and woo, as fallyng in to oure blyndnesse and oure pronyte,[5] yett be we suer and safe by the mercyfull kepyng of God that we perysch nott. But we be nott blyssefully safe in havyng of oure endlesse joye tyll we be all in pees and in love, that is to sey, full plesyd with God and with alle his werkes and with alle his domys, and lovyng and plesabyll[6] with oure selfe and with oure evyn Cristen and with alle that God lovyth, as love lykyth. And this doth Goddes goodnes in us. Thus saw I that God is our very peas, and he is oure suer keper when we be oure selfe at unpeas, and he contynually werkyth to bryng us into endlesse peas. And thus when by the werkyng of mercy and grace we be made meke and mylde, than be we full safe.

Sodenly is the soule onyd to God when she is truly peesyd[7] in her selfe, for in hym is founde no wrath. And thus I saw whan we be alle in peas and in love, we fynde no contraryousnes in no manner of lettyng.[8] And that contraryousnes whych is now in us oure Lorde God of hys goodnes makyth it to us fulle profytable. For contraryousnes is cause of alle oure tribulation and alle oure woo. And oure Lorde Jhesu takyth them and sendyth them uppe to hevyn, and then they ar made more swete and delectable than hart may thyngke or tonge can tell. And when we come theder[9] we shalle fynde them redy, alle turnyd in to very feyernesse and endlesse wurschype. Thus is God oure stedfast ground and shall be oure full blysse and make us unchaungeable as he is when we be ther.

Chapter 50

And in this dedely lyfe mercy and forgevenesse is oure way that evyr more ledyth us to grace. And by the tempest and the sorow that

3. In his kindness, and in his graciousness.
4. Negotiates, entreats.
5. Inclination. "Be wrath": are angry.
6. Capable of being pleased.
7. Reconciled.
8. Hindering.
9. Thither, there.

we fall in on oure perty, we be ofte deed as to mannes dome in erth. But in the syght of God the soule that shall be safe was nevyr deed, ne nevyr shall. But yet here I wondryde and merveylyd with alle the dylygence of my soule, menyng thus, "Goode Lorde, I see the that thou arte very truth, and I know truly that we syn grevously all day and be moch blame wurthy. And I may neyther leve the knowyng of this sooth, nor I se nott the shewyng to us no manner of blame. How may this be?"

For I knew be the comyn techyng of holy church and by my owne felyng that the blame of oure synnes contynually hangyth uppon us, fro the furst man in to the tyme that we come uppe in to hevyn. Then was this my merveyle, that I saw oure Lorde God shewyng to us no more blame then if we were as clene and as holy as angelis be in hevyn. And betwene theyse two contraryes my reson was grettly traveyled by my blyndnes and culde have no rest for drede that his blessed presens[1] shulde passe fro my syght, and I to be lefte in unknowyng how he beholde us in oure synne. For eyther me behovyd to se in God that synne were alle done awey, or els me behovyd to see in God how he seeth it, wher by I myght truly know how it longyth to me to see synne and the manner of oure blame.

My longyng endured, hym contynuantly beholdyng, and yet I culde have no pacience for grett feer and perplexite, thyngkyng, "Yf I take it thus, that we be no synners nor no blame wurthy, it semyth as I shulde erre and faile of knowyng of this soth.[2] And yf it be tru that we be synners and blame wurthy, good Lorde, how may it than be that I can nott see this truth in the, whych arte my God, my maker in whom I desyer to se alle truth?"

For thre poyntes make me hardy[3] to aske it. The furst is for it is so lowe athyng, for if it were an hye, I shulde be adred. The secunde is that it is so comon, for if it were specyall and prevy, also I shulde be adred.[4] The thyrde is that it nedyth me to wytt, as me thyngkyth, if I shall lyve here, for knowyng of good and evyll, wher by I may be reson and by grace the more deperte them a sonder[5] and love goodnesse and hate evyll as holy chyrch techyth. I cryde inwardly with all my myght, sekyng in to God for helpe, menyng thus, "A, Lorde Jhesu, kyng of blysse, how shall I be esyde? Who shall tell me and tech me that me nedyth to wytt, if I may nott at this tyme se it in the?"

1. Presence.
2. Truth.
3. Bold.
4. Afraid.
5. Separate them apart.

Chapter 51

And then oure curteyse Lorde answeryd in shewyng full mystely[6] by a wonderfull example of a lorde that hath a servaunt and gave me syght to my understandyng of both. Whych syght was shewed double[7] in the lorde, and the syght was shewed double in the servaunt. That one perty was shewed gostly in bodely lycknesse. That other perty was shewed more gostly withoute bodely lycknes. For the furst thus I sawe: two persons in bodely lycknesse, that is to sey, a lorde and a servaunt. And therwith God gave me gostly understandyng. The lorde syttyth solempnely in rest and in pees. The servaunt stondyth before his lorde, reverently redy to do his lordes wylle. The lorde lokyth uppon his servaunt full lovely and swetly and mekely. He sendyth hym in to a certeyne place to do his wyll. The servaunt nott onely he goyth, but sodenly he stertyth and rynnyth in grett hast[8] for love to do his lordes wylle. And anon he fallyth in a slade[9] and takyth ful grett sorow. And than he gronyth and monyth and wallowyth and wryeth,[1] but he may nott ryse nor helpe hym selfe by no manner of weye.

And of all this the most myschefe that I saw hym in was feylyng of comfort, for he culde nott turne his face to loke uppe on his lovyng lorde, whych was to hym full nere, in whom is full comfort. But as a man that was full febyll and unwyse for the tyme, he entendyd[2] to his felyng and enduryng in woo, in whych woo he sufferyd vii grett paynes. The furst was the soore brosyng[3] that he toke in his fallyng, whych was to hym moch payne. The seconde was the hevynesse of his body. The thyrde was fybylnesse that folowyth of theyse two. The iiii was that he was blyndyd in his reson and stonyd[4] in his mynde so ferforth that allmost he had forgeten his owne love. The v was that he myght nott ryse. The vi was payne most mervelous to me, and that was that he leye aloone. I lokyd alle about and behelde, and ferre ne nere ne hye ne lowe I saw to hym no helpe.[5] The vii[th] was that the place whych he ley in was alang, harde, and grevous.[6]

I merveyled how this servaunt myght thus mekely suffer all this woo. And I behelde with avysement to wytt yf I culde perceyve in

---

6. Very obscurely and figuratively.
7. Showed double. I.e., spiritually with a bodily likeness and spiritually without a bodily likeness. The showings Julian describes in Revelation XIV have little or no sensory manifestation.
8. Starts and runs in great haste.
9. At once he falls into a valley.
1. Groans and moans and wallows and twists.
2. Paid attention to.
3. Painful bruising.
4. Stunned, bewildered.
5. Neither far nor near, high nor low saw I any help for him.
6. Lonely, hard, and oppressive.

hym ony defaughte,[7] or yf the lorde shuld assigne in hym ony maner of blame. And verely there was none seen, for oonly hys good wyll and his grett desyer was cause of his fallyng. And he was as unlothfull[8] and as good inwardly as he was when he stode before his lorde redy to do his wylle.

And ryght thus contynuantly his loveyng lorde full tenderly beholdyth hym. And now wyth a doubyll chere: oone owtwarde, full mekly and myldely with grett rewth and pytte, and this was of the furst; another inwarde, more gostly, and this was shewed with a ledyng of my understandyng in to the lorde, in restoryng whych[9] I saw hym hyely enjoy for the wurschypfull restyng and noble that he wyll and shall bryng his servaunt to by his plentuous grace. And this was of that other shewyng. And now was my understandyng ledde ageyne in to the furst, both kepyng in mynd.

Than seyde this curteyse lorde in his menyng, "Lo, my belovevyd servant, what harme and dysses he hath had and takyn in my servys for my love, yea, and for his good wylle. Is it nott reson that I reward hym his frey and his drede, his hurt and his mayme[1] and alle his woo? And nott only this, but fallyth it nott to me to geve hym a gyfte that be better to hym and more wurschypfull than his owne hele[2] shuld have bene? And ells me thyngkyth I dyd hym no grace."[3] And in this an inwarde goostely shewyng of the lordes menyng descendyd in to my soule, in whych I saw that it behovyth nedys to be, standyng his grett goodnes and his owne wurschyppe, that his deerworthy servaunt, whych he lovyd so moch, shulde be hyely and blessydfully rewardyd withoute end, above that he shulde have be yf he had nott fallen, yea, and so ferforth that his fallyng and alle his wo that he hath takyn there by shalle be turnyd in to the hye ovyrpassyng wurschyppe and endlesse blesse.[4]

And at this poynt the shewyng of the example vanysschyd, and oure good Lorde ledde forth my understandyng in syght and in shewyng of the revelacion to the ende. But nott withstandyng all thys forthledyng, the marveylyng of the example went nevyr fro me, for me thoght it was gevyn me for answere to my desyer. And yet culde I nott take there in full understandyng to my ees in that tyme. For in the servaunt that was shewed for Adam, as I shall sey, I sawe many dyverse properteys that myght by no manner be derecte to syngell Adam.[5]

7. And I beheld with due consideration to know if I could perceive in him any default, failure.
8. Undeserving of hate.
9. In restoring which (his servant). "Chere": facial expression.
1. Is it not reasonable that I reward him for his fright and his dread, his hurt and his injury?
2. Health.
3. Otherwise I think I did him no favor.
4. High, surpassing honor and endless bliss. Julian expresses the view that Adam's fall was fortunate (*felix culpa*) because it resulted in the greater gift of redemption.
5. Be directed to, refer to Adam alone.

And thus in that tyme I stode mykylle[6] in thre knowynges, for the full understandyng of this mervelouse example was nott gevyn me in that tyme, in whych mysty example the pryvytes of the revelacyon be yet moch hyd.[7] And nott withstandyng this, I sawe and understode that every shewyng is full of pryvytes. And there fore me behovyth now to tell thre propertes in whych I am som dele esyd. The furst is the begynnyng of techyng that I understode ther in in the same tyme. The secunde is the inwarde lernyng that I have understonde there in sythen.[8] The thyrd is alle the hole revelation fro the begynnyng to the ende whych oure Lorde God of his goodnes bryngyth oftymes frely to the syght of my understondyng. And theyse thre be so onyd, as to my understondyng, that I can nott nor may deperte[9] them. And by theyse thre as one I have techyng wherby I ow[1] to belyve and truste in oure Lorde God, that of the same goodnesse that he shewed it and for the same end, ryght so of the same goodnes and for the same end he shall declare it to us when it is his wyll.

For twenty yere after the tyme of the shewyng save thre monthys I had techyng inwardly as I shall sey: "It longyth to the to take hede to alle the propertes and the condescions that were shewed in the example though ye thyngke that it be mysty and indefferent[2] to thy syght." I assentyd wylfully with grett desyer, seeing inwardly with avysement all the poyntes and the propertes that were shewed in the same tyme, as ferforth as my wytt and my understandyng wylle serve, begynnyng my beholdyng at the lorde and at the servaunt: at the manner of syttyng of the lorde, and the place he satt on, and the coloure of his clothyng, and the manner of shape, and his chere withoute, and his nobley and his goodnes within; and the manner of stondyng of the servaunt, and the place where and how, and his manner of clothyng, the coloure and the shape, at his outwarde behavyng, and at his inwarde goodnes and his unlothfulnesse.[3] The lorde that satt solemply in rest and in peas, I understonde that he is God. The servaunt that stode before hym, I understode that he was shewed for Adam, that is to sey, oone man was shewed that tyme and his fallyng to make there by to be understonde how God behold-yth alle manne and his fallyng. For in the syghte of God alle man is oone man, and oone man is alle man.

This man was hurte in his myghte and made fulle febyll, and he was stonyd[4] in his understandyng. For he was turnyd fro the behold-

6. I remained to a great degree.
7. In which obscure and figurative example the secrets of the revelations are yet much hidden.
8. Since.
9. Separate.
1. Ought.
2. Obscure and indistinct.
3. Lack of loathsomeness.
4. Stunned, bewildered.

yng of his lorde, but his wylle was kepte in God's syght. For his wylle I saw oure Lorde commende and aprove, but hym selfe was lettyd[5] and blyndyd of the knowyng of this wyll. And this is to hym grett sorow and grevous dysses, for neyther he seeth clerly his lovyng lorde, whych is to hym full meke and mylde, nor he seeth truly what hym selfe is in the syght of his lovyng lord. And welle I wott when theyse two be wysely and truly seen we shall gett rest and peas, here in party and the fulsomnesse[6] in the blysse in hevyn by his plentuous grace. And this was a begynnyng of techyng whych I saw in the same tyme, wherby I myght come to knowyng in what manner he beholdeth us in oure synne. And then I saw that oonly payne blamyth and ponyschyth, and oure curteyse Lorde comfortyth and socurryth,[7] and evyr he is to the soule in glad chere, lovyng and longyng to bryng us to his blysse.

The place that the lorde satt on was symply on the erth, bareyn and deserte, aloone in wyldernesse. His clothyng was wyde and syde and full semely as fallyth[8] to a lorde. The colour of the clothyng was blew as asure, most sad and feyer.[9] His chere was mercifull. The colour of his face was feyer brown whyt with full semely counte-naunce.[1] His eyen were blake, most feyer and semely, shewyng full of lovely pytte; and within hym, an hey ward, long and brode, all full of endlesse hevynlynes.[2] And the lovely lokyng that he lokyd on his servaunt contynually, and namely, in his fallyng, me thought it myght melt oure hartys for love and brest them on twoo for joy. This feyer lokyng shewed of a semely medelur[3] whych was marvelous to beholde. That one was rewth and pytte; that other, joy and blysse. The joy and blysse passyth as ferre the rewth and the pytte as hevyn is above erth. The pytty was erthly and the blysse, hevynly.

The rewth and the pytty of the Fader was of the fallyng of Adam, whych is his most lovyd creature. The joy and the blysse was of the fallyng of his deerwurthy Son, whych is evyn[4] with the Fader. The mercyfull beholdyng of his lovely chere fulfyllyd all erth and de-scendyd downe with Adam into helle, with whych countynuant[5] pytte Adam was kepte fro endlesse deth. And this mercy and pytte dwellyth with mankynde in to the tyme that we come uppe in to hevyn. But man is blyndyd in this life, and therefore we may nott se oure Fader God as he is. And what tyme that he of hys goodnesse wyll shew hym

---

5. Prevented.
6. Fullness.
7. Relieves. "Ponyschyth": punishes.
8. Roomy and ample and very pleasing as befalls.
9. Blue as azure, most dignified and fair.
1. Very dignified features.
2. A high stronghold or citadel, long and broad, all full of endless heavenliness.
3. Proper mixture. "Brest": burst.
4. Equal.
5. Continuous.

to man, he shewyth hym homely as man, not withstondyng that I saw verely we ought to know and beleve that the Fader is nott man.

But his syttyng on the erth, bareyn and desert, is thus to mene: he made mannes soule to be his owne cytte[6] and his dwellyng place, whych is most pleasyng to hym of all his workes. And what tyme man was fallyn in to sorow and payne, he was not all semely to serve of that noble offyce.[7] And therfore oure kynde Fader wolde have dyght hym noon other place but to sytt uppon the erth, abydyng man kynde whych is medlyd with erth,[8] tyll what tyme by his grace hys deerwurthy Sonne had brought agayne hys cytte in to the nobyll feyernesse with his harde traveyle.

The blewhed of the clothyng betokenyth his stedfastnesse. The brownhed of his feyer face with the semely blackhede of the eyen was most accordyng to shew his holy sobyrnesse.[9] The largnesse of his clothyng, whych was feyer, flammyng about,[1] betokenyth that he hath beclosyd in hym all hevyns and all endlesse joy and blysse. And this was shewed in a touch,[2] wher I saw that my understandyng was led in to the lorde, in whych I saw hym heyly enjoye for the worschypfull restoryng that he wyll and shall bryng hys servaunt to by hys plentuous grace.

And yet I marveyled, beholdyng the lorde and the servaunt before seyde. I saw the lorde sytt solemply and the servant standyng reverently before his lorde, in whych servant is doubyll understandyng, one without, another within. Outward he was clad symply as a laborer whych was dysposyd to traveyle, and he stod full nere the lorde, nott evyn for anenst hym, but in perty a syde,[3] and that on the lefte syde. Hys clothyng was a whyt kyrtyll, syngell, olde, and alle defautyd, dyed with swete of his body, streyte fyttyng to hym and shorte, as it were an handfull beneth the knee, bare, semyng as it shuld sone be worne uppe, redy to be raggyd and rent.[4] And in this I marvelyd gretly, thynkyng, "This is now an unsemely[5] clothyng for the servant that is so heyly lovyd to stond in before so wurschypfull a lord."

And inward in hym was shewed a ground of love, whych love he had to the lorde that was evyn lyke to the love that the lord had to

6. City.
7. Not all appropriate to serve in that noble office or duty.
8. Awaiting mankind that is mixed with earth. "Dyght": prepared.
9. Seriousness.
1. Amplitude of his clothing, which was fair, shining(?) or radiating(?) about. The meaning of *flammyng* is not known.
2. Brief contact.
3. Not even in relation to him but partly aside.
4. His clothing was a white tunic, alone (without a covering garment), old, and all defective, dyed with the sweat of his body, tight-fitting and short, about a hand's width beneath the knee, bare, seeming as if it should soon be worn out, ready to be torn into rags and ripped into pieces
5. Inappropriate.

hym. The wysdom of the servaunt sawe inwardly that ther was one thyng to do whych shuld be wurshyppe to the lord. And the servaunt for love, havyng no regarde to hym selfe nor to nothyng that myght fall of hym, hastely deed sterte and rynne[6] at the sendyng of his lorde to do that thyng whych was hys wylle and his wurshyppe. For it semyd by his outwarde clothyng as he had ben a contynuant[7] laborer and an hard traveler of long tyme. And by the inward syght that I had, both in the lorde and in the servant, it semyd that he was a newyd, that it to sey, new begynnyng for to traveyle, whych servaunt was nevyr sent out before.

Ther was a tresoure in the erth whych the lorde lovyd. I merveyled and thought what it myght be. And I was answeryd in my under-standyng, "It is a mete whych is lovesom[8] and plesyng to the lorde." For I saw the lorde sytt as a man, and I saw neyther meet nor drynke wher with to serve hym. Thys was one merveyle. A nother merveyle was that this solempne lorde had no servant but one, and hym he sent out. I beheld, thyngkyng what manner labour it may be that the servaunt shulde do. And then I understode that he shuld do the grettest labour and the hardest traveyle that is. He shuld be a gar-dener, delvyng and dykyng and swetyng[9] and turnyng the erth up and down, and seke the depnesse, and water the plantes in tyme. And in this he shulde contynue his traveyle and make swete flodys to rynne and nobylle plentuousnesse fruyte to spryng, whych he shulde bryng before the lorde and serve hym therwith to his lykynk. And he shulde nevyr turne ageyne tyll he had dyghte this mett[1] alle redy as he knew that it lykyd to the lorde. And than he shulde take thys mett with the dryngke and bere it full wurschypply before the lorde. And all thys tyme the lorde shulde sytt ryght on the same place, abydyng the servant whom he sent oute.

And yett I merveylyd fro whens[2] the servant came. For I saw in the lord that he hath within hym selfe endlesse lyfe and all manner of goodnes, save the tresure that was in the erth, and that was groundyd with in the lord in mervelous depnesse of endlesse love. But it was nott alle to his wurschypp tyll his servant hath thus nobly dyghte it and brought it before hym in hym selfe present. And with out the lorde was ryght noght but wyldernysse. And I understode nott alle what this exampyll ment, and therfore I marveylyd from wens the servant came.

In the servant is comprehendyd[3] the Seconde Person of the Tryn-

---

6. Did start and run.
7. Continual.
8. A food that is lovable.
9. Digging and making dikes and sweating. Julian is alluding to the punishment of Adam, but she regards it much more positively than Genesis does.
1. Prepared this food.
2. Whence, where.
3. Included and understood. Combining divine and human natures, Jesus is both the Second

yte, and in the servaunt is comprehendyd Adam, that is to sey, all men. And, therfore, whan I sey the Sonne, it menyth the Godhed, whych is evyn with the Fader. And whan I sey the servaunt, it menyth Crystes manhode, whych is ryghtfull Adam. By the nerehede of the servaunt is understand the Sonne, and by the stondyng of the lyft syde is understond Adam. The lorde is God the Father, the servant is the Sonne Jesu Cryst, the Holy Gost is the evyn love whych is in them both.

When Adam felle, Godes Sonne fell. For the ryght onyng whych was made in hevyn,[4] Goddys Sonne myght nott be seperath from Adam, for by Adam I understond alle man. Adam fell fro lyfe to deth in to the slade of this wrechyd worlde and aftyr that in to hell.[5] Goddys Son fell with Adam in to the slade of the meyden's wombe,[6] whych was the feyerest doughter of Adam, and that for to excuse Adam from blame in hevyn and in erth; and myghtely he fechyd hym out of hell.[7] By the wysdom and the goodnesse that was in the servaunt is understond Goddys Son. By the pore clothyng as a laborer stondyng nere the lyft syde is understonde the manhode of Adam with alle the myschefe and febylnesse that folowyth. For in alle this oure good Lorde shewed his owne Son and Adam but one man. The vertu and the goodnesse that we have is of Jesu Crist, the febilnesse and blyndnesse that we have is of Adam, which two were shewed in the servant.

And thus hath oure good Lorde Jhesu taken uppon hym all oure blame, and therfore oure Fader may nor wyll no more blame assigne to us than to hys owne derwurthy Son Jhesu Cryst. Thus was he the servant before hys comyng in to erth, stondyng redy before the Father in purpos tyll what tyme he wolde sende hym to do the wurschypfull deede by whych mankynde was brought agayn in to hevyn. That is to sey, nott withstondyng that he is God, evyn with the Fader as anenst the Godhede, but in his forseyng purpos[8] that he woulde be man to save man in fulfyllyng of the wyll of his Fader, so he stode before his Fader as a servant, wylfully takyng uppon hym alle oure

---

Person of the Trinity and the second Adam. What Adam lost through a tree, Christ restored through the tree of the cross.

4. For the just union which was made in heaven. Julian describes the ontological union between the Second Person of the Trinity and humankind in Revelation XIV, chapters 53–56.

5. Adam fell from life to death into the valley of this wretched world and afterward into hell. Julian's concept of creation is influenced by Christian Neoplatonism. She believes that the substance or higher part of the soul subsists in the divine substance until it falls to earth to be joined to the lower part of the soul, the sensuality, and the body.

6. Valley of the maiden's womb. At the incarnation, the Son of God took on human form in Mary's womb.

7. And mightily he (Christ) fetched him (Adam) out of hell. Julian is referring to the harrowing of hell, the belief that Jesus descended to hell between his death on the cross and his resurrection to free the souls of the just, including Adam, who could not be saved before Jesus' atonement to the Father for original sin.

8. Equal with the Father in respect of the Godhead but in his foreseeing purpose.

charge. And than he sterte full redely at the Fader's wyll. And anon
he fell full lowe in the maydyn's wombe, havyng no regarde to hym
selfe ne to his harde paynes. The wyth kyrtyll[9] is his fleshe. The
singlehede[1] is that ther was ryght noght betwen the Godhede and
the manhede. The strayght nesse is povyrte, the elde is of Adam's
weryng, the defautyng is the swete of Adam's traveyle, the shortnesse
shewyth the servant laborar.[2]

And thus I saw the Sonne stonde, seyng in his menyng, "Lo, my
dere Fader, I stonde before the in Adam's kyrtylle alle redy to sterte
and to rynne. I wolde be in the erth to thy worschyppe whan it is thy
wyll to send me. How long shall I desyer it?" Full truly wyst the Son
whan it was the Fader's wyll and how long he sholde desyer, that is
to sey, as a nemptes the Godhed,[3] for he is the wysdom of the Fader.
Wher fore this menyng was shewed in understandyng of the manhod
of Crist. For all mankynde that shall be savyd by the swete incarnacion and the passion of Crist, alle is the manhode of Cryst. For
he is the heed, and we be his membris,[4] to whych membris the day
and the tyme is unknowyn whan every passyng wo and sorow shall
have an eende and the everlastyng joy and blysse shall be fulfyllyd,
whych day and tyme for to see all the company of hevyn longyth or
desyreth. And all that be under hevyn whych shall come theder,[5]
ther wey is by longyng and desyeryng, whych desyeryng and longyng
was shewed in the servant stondyng before the lorde, or ellys thus
in the Son stondyng afore the Fadyr in Adam kyrtyll. For the longyng
and desyer of all mankynd that shall be safe aperyd in Jhesu. For
Jhesu is in all that shall be safe, and all that is savyd is in Jhesu,
and all of the charyte of God with obedience, mekenesse, and
paciens, and vertuous that longyth to us.

Also in thys merveylous example I have techyng with in me, as it
were the begynnyng of an A B C, wher by I may have some understondyng of oure Lordys menyng. For the pryvytes of the revelacion
be hyd ther in, not withstondyng that alle the shewyng be full of
prevytes.

The syttyng of the Fader betokynnyth the Godhede, that is to sey,
for shewyng of rest and pees, for in the Godhed may be no traveyle.
And that he shewyth hym selfe as lorde betokynnyth to oure manhod.
The standyn of the servant betokynnyth traveyle, and on the lyfte

9. White tunic.
1. Singleness. Adam is wearing no other garment
2. The age is because of Adam's wearing, the defectiveness is due to the sweat of Adam's
   toil, the shortness shows the servant a laborer.
3. In respect of the Godhead.
4. For he is the head, and we are his members. Julian is referring to the concept of the
   Mystical Body of Christ that regards Christ and Christians as a figurative body; the idea
   derived from 1 Corinthians 12:27, where St. Paul writes: "Now ye are the body of Christ,
   and members in particular."
5. Thither, there.

syde betokynnyth that he was nott alle wurthy to stonde evyn ryght before the lorde. His stertyng was the Godhed, and the rennyng was the manhed. For the Godhed sterte fro the Fader in to the maydyn's wombe, fallyng in to the takyng of oure kynde. And in this fallyng he toke grete soore.[6] The soore that he toke was oure flessch, in whych as Sone he had felyng of dedely paynes. By that that he stode dredfully before the lorde and nott evyn ryghte betokynnyth that his clothyng was not honest[7] to stonde evyn ryght before the lorde, nor that myght nott nor shulde nott be hys offyce whyle he was a laborer. Nor also he myght nott sytt with the lord in rest and pees tyll he had wonne his peece ryghtfully with hys hard traveyle. And by the lefte syde, that the Fader lefte his owne Son wylfully in this manhed to suffer all man's payne without sparyng of hym. By that his kertyll was at the poynt to be ragged and rent is understond the roddys and scorgys, the thornes and the naylys, the drawyng and the draggyng, his tendyr flessch rentyng,[8] as I saw in some party. The flessch was rent fro the head panne, fallyng on pecys unto the tyme the bledyng feylyd, and than it beganne to dry agayne, clevyng to the bone. And by the walowyng and wrythyng, gronyng and mornyng is understonde that he myght nevyr ryse all myghtly fro that tyme that he was fallyn in to the maydyn's wombe tyll his body was sleyne and dede, he yeldyng the soule in to the Fadyr's hand with alle mankynde for whome he was sent.[9]

And at this poynt he beganne furst to show his myght, for then he went in to helle. And whan he was ther, than he reysyd uppe the grett root oute of the depe depnesse,[1] whych ryghtfully was knyt to hym in hey hevyn. The body ley in the grave tyll Ester morow, and fro that tyme he ley nevyr more. For ther was ryghtfully endyd the walowyng and the wrythyng, the gronyng and the mornyng. And oure foule, dedely flessch that Goddys Son toke uppon hym, whych was Adam's olde kyrtyll, streyte, bare, and shorte, then by oure Savyoure was made feyer, new, whyt, and bryght, and of endlesse clennesse, wyde and seyde, feyer and rychar[2] than was the clothyng whych I saw on the Fader. For that clothyng was blew, and Crystes clothyng

6. Sore, bodily pain.
7. Respectable.
8. By (the fact) that his tunic was at the point to be made into rags and torn is understood the rods and the scourges, the thorns and the nails, the pulling and the dragging, his tender flesh tearing.
9. The flesh was torn from the skull, falling in pieces until the time the bleeding stopped, and then it began to dry again, clinging to the bone. And by the wallowing and writhing, groaning and mourning is understood that he might never rise all powerfully from the time that he fell into the maiden's womb until his body was slain and dead, he yielding the soul with all mankind for whom he was sent into the Father's hand.
1. Then he raised up the great rout or company out of the deep deepness (the harrowing of hell).
2. Roomy and ample, fair and richer.

is now of feyer, semely medolour,[3] whych is so mervelous that I can it nott discryve,[4] for it is all of very wurschyppe.

Now sittyth nott the lorde on erth in wyldernesse, but he syttyth on hys ryche and nobyll seet, whych he made in hevyn most to his lykyng. Now stondyth nott the Son before the Fader as a servant before the lorde, dredfully clothyd, in perty nakyd, but he stondyth before the Fader evyn ryghte rychely clothyd in blyssefull largenesse with a crowne upon his hed of precyous rychenes. For it was schewede that we be his crowne,[5] whych crowne is the Fader's joy, the Sonnes wurshyppe, the Holy Gostys lykyng, and endlesse mervelous blysse to alle that be in hevyn.

Now stondyth not the Sonne before the Fader on the lyfte syde as a laborer, but he syttyth on the Fader's ryght hande in endlesse rest an pees. But it is nott ment that the Sonne syttyth on the ryght hand besyde as one man syttyth by an other in this lyfe, for ther is no such syttyng, as to my syght, in the Trynyte. But he syttyth on his Fader's ryght honde, that is to sey, ryght in the hyest nobylyte of the Fader's joy. Now is the Spouse, Goddys Son, in pees with this lovyd wyfe,[6] whych is the feyer maydyn of endlesse joy. Now syttyth the Son, very God and very man, in his cytte in rest and in pees, whych his Fader hath dyghte to[7] hym of endlesse purpose, and the Fader in the Son, and the Holy Gost in the Fader and in the Son.

Chapter 52

And thus I saw that God enjoyeth that he is our Fader, and God enjoyeth that he is our Moder, and God enjoyeth that he is our very Spouse and our soule his lovyd wyfe. And Crist enjoyeth that he is our Broder, and Jhesu enjoyeth that he is our Savyour. Theyse be v hye joyes, as I understonde, in whych he wylle that we enjoye, hym praysyng, thankyng, hym lovyng, hym endlessly blessing.

Alle that shall be savyd, for the tyme of this lyfe we have in us a mervelous medelur[8] both of wele and of woo. We have in us oure Lorde Jhesu Cryst up resyn, and we have in us the wrechydnesse and the myschef of Adam's fallyng. Dyeng by Cryst, we be lastynly kept, and by hys gracyous touchyng we be reysed in to very trust of salvacyon. And by Adam's fallyng we be so broken in oure felyng on dyverse manner by synne and by sondry paynes, in whych we be made derke and so blynde that unnethys[9] we can take any comforte. But

---

3. Decorous medley cloth, cloth made of wools dyed and mingled before being spun, either of one color or of different shades or colors.
4. Describe.
5. Revelation IX, chapter 22.
6. This beloved wife. As Queen of Heaven, Mary is Christ's wife as well as his mother.
7. Prepared for.
8. Mixture.
9. Scarcely.

in oure menyng[1] we abyde God and feythfully trust to have mercy and grace. And this is his owne werkyng in us, and of his goodnesse openyth the ey of oure understanding, by whych we have syght, some tyme more and somtyme lesse, after that God gevyth abylte[2] to take. And now we be reysyde[3] in to that one, and now we are sufferyd to fall in to that other.

And thus is that medle so mervelous in us that unnethis we knowe of oure selfe or of oure evyn Crysten in what wey we stonde for the mervelousnes of this sondrye felyng, but that ech holy assent that we assent to God[4] when we fele hym truly, wyllyng to be with hym with all oure herte, with all oure soule, and with all oure myghte. And than we hate and dyspise oure evyll steryng and all that myghte be occasion of synne, gostely and bodely. And yett nevyr thelesse whan this swetnesse is hyd, we fall ayeen in to blyndnesse and so in to woo and trybulacion on dyverse manners. But than is this oure comfort, that we knowe in oure feyth that by the vertu of Crist, whych is oure keper, we assent nevyr therto, but we groge ther agenst[5] and endure in payne and in woo, prayeng in to that tyme that he shewede hym ayeen to us.

And thus we stonde in this medelur all the dayes of oure lyfe, but he wyll we trust that he is lastyngly with us and that in thre manner. He is with us in hevyn, very man in his owne person, us updrawyng; and that was shewd in the gostely thyrst.[6] And he is with us in erth, us ledyng; and that was shewde in the **thyrde**, wher I saw God in a poynt. And he is with us in oure soule, endlesly wonnyng, rewlyng, and gydyng us;[7] and that was shewde in the **xvi**, as I shalle sey.

And thus in the servant was shewde the blyndnesse and the mys-chefe of Adam's fallyng, and in the servant was shewde the wysdom and the goodnesse of Goddys Son. And in the lorde was schewde the rewth and the pytte of Adam's woo, and in the lorde was shewde the hye noblyte and the endlesse wurschyppe that mankynde is come to by the vertu of the passyon and the deth of his deerwurthy Son. And therfore myghtely he enjoyeth in his fallyng, for the hye reysyng and fulhed of blysse that mankynde is come to, ovyr passyng that we shuld have had yf he had nott fallyn. And thus to se this ovyrpassyng noblete was my understondyng leed in to God in the same tyme that I saw the servant falle.

And thus we have mater of mornyng, for oure synne is cause of

---

1. Understanding.
2. Gives ability.
3. Are raised.
4. And thus is that mixture so marvelous in us that we scarcely know about our self or our fellow Christians which way we stand for the marvelousness of these different feelings, except that (we know) each holy assent that we give to God.
5. Grouch there against.
6. Spiritual thirst (see Revelation XIII, chapter 31).
7. Dwelling in, ruling, and guiding us.

Cristes paynes. And we have lastyngly mater of joy, for endlesse love made hym to suffer. And therfore the creature that seeth and felyth the workyng of love by grace hatyth nought but synne, for of alle thyng, as to my syght, love and hate be hardest and most unmesurable contrarys. And nott withstondyng all this, I sawe and understode in oure Lordys menyng that we may nott in this lyfe kepe us fro synne, alle holy in full clenesse as we shall be in hevyn. But we may wele by grace kepe us fro the synnes whych wolde lede us to endlesse payne, as holy chyrch techyth us, and eschewe venyall resonably uppe oure myght.[8] And if we by oure blyndnesse and oure wrechydnesse ony tyme falle, that we redely ryse, knowyng the swete touchyng of grace, and wylfully amend us upon techyng of holy chyrch after that the synne is grevous,[9] and go forth with God in love, and neyther on that one syde fall ovyr lowe, enclynyng to dyspeyrs, ne on that other syde be ovyr rechelesse, as yf we geve no forse,[1] but mekely know oure febylnes, wyttyng that we may nott stonde a twynglyng of an ey but with kepyng of grace, and reverently cleve[2] to God, in hym oonly trustyng.

For other wyse is the beholdyng of God, and other wyse is the beholdyng of man. For it longyth to man mekely to accuse hym selfe, and it longyth to the propyr goodnesse of oure Lorde God curtesly to excuse man. And theyse be two partyes that were shewde in the doubyll chere in whych the lorde behelde the fallyng of hys lovyd servant. That oone was shewde outward, full mekely and myldely, with gret rewth and pytte; and that other, of inwarde endlesse love and ryght. Thus wylle oure good Lorde that we accuse oure selfe wylfully and truly se and know his evyrlastyng love that he hath to us and his plentuous mercy. And thus gracyously to se and know both to geder is the meke accusyng that oure good Lorde askyth of us. And hym selfe wurkyth there it is, and this is the lower party of mannys lyfe.[3] And it was shewde in the outwarde chere, in whych shewyng I saw two partes. The one is the rufull fallyng of man. That other is the wurshypfull asseth[4] that oure Lorde hath made for man. That other chere was shewde inwarde, and that was more hyly and all one. For the lyfe and the vertu that we have in the lower perty is of the hyer, and it comyth downe to us of the kynde love of the selfe

---

8. Avoid venial sin in accordance with our power. Julian distinguishes between two kinds of sin: mortal or deadly sin, which is so serious an offense that one dying in this state is condemned to hell, and venial or minor infractions, which do not result in eternal damnation. All sin, mortal or venial, can be absolved through the sacrament of penance as alluded to in the following sentence.
9. According to the degree of severity of the sin. I.e., mortal or venial.
1. Neither on that one side fall too low, inclining to despair, nor on that other side be overly careless, as if we give it no importance.
2. Twinkling of an eye except with the protection of grace, and reverently cling.
3. The lower part of man's life. I.e., the physical and temporal being (which is the concern of the lower part of the soul, the sensuality).
4. Amends, reparation.

by grace. Betwene that one and that other is ryght nought, for it is all one love, whych one blessyd love hath now in us doubyll werkyng. For in the lower perty be payns and passions, ruthis and pyttes, mercis and forgevenesse and such other, whych be profytable. But in the hyer perty be none of theyse, but all one hye love and mervelous joy, in whych marvelous joy all paynes be holy dystroyed.[5] And in this nott only oure good Lorde shewde our excusyng, but also the wurschypfulle noblyte that he shall breng us to, tornyng all oure blame into endlesse wurschyppe.

Chapter 53

And thus I saw that he wyll that we know he takyth no herder the fallyng of any creatur that shalle be savyd than he tok the fallyng of Adam, whych we know was endlessly lovyd and suerly kepte in the tyme of all his nede and now is blyssydfully restoryd in hye ovyr passyng joyes. For oure Lorde God is so good, so gentyll, and so curtesse that he may never assigne defaughte finall[6] in whome he shall be evyr blessyd and praysyd. And in this that I have now seyde was my desyer in perty answeryd and my grete fere somdele esyd[7] by the lovely, gracious shewyng of oure Lorde God. In whych shewyng I saw and understode full suerly that in ech a soule that shall be safe is a godly wylle[8] that nevyr assentyd to synne ne nevyr shall, whych wyll is so good that it may nevyr wylle evyll, but evyr more contynuly it wyllyth good and werkyth good in the syght of God.

There fore oure Lorde wylle we know it in the feyth and the beleve, and namly and truly that we have all this blessyd wyll hoole and safe in oure Lorde Jhesu Crist, for that ech kynde that hevyn shall be fulfyllyd with behovyd nedys of Goddys ryghtfulnes so to be knytt and onyd in hym that there in were kepte a substaunce whych myght nevyr nor shulde be partyd from hym, and that thorow his awne good wyll in his endlesse forseing purpose.[9] And nott withstonding this

---

5. For in the lower part (the physical and temporal existence governed by the sensuality) are (human) pains and passions, (God's) compassion and pity, mercy and forgiveness and such other, which are profitable. But in the higher part (the spiritual life governed by the substance of the soul) are none of these, but all one high love and marvelous joy, in which marvelous joy all pains are wholly destroyed.

6. Final default, failure. Dying in a state of mortal sin would result in eternal damnation.

7. Was my desire in part answered and my great fear somewhat eased. Julian is referring to the questions she asked at the end of chapter 50 about the discrepancies between her showings and the teachings of the church.

8. Godly will. This concept, introduced in Revelation XIII, chapter 37, is Julian's ultimate solution to the apparent discrepancy between the revelation that all shall be well and the church's teachings about damnation. Influenced by Christian Neoplatonism, Julian describes the ontological union between the substance of the soul and the Second Person of the Trinity that has been foreseen from all eternity and that exists before the substance's union with the sensuality and body at birth. Because every person participates in this union of the divine substance and the human soul, Julian implies that all will be saved. See also chapter 58.

9. For each kind or natural being that heaven shall be made full with must of God's right-

ryghtfull knyttyng and this endlesse oonyng, yett the redempcion and the agayne byeng of mannekynde is nedfull and spedfull in every thyng, as it is done for the same entent and the same ende that holy chyrch in oure feyth us techyth.

For I saw that God began nevyr to love mankynde. For ryghte the same that mankynd shall be in endlesse blesse, fulfyllyng the joy of God as anemptis[1] his werkys, ryghte so the same mankynd hath be in the forsyghte of God knowen and lovyd fro without begynnyng in his ryghtfull entent. And by the endlesse entent and assent and the full acorde of all the Trynyte, the myd person wolde be ground and hed of this feyer kynde out of whom we be all come, in whom we be alle enclosyd, in to whom we shall all goo, in hym fyndyng oure full hevyn in everlastyng joy by the forseing[2] purpose of alle the blessyd Trynyte fro without begynnyng. For or[3] that he made us, he lovyd us. And when we were made, we lovyd hym. And this is a love made of the kyndly substauncyall goodnesse of the Holy Gost, myghty in reson of the myghte of the Fader, and wyse in mynde of the wysdom of the Son. And thus is mannys soule made of God and in the same poynte knyte to God.[4]

And thus I understode that mannes soule is made of nought, that is to sey, it is made but of nought that is made, as thus: Whan God shulde make mannes body, he toke the slyme of the erth, whych is a mater medelyd and gaderyd of[5] alle bodely thynges, and therof he made mannes body. But to the makyng of mannys soule he wolde take ryght nought, but made it. And thus is the kynde made ryghtfully onyd to the maker, whych is substauncyall kynde unmade, that is God.[6] And therfore it is that ther may ne shall be ryght noughte betwene God and mannis soule. And in this endlesse love mannis soule is kepte hole, as all the mater of the revelacion menyth and shewyth, in whych endlesse love we be ledde and kepte of God and nevyr shalle be lost.

For he wyll that we know that oure soule is a lyfe, whych lyfe of hys goodnesse and his grace shall last in hevyn without ende, hym lovyng, hym thangkyng, hym praysyng. And right the same that we

---

eousness be so knit and united in him (Christ) that therein remains a substance (the higher part of the soul) that never might nor never should be separated from him and that through his own good will in his endless, foreseeing purpose. Corrected from S1; P has *forseyde*, foresaid.

1. As regards.
2. Foreseeing. Corrected from S1; P has *forseyeng*. "Myd person": Second Person, or Son.
3. Before.
4. And thus is man's soul made of God and in the same point knit to God. Julian refers to the concept of the highest point or apex of the soul, that part of the substance that remains grounded in God's substance. She sees God in this highest point of the soul in Revelation III, chapter 11.
5. Mixed and gathered from.
6. And thus is the nature (of humankind) created rightfully united with the maker, who is substantial nature uncreated, that is, God. "Ryght nought": nothing whatsoever.

shulde be without end, the same we ware tresured in God and hyd, knowen and lovyd fro without begynnyng. Wherfore he wyll we wytt that the nobelest thyng that evyr he made is mankynde, and the fulleste substaunce and the hyest vertu is the blessyd soule of Crist. And ferthermore, he wyll we wytt that this deerwurthy soule was preciously knytt to hym in the makyng, whych knott is so suttell[7] and so myghty that it is onyd in to God, in whych onyng it is made endlesly holy. Farthermore, he wyll we wytt that all the soulys that shalle be savyd in hevyn with out ende be knytt in this knott, and onyd in this oonyng, and made holy in this holynesse.

Chapter 54

Ande for the grete endlesse love that God hath to alle mankynde, he makyth no depertyng[8] in love betwen the blessyd soule of Crist and the lest soule that shall be savyd. For it is full esy to beleve and truste that the dwellyng of the blessyd soule of Crist is full hygh in the glorious Godhede. And truly, as I understode in oure Lordes menyng, where the blessyd soule of Crist is, there is the substance of alle the soules that shall be savyd by Crist.

Hyely owe[9] we to enjoye that God dwellyth in oure soule, and more hyly we owe to enjoye that oure soule dwellyth in God. Oure soule is made to be Goddys dwellyng place, and the dwellyng of oure soule is God, whych is unmade.[1] A hye understandyng it is inwardly to se and to know that God, whych is oure maker, dwellyth in oure soule. And a hygher understandyng it is and more inwardly to se and to know oure soule that is made dwellyth in God in substance, of whych substance by God we be that we be.

And I sawe no dyfference betwen God and oure substance, but as it were all God. And yett my understandyng toke that oure substance is in God, that is to sey, that God is God and oure substance is a creature in God.[2] For the almyghty truth of the Trynyte is oure Fader, for he made us and kepyth us in hym. And the depe wysdome of the Trynyte is our Moder, in whom we be closyd. And the hye goodnesse of the Trynyte is our Lord, and in hym we be closyd and he in us. We be closyd in the Fader, and we be closyd in the Son, and we are closyd in the Holy Gost. And the Fader is beclosyd in us, the Son is

---

7. Subtle, both cleverly made and difficult to understand.
8. Separating.
9. Greatly ought.
1. The *imago Dei* or image of God, according to Augustine's interpretation of Genesis 1:27, resides in the higher part of the soul, what Julian calls the substance, a portion of which, in turn, remains within God's substance or uncreated being.
2. In distinguishing between God's substance and the part of the human soul that remains within it, Julian is disavowing the heretical claim that God and the human soul are one and the same.

beclosyd in us, and the Holy Gost is beclosyd in us, all myghty, alle wysdom, and alle goodnesse, one God, one Lorde.

And oure feyth is a vertu that comyth of oure kynde substaunce in to oure sensuall soule by the Holy Gost, in whych vertu alle oure vertues comyn to us, for without that no man may receyve vertues. For it is nought eles but a ryght understandyng with trew beleve and suer truste of oure beyng that we be in God and he in us, whych we se nott. And this vertu with all other that God hath ordeyned to us comyng ther in werkyth in us grete thynges. For Cryst marcyfully is werkyng in us, and we gracyously accordyng to hym thorow the yefte[3] and the vertu of the Holy Gost. This werkyng makyth that we be Crystes chyldren and Cristen in lyvyng.

Chapter 55

And thus Crist is oure wey, us suerly ledyng in his lawes. And Crist in his body myghtely beryth us up in to hevyn. For I saw that Crist, us alle havyng in hym that shall be savyd by hym, wurschypfully presentyth his Fader in hevyn with us. Whych present fulle thangk-fully hys Fader receyvyth and curtesly gevyth it unto his Sonne Jhesu Crist. Whych gyfte and werkyng is joy to the Fader, and blysse to the Son, and lykyng to the Holy Gost. And of alle thyng that to us long-yth, it is most lykyng to oure Lorde that we enjoye in this joy, whych is in the blessyd Trynyte of oure salvacion. And this was sene in the **nyneth** shewyng, where it spekyth more of this matere.

And nott withstondyng all oure felyng, woo or wele, God wyll we understond and beleve that we be more verely in hevyn than in erth. Oure feyth comyth of the kynde love of oure soule, and of the clere lyghte of oure reson, and of the stedfaste mynde, whych we have of God in oure furst makyng. And what tyme oure soule is enspyred in oure body, in whych we be made sensuall,[4] as soone mercy and grace begynne to werke, havyng of us cure and kepyng with pytte and love. In whych werkyng the Holy Gost formyth in oure feyth hope that we shall come agayne up abovyn to oure substaunce, in to the vertu of Crist, encresyd and fulfyllyd throw the Holy Gost.

Thus I understode that the sensuallyte is groundyd in kynde, in mercy, and in grace, whych ground ablyth us to receyve gyftes that leed us to endlesse lyfe. For I saw full suerly that oure substaunce is in God, and also I saw that in oure sensualyte God is. For in the same poynt that oure soule is made sensuall, in the same poynt is the cytte of God,[5] ordeyned to hym fro without begynnyng, in whych

---

3. Gift.
4. And at the time our soul is breathed into our body, by which we are made sensual or physical.
5. For at the same point that our soul is made sensual (i.e., the substance is united to the sensuality to inform the body) at the same point is the city of God. Julian is referring to

cytte he comyth and nevyr shall remeve[6] it. For God is nevyr out of
the soule, in whych he shalle dwell blessydly without end. And this
was seyd in the **xvi** shewyng where it seyth the place that Jhesu takyth
in oure soule, he shall nevyr remeve it. And all the gyftes that God
may geve to the creature he hath gevyn to his Son Jhesu for us,
whych gyftes he, wonnyng[7] in us, hath beclosyd in hym in to the
tyme that we be waxyn and growyn, oure soule with oure body and
oure body with oure soule. Eyther of them take helpe of other tylle
we be broughte up in to stature as kynde werkyth. And than in the
ground of kynd with werkyng of mercy the Holy Gost gracyously
enspirith in to us gyftes ledyng to endlesse lyfe.

And thus was my understandyng led of God to se in hym and to
wytt, to understonde and to know that oure soule is a made trynyte
lyke to the unmade blessyd Trynyte,[8] knowyn and lovyd fro with out
begynnyng, and in the makyng onyd to the maker, as it is before
seyde. Thys syght was fulle swete and mervelous to beholde, pesyble
and restfull, suer and delectabyll. And for the worschypfull oonyng
that was thus made of God between the soule and the body, it
behovyd nedys to be that mankynd shuld be restoryd fro doubyll
deth, whych restoryng myght nevyr be in to the tyme that the
Seconde Person in the Trynyte had takyn the lower party of mankynd, to whome that hyest was onyd in the furst makyng.[9] And theyse
two pertyes were in Crist, the heyer and the lower, whych is but one
soule. The hyer perty was evyr in pees with God in full joy and blysse.
The lower perty, whych is sensualyte, sufferyd for the salvacion of
mankynd. And theyse two pertyes were seene and felte in the **viii**
shewyng, in whych my body was fulfyllyd of felyng and mynd of
Cristes passion and his dyeng. And ferthermore, with this was a suttell felyng and a prevy inwarde syghte of the hye partys, and that was
shewed in the same tyme wher I myghte nott for the mene profer[1]
loke up in to hevyn. And that was for that ech myghty beholdyng[2] of
the inwarde lyfe, in whych inward lyfe is that hye substaunce, that
precious soule, whych is endlessly enjoyeng in the Godhede.

---

the image of God in the soul, which she associates with the joining of the preexistent
substance to the sensuality and a physical, temporal body.

6. Leave.
7. Dwelling.
8. Our soul is made a trinity like the uncreated blessed Trinity. In *The Trinity* Augustine
   compares the soul's triad of powers to the three persons of the Trinity.
9. Until the Second Person of the Trinity, to whom the highest part of human nature (the
   substance of the soul) was united in the first creation, had taken the lower part of human
   nature (the sensuality or physicality). "Doubyll deth": double death. I.e., physical and
   spiritual damnation.
1. For the offer of a means. Julian is alluding to Revelation VIII, chapter 19, when she could
   not take her eyes from the cross. "Suttell": subtle.
2. Because each powerful sight (in contemplation).

Chapter 56

And thus I saw full suerly that it is redyer to us and more esy[3] to come to the knowyng of God then to know oure owne soule. For oure soule is so depe growndyd in God and so endlesly tresoryd that we may nott come to the knowyng ther of tylle we have furst knowyng of God, whych is the maker to whome it is onyd. But not withstondyng, I saw that we have kyndly of fulhed to desyer wysely and truly to know oure owne soule, wherby we be lernyd[4] to seke it ther it is, and that is in to God. And thus by the gracious ledyng of the Holy Gost we shall know hym both in oone. Whether we be steryd to know God or oure soule, it is both good and trew. God is more nerer to us than oure owne soule, for he is grounde in whome oure soule standyth, and he is mene that kepyth the substaunce and the sensualyte to geder so that it shall nevyr departe.[5] For oure soule syttyth in God in very rest, and oure soule stondyth in God in suer strenght, and oure soule is kyndely rotyd in God in endlesse love. And therfore if we wylle have knowyng of oure soule and comenyng and dalyance[6] ther with, it behovyth to seke in to oure Lord God in whom it is enclosyd.

And of this enclosyng I saw and understode more in the **xvi** shewyng, as I shall sey. And as anemptis[7] oure substaunce, it may ryghtly be callyd oure soule. And anemptis oure sensualite, it may ryghtly be callyd oure soule, and that is by the onyng that it hath in God. That wurschypfull cytte that oure Lorde Jhesu syttyth in, it is oure sensualyte, in whych he is enclosyd. And oure kyndly substance is beclosyd in Jhesu, with the blessyd soule of Crist syttyng in rest in the Godhed. And I saw full suerly that it behovyth nedys to be that we shulde be in longyng and in pennance into the tyme that we be led so depe in to God that we verely and trewly know oure owne soule. And suerly I saw that in to this hye depnesse our good Lorde hym selfe ledyth us in the same love he made us and in the same love he boughte us by mercy and grace thorow vertu of his blessyd passyon.

And not withstandyng all this, we may nevyr come to the full knowyng of God tylle we knowe furst clerely oure owne soule. For in to the tyme that it is in the full myghtis we may nott be alle holy, and that is that oure sensualyte, by the vertu of Cristes passion, be

3. We are readier and it is easier.
4. Taught.
5. For he is the ground in whom our soul stands, and he is the medium that keeps the substance and the sensuality together so that they shall never separate. Julian is referring to the two points at which the soul is knit to God: the preexisting substance subsists in God's substance from its creation and the Second Person unites the substance to the sensuality when the soul descends to earth (see Revelation XIV, chapters 53–55).
6. Communing and familiar conversation.
7. As regards.

brought up in to the substance with all the profytes of oure trybulacion that oure Lorde shall make us to gett by mercy and grace.[8]

I had in perty touchyng, and it is growndyd in kynd, that is to say,
oure reson is groundyd in God, whych is substauncyally kyndnesse.[9]
Of this substancyall kyndnesse mercy and grace spryngyth and spred-
yth in to us, werkyng all thynges in fulfyllyng of oure joy. Theyse be
oure groundys, in whych we have oure beyng, oure encrese, and oure
fulfyllyng. For in kynde we have oure lyfe and oure beyng, and in
mercy and grace we have oure encres and oure fulfyllyng. It be thre
propertes in one goodnes, and where that one werkyth alle werkyn
in the thynges whych be now longyng to us.

God wylle we understande, desyeryng with all oure hart and alle
oure strength to have knowyng of them evyr more and more in to
the tyme that we be fulfyllyd. For fully to know them and clerely to
se them is not elles but endles joy and blysse that we shall have in
hevyn, whych God wyll we begynne here in knowyng of his love. For
only by oure reson we may nott profyte, but yf we have evynly therwith mynde and love.[1] Ne onely in oure kyndly grounde that we have
in God we may not be savyd, but yf we have connyng of the same
grounde, mercy, and grace. For of these thre werkynges alle to geder
we receyve alle oure goodys, of whych the furst be goodys of kynde.[2]
For in oure furst making God gave us as moch good and as greate
good as we might receyve onely in oure spyryte, but his forseeyng
perpos in his endlesse wysdom wolde that we were doubyll.[3]

Chapter 57

And anemptys[4] oure substaunce, he made us so nobyll and so rych
that evyr more we werke his wylle and his worshyppe. Ther I sey *we*,
it menyth man that shall be savyd. For truly I saw that we be that he
lovyth and do that hym lykyth lastyngly withoute ony styntyng.[5] And
of this grete rychesse and of this hygh noble, vertues by mesure come
to oure soule what tyme that it is knytt to oure body, in whych knyt-

8. For until the time that it (the soul) achieves its full powers we may not be entirely holy,
   and that is when our sensuality, by virtue of Christ's Passion, is brought up into the
   substance with all the profits of our tribulation that our Lord shall allow us to gain by
   mercy and grace.
9. Substantially kindness. Both meanings of *kind* are relevant. God is essentially both nature
   and benevolence.
1. For we may not profit by our reason alone, unless we have equally therewith memory and
   love. Julian's triad of reason, memory, and love resembles the psychological trinity of
   understanding, memory, and love that Augustine elucidates in *The Trinity*, book 14.
2. We may not be saved only in our natural ground that we have in God, unless we have
   knowledge of the same ground, mercy, and grace. For of these three workings all together
   we receive all our goods, of which the first are goods of nature. In chapter 57 Julian
   identifies the other two goods as faith and the things that lead to salvation.
3. Double. I.e., a union of substance and sensuality.
4. In respect to.
5. Ceasing.

tyng we be made sensuall.[6] And thus in oure substaunce we be full and in oure sensualyte we feyle, whych feylyng God wylle restore and fulfyll by werkyng of mercy and grace, plentuously flowyng in to us of his owne kynde goodnesse. And thus this kynde goodnesse makyth that mercy and grace werkyth in us, and the kynde goodnesse that we have of hym ablyth us to receyve the werkyng of mercy and grace.

I saw that oure kynde is in God hoole, in whych he makyth dyversytes flowyng oute of hym to werke his wylle, whose kynde kepyth, and mercy and grace restoryth and fulfyllyth.[7] And of theyse none shalle be perysschyd.[8] For oure kynde, whych is the hyer party, is knytte to God in the making; and God is knytt to oure kynde, whych is the lower party, in oure flessch takyng. And thus in Crist oure two kyndys be onyd. For the Trynyte is comprehendyd in Crist, in whom oure hyer party is groundyd and rotyd; and oure lower party the Secund Parson hath taken, whych kynd furst to hym was adyght.[9] For I saw full trewly that alle the werkys that God hath done or evyr shall were full knowen to hym and before seen fro without begynnyng. And for love he made mankynd, and for the same love hym selfe wolde become man.

The nexte good[1] that we receyve is oure feyth, in whych oure profetyng begynnynth. And it comyth of the hye rychesse of oure kynde substaunce in to oure sensuall soule. And it is groundyd in us and we in that throw the kynde goodnes of God by the werkyng of mercy and grace. And therof come alle oure goodys by whych we be led and savyd. For the commawndementys[2] of God come there in, in whych we owe to have two manner of understandyng. That one is that we owe to understand and know whych by his byddynges, to love them and to kepe them. That other is that we owe to knowe his forbyddynges, to hate them and refuse them. For in theyse two is all oure werkyng comprehendyd. Also in oure feyth come the vii sacramentes,[3] eche folowyng other in order as God hath ordeyneth them to us, and all manner vertuse. For the same vertuse that we have receyvyd of oure substaunce gevyn to us in kynd of the goodnes of God, the same vertuse by the werkyng of mercy be gevyn to us in

---

6. And because of these great riches and because of this high nobility, virtues in proportion come to our soul at that time it is knit to our body, by which knitting we are made sensual, physical.

7. I saw that our nature is whole in God, into which nature he makes diverse qualities flowing out of him to work his will, which qualities protect nature, and mercy and grace restore and fulfill it. S1 has *whom* instead of P's *whose*.

8. And of these (substance and sensuality), none shall be destroyed.

9. Which nature was first appointed to him. It was decreed from the beginning that Christ should take on human nature. "Comprehendyd": understood and included.

1. The next good, after nature, in the list of three introduced at the end of chapter 56. The third follows: all the goods by which we are saved.

2. Commandments.

3. Seven sacraments or religious rites of the Catholic Church: baptism, penance, the Eucharist, confirmation, marriage, ordination to the priesthood, extreme unction (the last rites).

grace throw the Holy Gost renewed, which vertuse and gyftys are tresoured to us in Jhesu Criste. For in that same tyme that God knytt hym to oure body in the meyden's wombe, he toke oure sensuall soule. In whych takyng, he us all havyng beclosyd in hym, he onyd it to oure substance; in whych oonyng he was perfit man.[4] For Crist, havyng knytt in hym all man that shall be savyd, is perfete man.

Thus oure Lady is oure moder in whome we be all beclosyd and of hyr borne in Crist. For she that is moder of oure Savyoure is mother of all that ben savyd in our Savyour. And oure Savyoure is oure very Moder in whome we be endlesly borne and nevyr shall come out of hym. Plentuously, fully, and swetely was this shewde. And it is spoken of in the **furst**, wher it seyde we be all in hym beclosyd, and he is beclosyd in us. And that is spoken of in the xvi shewyng, where he seyth he syttyth in oure soule. For it is his lykyng to reigne in oure understandyng blessydfully, and syttyth in oure soule restfully, and to dwell in oure soule endlesly, us all werkyng in to hym.[5] In whych werkyng he wylle we be his helpers, gevyng to hym alle oure entent, lernyng his lawes, kepyng his lore,[6] desyeryng that alle be done that he doth, truly trustyng in hym. For verely I saw that oure substaunce is in God.

Chapter 58

God, the blyssydfull Trynyte whych is evyr lastyng beyng, ryght as he is endlesse fro without begynnyng, ryghte so it was in his purpose endlesse to make mankynde, whych feyer kynd furst was dyght[7] to his owne Son, the Second Person. And when he woulde, by full accorde of alle the Trynyte, he made us alle at onys.[8] And in oure makyng he knytt us and onyd us to hym selfe, by whych oonyng we be kept as clene and as noble as we were made. By the vertu of that ech precyous onyng[9] we love oure maker and lyke hym, prayse hym and thanke hym and endlesly enjoye in hym. And this is the werkyng whych is wrought contynually in ech soule that shalle be savyd, whych is the godly wylle before seyde.[1]

And thus in oure makyng God almyghty is oure kyndly Fader, and God alle wysdom is oure kyndly Mother, with the love and the goodnes of the Holy Gost, whych is alle one God, onne Lorde. And in the knyttyng and in the onyng he is oure very tru Spouse and we, his

---

4. In which taking (of a sensual soul), having enclosed us all in him, he united it to our substance; in which union he was perfect man.
5. Working us all into him.
6. Teachings.
7. Appointed.
8. At once. Julian believes in the preexistence of souls in the Second Person of the Trinity before the creation of individual bodies; this is the first creation in which Jesus is our Mother in nature in our substantial making or creation of the substance of the soul.
9. By virtue of each precious union.
1. Revelation XIII, chapter 37, and Revelation XIV, chapter 53.

lovyd wyfe and his feyer meydyn, with whych wyfe he was nevyr displesyd. For he seyeth, *I love the and thou lovyst me, and oure love shall nevyr parte in two.*

I beheld the werkyng of alle the blessyd Trynyte, in whych beholld-yng I saw and understode these thre propertes: the properte of the faderhed, and the properte of the mother hed, and the properte of the lordschyppe in one God. In oure Fader almyghty we have oure kepyng and oure blesse and a nemptys oure kyndely substaunce, whych is to us by oure makyng fro without begynnyng. And in the Seconde Person in wytt and wysdom we have oure kypyng and anemptys oure sensuallyte, oure restoryng and oure savyng, for he is oure Moder, Broder, and Savyoure. And in oure good Lorde the Holy Gost we have oure rewardyng and oure yeldyng for oure lyvyng and oure traveyle, and endlessly ovyrpassyng alle that we desyer in his mervelous curtesy of his hye plentuous grace. For alle oure lyfe is in thre: in the furst, oure beyng; and in the seconde we have oure encresyng; and in the thyrde we have oure fulfyllyng. The furst is kynde, the seconde is mercy, the thyrde is grace.

For the furst I saw and understode that the hygh myght of the Trynyte is oure Fader, and the depe wysdom of the Trynyte is oure Moder, and the grete love of the Trynyte is oure Lorde. And alle these have we in kynde and in oure substauncyall makyng. And fer-there more I saw that the Seconde Person, whych is oure Moder substauncyally, the same derewurthy Person is now become oure Moder sensuall, for we be doubell of God's makyng, that is to sey, substaunciall and sensuall. Oure substaunce is the hyer perty, whych we have in oure Fader God almyghty. And the Seconde Person of the Trynyte is oure Moder in kynd in oure substauncyall makyng in whom we be groundyd and rotyd, and he is oure Moder of mercy in oure sensualyte takyng.[2] And thus oure Moder is to us dyverse man-ner werkyng, in whom oure pertys be kepte undepertyd. For in oure Moder Cryst we profyt and encrese, and in mercy he reformyth us and restoryth and, by the vertu of his passion, his deth, and his upry-syng, onyd us to oure substaunce. Thus workyth oure Moder in mercy to all his belovyd chyldren whych be to hym buxom[3] and obed-yent. And grace werkyth with mercy, and namely, in two propertes, as it was shewde, whych werkyng longyth to the Thurde Person, the Holy Gost. He werkyth rewardyng and gevyng. Rewardyng is a gyfte of trust that the Lorde doth to them that hath traveyled, and gevyng

---

2. And he is our Mother of mercy in taking our sensuality (physical and temporal existence in his assumption of human nature). By assuming human nature to atone for original sin, Jesus made mercy available to humankind.
3. Submissive.

is a curtesse werkyng whych he doth frely of grace, fulfyllyng and ovyr passyng alle that is deservyd of creaturys.[4]

Thus in oure Fader God almyghty we have oure beyng. And in oure Moder of mercy we have oure reformyng and oure restoryng, in whom oure partys be onyd and all made perfyte man. And by yeldyng and gevyng in grace of the Holy Gost we be fulfyllyde. And our substaunce is in oure Fader God almyghty, and oure substaunce is in oure Moder God all wysdom, and oure substaunce is in oure Lorde God the Holy Gost all goodnes. For oure substaunce is hole in ech Person of the Trynyte, whych is one God. And oure sensuallyte is only in the Seconde Person, Crist Jhesu, in whom is the Fader and the Holy Gost. And in hym and by hym we be myghtly takyn out of hell and oute of the wrechydnesse in erth, and wurschypfully brought up in to hevyn, and blyssydfully onyd to oure substaunce, encresyd in rychesse and nobly by all the vertu of Crist and by the grace and werkyng of the Holy Gost.

Chapter 59

And all this blysse we have by mercy and grace, whych manner blysse we myght nevyr have had and knowen but yf that properte of goodnesse whych is in God had ben contraryed, wher by we have this blysse. For wyckydnesse hath ben sufferyd to ryse contrary to that goodnesse, and the goodnesse of mercy and grace contraryed agaynst that wyckydnesse and turnyd all to goodnesse and wurshyppe to all that shall be savyd. For it is that properte in God whych doth good agaynst evylle. Thus Jhesu Crist, that doth good agaynst evyll, is oure very Moder. We have oure beyng of hym, where the ground of moderhed begynnyth with alle the swete kepyng of love that endlesly folowyth.

As verely as God is oure Fader, as verely is God oure Moder. And that shewde he in all, and namely, in theyse swete wordys there he seyth, *I it am.*[5] That is to sey, *I it am, the myght and the goodnes of faderhode. I it am, the wysdom and the kyndnes of moderhode. I it am, the lyght and the grace that is all blessyd love. I it am, the Trynyte. I it am, the unyte. I it am, the hye sovereyn goodnesse of all manner thyng. I it am that makyth the to long. I it am, the endlesse fulfyllyng of all true desyers.*[6] For ther the soule is hyest, noblyest, and wurschypfullest, yett it is lowest, mekest, and myldest.

And of this substauncyall grounde we have all oure vertuse in oure sensualyte by gyft of kynd and by helpyng and spedyng of mercy and grace, with oute whych we may nott profyte. Oure hye Fader

---

4. And giving is a courteous working which he does freely of grace, fulfilling and surpassing all that creatures deserve.
5. Revelation XII, chapter 26.
6. These attributes are different from those listed in chapter 26.

almyghty God, whych is beyng, he knowyth us and lovyd us fro before ony time. Of whych knowyng in his full mervelous depe charyte by the forseeng endlesse councell of all the blessyd Trynyte, he woulde that the Seconde Person shulde become oure Moder, oure Brother, and oure Savyoure. Where of it folowyth that as verely as God is oure Fader, as verely God is oure Mother. Oure Fader wyllyth, oure Mother werkyth, oure good Lorde the Holy Gost confyrmyth. And therfore it longyth to us to love oure God in whome we have oure beyng, hym reverently thankyng and praysyng of oure makyng, myghtly prayeng to oure Moder of mercy and pytte, and to oure Lorde the Holy Gost of helpe and grace. For in these iii is alle oure lyfe—kynd, mercy, and grace—werof we have myldeheed, pacyence and pytte, and hatyng of synne and wyckydnesse. For it longyth properly to vertuse to hat[7] synne and wyckydnesse.

And thus is Jhesu oure very Moder in kynd of oure furst makyng, and he is oure very furst Moder in grace by takyng of oure kynde made. Alle the feyer werkyng and all the swete, kyndly officis of dereworthy motherhed is in propred to[8] the Seconde Person, for in hym we have this goodly wylle,[9] hole and safe without ende, both in kynde and grace, of his owne propyr goodnesse. I understode thre manner of beholdynges of motherhed in God. The furst is grounde of oure kynde makyng. The seconde is takyng of oure kynde, and ther begynnyth the moderhed of grace. The thurde is moderhed in werkyng, and therin is a forth spredyng[1] by the same grace of lenght and brede, of hygh and of depnesse without ende. And alle is one love.

Chapter 60

But now me behovyth to seye a lytyll more of this forth spredyng, as I understode in the menyng of oure Lord: how that we be brought agayne by the motherhed of mercy and grace in to oure kyndly stede,[2] where that we ware in made by the moderhed of kynd love, whych kynde love nevyr leevyth us.

Oure kynde Moder, oure gracious Modyr, for he wolde alle hole[3] become oure Modyr in alle thyng, he toke the grounde of his werke full lowe and full myldely in the maydyn's wombe. And that shewde he in the **furst**, wher he broughte that meke maydyn before the eye of my understondyng in the sympyll stature as she was whan she conceyvyd. That is to sey, oure hye God, the sovereyn wysdom of all,

7. Hate.
8. The duties of beloved motherhood are reserved or appropriated to.
9. Goodly will. The same concept as the godly will in Revelation XIV, chapter 53.
1. Spreading forth.
2. Natural place.
3. Entirely.

in this lowe place he arayed hym and dyght hym all redy in oure poure flessch,[4] hym selfe to do the servyce and the officie of moderhode in alle thyng.

The moder's servyce is nerest, rediest, and suerest. Nerest for it is most of kynd, redyest for it is most of love, and sekerest for it is most of trewth. This office ne myght nor coulde nevyr none done to the full, but he allone.[5] We wytt that alle oure moders bere us to payne and to dyeng. A, what is that? But oure very Moder Jhesu, he alone beryth us to joye and to endlesse levyng, blessyd mot he be. Thus he susteyneth us with in hym in love and traveyle in to the full tyme that he wolde suffer the sharpyst thornes and grevous paynes that evyr were or evyr shalle be and dyed at the last. And whan he had done and so borne us to blysse, yett myght nott all thys make a seeth[6] to his mervelous love. And that shewd he in theyse hye ovyrpassyng wordes of love, *If I myght suffer more, I wold suffer more.*[7] He myght no more dye, but he wolde nott stynte werkyng. Wherfore hym behovyth to fynde us, for the deerworthy love of moderhed hath made hym dettour[8] to us.

The moder may geve her chylde sucke hyr mylke, but oure precyous Moder Jhesu, he may fede us with hym selfe and doth full curtesly and full tendyrly with the blessyd sacrament that is precyous fode[9] of very lyfe. And with all the swete sacramentes he susteynyth us full mercyfully and graciously. And so ment he in theyse blessyd wordys where he seyde, *I it am that holy chyrch prechyth the and techyth the.*[1] That is to sey, all the helth and the lyfe of sacramentyes, alle the vertu and the grace of my worde, alle the goodnesse that is ordeynyd in holy chyrch to the, I it am. The moder may ley hyr chylde tenderly to hyr brest, but oure tender Mother Jhesu, he may homely lede us in to his blessyd brest by his swet opyn syde and shewe us there in perty of the Godhed[2] and the joyes of hevyn with gostely suernesse of endlesse blysse. And that shewde he in the x[3] revelation, gevyng the same understandyng in thys swet worde where he seyth, *Lo, how I love thee.*

Beholde in to his blyssyd syde, enjoyeng thys feyer, lovely worde, *moder.* It is so swete and so kynde in it selfe that it may not verely be seyde of none ne to none but of hym and to hym that is very Mother of lyfe and of alle. To the properte of moderhede longyth

---

4. Attired himself and made himself all ready in our poor flesh.
5. These duties no one else might or could ever perform to the fullest except he alone.
6. Make satisfaction.
7. Revelation IX, chapter 22.
8. Debtor.
9. The blessed sacrament (the Eucharist) that is precious food.
1. Revelation XII, chapter 26.
2. He may lead us intimately into his blessed breast through his sweet open side and show us there in part the Godhead
3. Corrected from S1; P has *ix.*

kynd love, wysdom, and knowyng; and it is God. For though it be so that oure bodely forthbryngyng be but lytle, lowe, and symple in regard of oure gostely forth brynggyng, yett it is he that doth it in the creaturys by whom that it is done. The kynde, lovyng moder that woot[4] and knowyth the nede of hyr chylde, she kepyth it full tenderly, as the kynde and condycion of moderhed wyll. And evyr as it waxyth in age and in stature, she chaungyth her werkes but nott her love. And when it is wexid of more age, she sufferyth it that it be chastised in brekyng downe of vicis to make the chylde receyve vertues and grace. This werkyng with all that be feyer and good oure Lord doth it in hem by whome it is done. Thus he is our Moder in kynde by the werkyng of grace in the lower perty for love of the hyer. And he wylle that we knowe it, for he wylle have alle oure love fastenyd to hym. And in this I sawe that alle dett that we owe by God's byddyng to faderhod and moderhod is fulfyllyd in trew lovyng of God, whych blessyd love Cryst werkyth in us. And this was shewde in alle, and namely, in the hye plentuous wordes wher he seyth, *I it am that thou lovest.*[5]

Chapter 61

Ande in oure gostly forth bryngyng he usyth more tendernesse in kepyng, without ony comparyson, by as moch as oure soule is of more pryce in his syght. He kyndelyth oure understondyng. He prepareth oure weyes. He esyth oure consciens. He confortyth oure soule. He lyghteth oure harte and gevyth us in party knowyng and lovyng in his blessydfull Godhede with gracyous mynde in his swete manhode and his blessed passyon, with curtesse mervelyng in his hye ovyr passyng goodnesse, and makyth us to love all that he lovyth for his love and to be well apayde[6] with hym and with alle his werkes. And whan we falle, hastely he reysyth us by his lovely beclepyng[7] and his gracyous touchyng. And when we be strenthyd by his swete werkyng, than we wylfully chose hym by his grace to be his servauntes and hys lovers lestyngly[8] without ende.

And yett aftyr thys he sufferyth some of us to falle more hard and more grevously then evyr we dyd before, as us thyngkyth. And than ween[9] we that be nott alle wyse that all were noughte that we have begonne. But it is nott so. For it nedyth us to falle, and it nedyth us to see it. For yf we felle nott, we shulde nott knowe how febyll and

---

4. Understands.
5. Revelation XII, chapter 26.
6. Pleased.
7. Calling.
8. Lastingly.
9. Believe.

how wrechyd we be of oure selfe, nor also we shulde not so fulsomly know the mervelous love of oure maker.

For we shalle verely see in hevyn without ende that we have grevously synned in this lyfe. And notwithstondyng this, we shalle verely see that we were nevyr hurt in his love, nor we were nevyr the lesse of pryce[1] in his syght. And by the assey[2] of this fallyng we shalle have an hygh and a mervelous knowyng of love in God without ende. For hard and mervelous is that love whych may nott nor wyll not be broken for trespas.[3] And this was one understandyng of profyte.

And other is the lownesse and mekenesse that we shall get by the syght of oure fallyng, for therby we shall hyely be reysyd in hevyn, to whych rysyng we myghte nevyr have comyn without that meknesse. And therfor it nedyt us to see it. And if we se it not, though we felle, it shuld not profyte us. And comonly furst we falle and sethen[4] we se it, and both is of the mercy of God.

The moder may ~~suffer~~ the chylde to fall some tyme and be dyssesyd on dyverse manner for the one profyte,[5] but she may nevyr suffer that ony manner of perell come to her chylde for love. And though oure erthly moder may suffer hyr chylde to peryssch, oure hevynly Moder Jhesu may nevyr suffer us that be his chyldren to peryssch, for he is almyghty, all wysdom, and all love, and so is none but he, blessyd motte he be. But oft tymes when oure fallyng and oure wrechydnes is shewde us, we be so sore adred and so gretly ashamyd of oure selfe that unnethis we witt wher that we may holde us.[6] But then wylle nott oure curtesse Moder that we flee away, for hym were nothing lother.[7] But he wyll than that we use the condicion of a chylde. For when it is dissesyd and a feerd, it rynnyth hastely to the moder. And if it may do no more, it cryeth on the mother for helpe with alle the myghtes. So wyll he that we done as the meke chylde, seyeng thus, "My kynd Moder, my gracyous Moder, my deerworthy Moder, have mercy on me. I have made my selfe foule and unlyke to thee, and I may not nor canne amende it but with thyne helpe and grace."

And if we feele us nott than esyd, as sone be we suer that he usyth the condycion of a wyse moder. For yf he see that it be for profyte to us to morne and to wepe, he sufferyth with ruth and pytte in to the best tyme for love. And he wylle then that we use the properte of a chylde that evyr more kyndly trustyth to the love of the moder in wele and in woo. And he wylle that we take us myghtly to the feyth

1. Of less value.
2. Test.
3. Offense, sin.
4. Then.
5. (His or her) own profit.
6. Scarcely we know where we may protect ourselves.
7. More loathsome, hateful.

of holy chyrch and fynd there oure deerworthy mother in solas and trew understandyng with all the blessyd comoun.[8] For one singular person may oftyn tymes be broken, as it semyth to the selfe, but the hole body of holy chyrch was nevyr broken nor nevyr shall be without ende. And therfore a suer thyng it is, a good and a gracious, to wylle mekly and myghtly be fastenyd and onyd to oure moder holy church, that is Crist Jhesu. For the flode of mercy that is his deerworthy blode and precious water is plentuous to make us feyer and clene. The blessed woundes of oure Saviour be opyn and enjoye to hele us. The swet gracious handes of oure Moder be redy and diligent a bout us. For he in alle this werkyng usyth the very office of a kynde norysse[9] that hath nott elles to done but to entendd about the salvation of hyr chylde. It is his office to save us, it is his worshyppe to do it, and it is hys wylle we know it. For he wyll we love hym swetely and trust in hym mekely and myghtly. And this shewde he in these gracious wordes, *I kepe the fulle suerly.*[1]

Chapter 62

For in that tyme he shewde oure fraylte and oure fallyng, oure brekynges and oure noughtynges, oure dispytes and oure chargynges,[2] and alle oure woo as farre forth as me thought that it myght falle in thys lyfe. And therwith he shewde his blyssyd myght, his blessyd wysdome, his blessyd love, that he kepyth us in this tyme as tendyrly and as swetely to hys wurshyppe and as suerly to oure salvacion as he doth when we be in most solace and comfort, and ther to reysyth us gostly and hyely in hevyn, and turnyth alle to his wurshypp and to oure joye with out ende. For his precious love he sufferyth us nevyr to lese tyme. And all this is of the kynde goodnes of God by the werkyng of grace.

God is kynd in his being. That is to sey, that goodnesse that is kynd, it is God. He is the grounde, he is the substaunce, he is the same thyng that is kyndnesse, and he is very Fader and very Modyr of kyndys. And alle kyndes that he hath made to flowe out of hym to werke his wylle, it shulde be restoryd and brought agayne in to hym by salvacion of man throw the werkyng of grace. For of all kyndys that he hath sett in dyverse creatures by party, in man is alle the hole in fullheed and in vertu, in feyerheed and in goodheed, in ryalte and in noblye, in alle manner of solempnyte, of preciousnesse, and wurschyppe.

Here may we see that we be all bounde to God for kynd, and we be bounde to God for grace. Her may we see that us nedyth nott

---

8. In common with all the blessed. "Mother": the church is often referred to as a holy mother.
9. Nurse.
1. Revelation XIII, chapters 37 and 40.
2. Our being made worthless, our scorns, and our burdens.

gretly to seke ferre out to know sondry kyndys, but to holy church, into oure moder's brest, that is to sey, in to oure owne soule, wher oure Lord dwellyth. And ther shulde we fynde alle, now in feyth and in understandyng, and after verely in hym selfe clerely in blysse. But no man ne woman take this syngulary[3] to hym selfe, for it is not so. It is generall, for it is oure precious Moder Cryst. And to hym was this feyer kynde dyght[4] for the wurshyppe and the nobly of man's making and for the joye and the blysse of mannes salvacion, ryght as he saw, wyst, and knew fro with out begynnyng.

Chapter 63

Here may we see that we have verely of kynd to hate synne, and we have verely of grace to hate synne. For kynd is all good and feyer in it selfe, and grace was sent oute to save kynde, and kepe kynde, and dystroy synne, and bryng agayne feyer kynde in to the blessyd poynt from thens it cam, that is, God, with more noblynes and wurschyppe by the vertuse wurkyng of grace. For it shall be seen before God of all his holy in joy without end that kynd hath ben assayde[5] in the fyer of trybulation and ther in founde no lack nor no defaute.

Thus is kynd and grace of one accorde. For grace is God, as unmade kynde is God. He is two in manner werkyng and one in love, and neyther of them werkyth without other ne none be depertyd. And whan we by the mercy of God and with his helpe accorde us to kynde and to grace, we shall se verely that synne is wurse, vyler, and paynfuller than hell without ony lycknesse.[6] For it is contraryous to our feyer kynde. For as verely as synne is unclene, as trewly synne is unkynde. Al this is an horryble thyng to see to the lovyng soule that wolde be alle feyer and shynyng in the syght of God as kynd and grace techyth.

But be we nott a dred of thys, but in as moch as dred may spede.[7] But mekely make we oure mone to oure derewurthy Mother, and he shall all besprynkyl us in his precious blode, and make oure soule full softe and fulle mylde, and heele us fulle feyer by processe of tyme, ryght as it is most wurschype to hym and joye to us without ende. And of this swete, feyer werkyng he shalle nevyr ceese nor stynte tylle all his deerwurthy chyldren be borne and brought forth. And that shewde he where he gave the understandyng of the gostely thurst[8] that is the love longyng that shalle last tylle domys day.

Thus in oure very Moder Jhesu oure lyfe is groundyd in the for-

---

3. Individually.
4. Prepared.
5. Tried, tested.
6. Worse, more vile and painful than hell without any comparison.
7. Help.
8. Revelation XIII, chapter 31.

seeyng wysdom of hym selfe fro without begynnyng with the hye
myght of the Fader and the sovereyne goodnesse of the Holy Gost.
And in the takyng of oure kynd he quyckyd us, and in his blessyd
dyeng uppon the crosse he bare us to endlesse lyfe. And fro that
tyme and now and evyr shall in to domysday, he fedyth us and for-
dreth[9] us, ryght as the hye, sovereyne kyndnesse of moderhed wylle
and as the kyndly nede of chyldhed askyth. Feyer and swete is our
hevenly Moder in the syght of oure soule, precyous and lovely be the
gracyous chyldren in the syght of oure hevynly Moder with myld-
nesse and mekenesse and alle the feyer vertuse that long to chyldren
in kynde. For kyndly the chylde dyspeyreth[1] nott of the moder's love,
kyndely the chylde presumyth nott of it selfe, kyndely the chylde
lovyth the moder and eche one of them other. Theyse be as feyer
vertues with alle other that be lyke wher with oure hevynly Moder is
servyd and plesyd.

And I understode none hygher stature in this lyfe than chyldehode
in febylnesse and faylyng of myght and of wytte in to the tyme that
oure gracious Moder hath brought us upp to oure Fadyr's blysse.
And ther shall it verely be made knowen to us, his menyng in the
swete woordes wher he seyth, *Alle shalle be welle, and thou shalt see
it thy selfe that alle manner thyng shall be welle.* And than shalle the
blysse of oure moderheed in Crist be new to begynne in the joyes of
oure Fader God, whych new begynnyng shall last, without end new
begynnyng. Thus I understode that all his blessyd chyldren whych
be come out of hym by kynd shulde be brougt agayne in to hym by
grace.[2]

Revelation XV

Chapter 64

Afore this tyme I had grete longyng and desyer of Goddys gyfte to
be delyverde of this worlde and of this lyfe. For oft tymes I behelde
the woo that is here and the wele and the blessyd beyng that is there.
And yf there had no payne ben in this lyfe but the absens of oure
Lorde, me thought some tyme that it was more than I myght bere.
And this made me to morne and besely to longe, and also of my owne
wretchydnesse, slowth, and werynesse, that my lykyd not to lyve and
to traveyle as me felle to do.[3]

---

9. Furthers, supports.
1. Despairs.
2. Corrected from S1; these last two sentences appear at the beginning of Revelation XV,
   chapter 64, in P.
3. As it fell to me to do. "Besely": busily. "Slowth, and werynesse": sloth, laziness and
   weariness.

And to all this oure curteyse Lorde answeryd for comfort and pacyens and seyde these wordes, *Sodeynly thou shalte be taken from all thy payne, from alle thy sycknesse, from alle thy dyseses, and fro alle thy woo. And thou shalte come up above, and thou schalt have me to thy mede, and thou shalte be fulfyllyd of joye and blysse. And thou shalte nevyr more have no manner of paynne, no manner of sycknes, no manner mysselykyng, no wantyng of wylle,*[4] *but evyr joy and blysse withoute end. What shulde it than agrevyn thee to suffer a whyle sythen*[5] *it is my wylle and my wurschyppe?*

And in thys worde, *Sodeynly thou shalte be taken,* I saw that God rewardyd man of the pacience that he hath in abydyng Goddys wylle and of hys tyme, and that man lengyth[6] his pacyence ovyr the tyme of his lyvyng for unknowyng of hys tyme of passyng. This is a greate profyte. For yf man knew hys tyme, he shulde nott have pacience ovyr that tyme. And also God wylle that whyle the soule is in the body, it seeme to it selfe that it is evyr at the poynte to be takyn. For alle this lyfe and thys longyng that we have here is but a poynt, and when we be takyn sodeynly out of payne in to blesse, than payn shall be nought.

And in thys tyme I sawe a body lyeng on the erth, whych body shewde hevy and feerfulle and withoute shape and forme, as it were a swylge, stynkyng myrre.[7] And sodeynly oute of this body sprong a fulle feyer creature, a lyttylle chylld, full shapyn and formyd, swyft and lyfly and whytter then the lylye, whych sharpely glydyd[8] uppe in to hevyn. The swylge of the body betokenyth grette wretchydnesse of oure dedely flessch, and the lyttylnes of the chylde betokenyth the clennes and the puernesse of oure soule. And I thought with thys body blyveth[9] no feyernesse of thys chylde, ne of this chylde dwellyth no foulnes of the body.

It is fulle blesfulle, man to be taken fro payne, more than payne be taken fro man. For if payne be taken from us, it may come agayne. Therfore this is a sovereyne comfort and a blesful beholdyng in a longyng soule that we shall be taken fro payne. For in this behest I saw a mercyfulle compassion that oure Lorde hath in us for oure woo and a curtesse behytyng of cleene delyverance,[1] for he wylle that we be comfortyd in the ovyr passyng joy. And that he shewde in theyse wordes, *And thou shalte come uppe above, and thou shalte have me to thy mede, and thou shalt be fulfyllyd of joy and blysse.*

---

4. Uneasiness, no lacking of will.
5. Since. "Agrevyn": grieve, distress.
6. Prolongs.
7. A pit, a stinking bog. Figuratively, *mire* also refers to a state of sin from which it is difficult to escape. "Lyeng": lying.
8. Swiftly glided.
9. Remains.
1. Promise of pure deliverance. "Behest": promise.

It is Goddys wylle that we sett the poynt of oure thought in this blesfulle beholdyng as oftyme as we may and as long tyme kepe us ther in with his grace, for this is a blesfulle contemplacion to the soule that is ladde[2] of God and fulle moch to his wurschyppe for the tyme that it lastyth. And whan we falle agayne to oure selfe by hevynes and gostely blynesse and felynge of paynes gostely and bodely by oure fragylyte,[3] it is Goddys wylle that we know that he hath nott forgett us. And so menyth he in theys wordes and seyth for comforte, *And thou shalt nevyr more have payne in no manner nor no manner of sycknes, no manner of myslykyng, no wantyng of wyll, but evyr joy and blysse without ende. What shuld it than agrevyd the to suffer a whyle sythen it is my wylle and my wurschyppe?*

It is Goddys wylle that we take his behestes and his comfortyng as largely and as myghtly[4] as we may take them. And also he wylle that we take oure abydynges and oure dyssesys as lyghtely as we may take them and sett them at nought. For the lyghtlyer that we take them and the lesse pryce that we sett at them for love, lesse payne shalle we have in the feelyng of them, and the more thanke and mede shalle we have for them.

Chapter 65

And thus I understode that what man or woman wylfully chosyth God in this lyfe for love, he may be suer that he is lovyd without end with endlesse love that werkyth in him that grace. For he wylle we kepe this trustly, that we be as seker in hope of the blysse of hevyn whyle we are here as we shalle be in suerte when we ar there. And ever the more likyng and joye that we take in this sekernesse, with reverence and meekenes, the better lyketh him.

For as it was shewed, this reverence that I meane is a holy, curtious drede of our Lorde to which meekenes is knyt, and that is that a creatur see the Lord mervelous great and her selfe mervelous litle. For these vertues ar had endlesly to the lovyd of God. And it may now be seen and feelt in mesure by the gracious presence of oure Lord whan it is, which presence in all thyng is most desyrid, for it worketh that mervelous sekernesse in true faith and seker hope by greatnes of charitie in drede that is sweet and delectable.

It is God's wyll that I see my selfe as much bound to hym in love as if he had done for me all that he hath done, and thus shuld everie sowle thynke in regard of his lover. That is to say, the charyte of God makyth in us such a unitie that when it is truly seen, no man can parte them selfe from other. And thus ought ech sowle to thynke that God hath done for hym all that he hath done.

2. Led.
3. Fragility. "Gostely blynesse": spiritual blindness.
4. As generously and as powerfully.

And this shewith he to make us to love him, and likyn him, and nothyng dred but hym. For it is his wyll we know that all our myght of our enemy is loketh in our frindes handes.[5] And therfore the sowle that knoweth this sekerly, she shall nott dred but him that she lovyth. Alle other dredes she set them among passions and bodely sicknesse and imaginations. And therfore though we ben in so much payne, woo, and dysese that us thynkith we can thinke ryght nought but that we are in or that we feele, as soone as we may, passe we lightly over and sett we it at nought. And whi? For God will be knowen. For if we know him and love him and reverently drede him, we shall have patience and be in great rest. And it shuld bin great likyng to us, all that he doth. And this shewid our Lord in these wordes, *What shuld it than agrieve thee to suffre a while seeing it is my will and my worshipe?*

Now have I tolde you of xv shewynges, as God whytsafe to minyster them to my mynde, renewde by lyghtenynges and touchynges, I hope, of the same spiryte that shewyth them alle.[6] Of whych xv shewynges the furst beganne erly in the mornynge about the oure of iiii and it lastyd, shewyng by processe fulle feyer and soberly, eche folowyng other, tylle it was none of the day or paste.[7]

Revelation XVI

Chapter 66

Ande after this the goode Lorde shewde the xvi revelation on the nyght folowyng, as I shalle sey after, whych xvi was conclusyon and confirmation to all the xv. But furst me behovyth to telle yow as anenst[8] my febylnes, wretchydnes, and blyndnes. I have seyde at the begynnyng wher it seyth, "And in this sodeynly all my payne was taken fro me,"[9] of whych payne I had no grefe[1] ne no dysesses as long as the xv shewynges lastyd in shewyng. And at the ende alle was close and I saw no more. And soone I feelt that I should life longer. And anone my syckness cam agene, furst in my hed with a sownde and anoyse.[2] And sodeynly all my body was fulfyllyd with sycknes lyke as it was before, and I was as baryn and as drye as I had nevyr

---

5. Locked in our friend's hands.
6. Granted to impart them to my mind, renewed by the enlightening and influence, I hope, of the same spirit (the Holy Spirit) that showed them all.
7. Showing in the course of time very fair and quietly, each following the other, until it was the ninth hour of the day (from sunrise, about 3 P.M.) or past.
8. As regards.
9. Chapter 3.
1. Grief.
2. Sound and a noise.

had comfort but lytylle, and as a wrech mornyd hevyly for feelyng of my bodely paynes and for fautyng[3] of comforte gostly and bodely.

Then cam a relygyous person to me and askyd me how I faryd, and I seyde I had ravyd to day. And he loght lowde and inwardly.[4] And I seyde, "The crosee that stode before my face, me thought it bled fast." And with this worde the person that I spake to waxsed all sad and merveylyd. And anone I was sore ashamyd and astonyd for my rechelesnesse.[5] And I thought this man takyth sadly the lest worde[6] that I myght sey that sawe no more therof. And when I saw that he toke it so sadly and with so grete reverence, I waxsyd full grettly ashamyd and wolde a bene shryvyn.[7] But I cowlde telle it to no prest, for I thought, "How shulde a preste believe me when I, by seaying I raved, I shewed my selfe nott to belyve oure Lorde God?" Nott with-standing, I beleft hym truly for the tyme that I saw hym, and so was than my wylle and my menyng ever for to do without end. But as a fole I lett it passe oute of my mynde.

A, loo how wrechyd I was! This was a grett synne and a grett unkyndnesse, that I for foly of felyng of a lytylle bodely payne so unwysely left for the tyme the comfort of alle this blessyd shewyng of oure Lorde God. Here may yow se what I am of my selfe, but here in woulde oure curtesse Lorde nott leeve me. And I ley stylle tylle nyght, trustyng in his mercy, and than I began to slepe.

Chapter 67

Ande in my slepe at the begynnyng me thought the fende sett hym in my throte, puttyng forth a vysage fulle nere my face lyke a yonge man, and it was longe and wonder leen.[8] I saw nevyr none such. The coloure was reed lyke the tylle stone whan it is new brent, with blacke spottes there in lyke frakylles fouler than the tyle stone.[9] His here was rede as rust, not scoryd afore, with syde lockes hangyng on the thonwonges.[1] He grynnyd upon me with a shrewde loke, shewde me whyt teth and so mekylle[2] me thought it the more ugly. Body ne handes had he none shaply, but with hys pawes he helde me in the throte and woulde a stoppyd my breth and kylde[3] me, but he myght not.

This ugly shewyng was made slepyng, and so was none other. And

---

3. Failing.
4. Laughed loudly and heartily.
5. Astonished by my recklessness, carelessness.
6. Seriously the least word.
7. Would have been shriven, would have confessed and received absolution for sin.
8. Surprisingly lean. "Vysage": face.
9. A brick when it is newly fired, with black spots therein like freckles, speckles fouler than the brick.
1. His hair was red as rust, not parted in front, with side locks hanging on the temples.
2. Large.
3. Killed.

in all this tyme I trustyd to be savyd and kepte by the mercy of God. And oure curtesse Lorde gave me grace to wake and unnethys had ony lyfe.[4] The persons that were with me beheld me and wett my templys, and my harte beganne to comfort. And anon a lyttyll smoke cam in at the dorre with a greete heet and a foule stynch. And than I seyd, "Benedicite, Dominus! Is it alle on fyer that is here?" And I went[5] it had bene a bodely fyer that shuld aburne us all to deth. I asked them that were with me if they felt ony stynch. They seyde nay, they felt noone. I seyde, "Blessyd be God!" For than wyst[6] I wele it was the fende that was come only to tempte me. And anon I toke me to that oure Lorde had shewed me on the same daye with alle the feyth of holy church, for I behelde it as both in one and fled ther to as to my comfort. And anon alle vanysschyd awey, and I was brought to grete reste and peas without sycknesse of body or drede of conscience.

Chapter 68

And then oure good Lorde opynnyd my gostely eye and shewde me my soule in the myddys of my harte. I saw the soule so large as it were an endlesse warde[7] and also as it were a blessyd kyngdom. And by the condicions that I saw there in I understode that it is a wurschypfulle cytte. In myddes of that cytte, oure Lorde Jhesu, very God and very man, a feyer person and of large stature, hyghest bysschoppe, most solempne kynge, wurschypfullest lorde. And I saw hym clothyd solemply in wurschyppes. He syttyth in the soule evyn ryghte in peas and rest, and he rulyth and gemyth[8] hevyn and erth and all that is. The manhode with the Godhed syttyth in rest. The Godhede rulyth and gemeth withoutyn ony instrument or besynesse. And the soule is alle occupyed with the blessyd Godhed that is sovereyne myghte, sovereyne wisdom, and sovereyn goodnesse.

The place that Jhesu takyth in oure soule he shall nevyr remove withouten ende as to my syght. For in us is his homelyest home and his endlesse dwellyng. And in this he shewde the lykyng that he hath of the makyng of mannes soule. For as wele as the Fader myght make a creature, and as wele as the Son myght make a creature, so wele wolde the Holy Gost that mannys soule were made, and so it was done. And therfore the blessydfulle Trynyte enjoyeth without ende in the makyng of mannys soule, for he sawe without begynnyng what shulde lyke him without ende.

Al thyng that he hath made shewyth his lordschyppe, as under-

---

4. (I) scarcely had any life.
5. Believed.
6. Knew.
7. Stronghold, citadel.
8. Guards. Corrected from S1; P has *geveth,* gives.

standyng was gevyn in the same tyme by example of a creature that is led to se grete noblynesse and kyngdoms longyng to a lorde. And when it had sene alle the nobylnes beneth, than mervelyng it was steryd to seke uppe above to that hygh place where the lorde dwell-yth, knowyng by reson that hys dwellyng is in the wurthyest place. And thus I understonde truly that oure soule may never have rest in thyng that is beneth it selfe. And whan it comyth above alle creatures in to it selfe, yett may it not abyde in the beholdyng of it selfe. But alle the beholdyng is blyssydfully sett in God that is the maker dwell-yng ther in, for in mannes soule is his very dwellyng.

And the hyghest lyght and the bryghtest shynyng of the sytte[9] is the glorious love of oure Lorde God as to my syght. And what may make us more enjoye in God than to see in hym that he enjoyeth in us hyghest of all his werkes? For I saw in the same shewyng that yf the blessyd Trynyte myght a made mannes soule ony better, ony feyerer, ony nobeler than it was made, he shulde nott a been full plesyd with makyng of mannys soule. But for he made mannes soule as feyer, as good, as precious as he myght make it a creature, therfore the blessyd Trynyte is fulle plesyd withoute ende in the makyng of mannes soule. And he wylle that oure hartes be myghtly reysed above the depnesse of the erth and alle veyne[1] sorowes and enjoye in hym.

This was a delectable syghte and a restfulle shewyng that is with-out ende. And the beholdyng of this whyle we are here, it is fulle plesaunt to God and fulle grete sped to us. And the soule that thus beholdyth it makyth it lyke to hym that is beholde and onyd it in rest and in pease by hys grace. And this was a synguler joye and blysse to me that I saw hym syttyng, for the truth of syttyng shewde endlesse dwellyng. And he gave me knowyng truly that it was he that shewde me alle before.

And whan I had behold thys with avysement,[2] then shewed oure good Lordes wordes fulle mekely, without voyce and without open-yng of lyppes, ryght as he had done afore, and seyde full swetely, *Wytt it now wele, it was no ravyng that thou saw to day, but take it, and beleve it, and kepe thee there in, and comfort thee ther with, and trust therto, and thou shalt not be ovrycome*. Theyse last wordes were seyde for lernyng of full tru sykernesse that is oure Lorde Jhesu that shewed me alle. And ryght as in the furst worde that oure good Lorde shewde, menyng his blessyd passyon, *Here with is the fende ovyr come*,[3] ryght so he seyde in the last worde with full tru feytfullnes,[4] menyng us alle, *Thou shalt not be ovyr come*. And alle this lernyng

9. City.
1. Vain.
2. With due consideration.
3. Revelation V, chapter 13.
4. Faithfulness.

and this tru comfort, it is generalle to alle myne evyn Crysten, as it
is afore sayde, and so is God's wylle.

And this worde, *Thou shalt nott be ovyrcom*, was seyde fulle
sharply[5] and full myghtly for sekernesse and comfort agaynst all tryb-
ulacyons that may come. He seyde nott thou shalt not be trobelyd,
thou shalt not be traveyled, thou shalte not be dyssesyd; but he seyde,
Thou shalt not be ovyrcom. God wylle that we take hede at this worde
and that we be evyr myghty in feytfull trust, in wele and wo, for he
lovyth us and lykyth us. And so wylle he that we love hym and lyke
hym and myghtely trust in hym, and all shall be welle.

And sone all was close and I saw no more afftyr this.

Chapter 69

The feende came agayne with his heet and with his stynch and
made me fulle besy. The stynch was so vyle and so paynfulle, and
bodely heet also dredfull and traveylous.[6] Also I harde a bodely talk-
yng as it had been of two bodyes and both, to my thyngkyng, talkyd
at one tyme as they had holde a perlement with greate besynes.[7] And
all was softe whystryn,[8] and I understode nott what they seyd. And
alle this was to stere me to dyspere,[9] as me thought, semyng to me
as they scornyd byddyng of bedys whych are seyde boystosly with
moch faylyng devout intendyng and wyse diligence,[1] the whych we
owe to God in oure prayer.

And oure good Lorde God gave me grace myghtly to trust in hym
and to comfort my soule with bodely spech, as I shulde a done to a
nother person that had been traveyled. Me thought that besynes
myght nott be lykened to no bodely lykenesse.

Chapter 70

Mi bodely eye I sett in the same crosse there I had seen in comforte
afore that tyme, my tong with spech of Cristes passion and rehersyng
the feyth of holy church, and my harte to fasten on God with alle
the truste and the myghte, that I thought to my selfe, menyng, "Thou
hast nowe great besenes to kepe the in the feyth, for that thou shuldest nott be taken of thyne enemys. Woldest thou now fro this tyme
evyr more be so besy to kepe the fro synne, this were a good and a
sovereyne occupacion." For I thought faythfully, were I safe fro

5. Very sternly.
6. Perilous.
7. Parliament or discussion with great business. "Harde": heard.
8. Whispering.
9. Move me to despair.
1. As if they scorned the praying of the rosary, which is said rudely with much lack of devout
   intention and wise attention.

synne, I were fullle safe fro alle the feendys in helle and enemys of my soule.

And thus he occupyed me alle that nyght and on the morow tylle it was about pryme day.[2] And anon they were alle goone and passyd, and there lefte nothyng but stynke and that lastyd styll a whyle. And I scornede hym. And thus was I delyvred of hym by the vertu of Crystes passion, for ther with is the feend ovyrcome, as oure Lorde Jhesu Cryst seyde afore.[3]

In alle this blessyde shewyng oure good Lorde gave understandyng that the syght shulde passe, whych blessyd shewyng the feyth kepyth with his owne good wylle and his grace, for he lefte with me neyther sygne ne tokyn where by I myght know it. But he lefte with me his owne blessyd worde in tru understandyng, byddyng me fulle myghtly that I shulde beleve it, and so I do, blessyd mott he be. I beleve that he is oure Savyoure that shewed it, and that it is in the feyth that he shewde, and therfore I love it evyr joyeng. And therto I am bounde by alle hys owne menyng, with the nexte wordes that folowen, *Kepe thee there in, and comforte thee ther with, and truste therto*. Thus I am beholdyng to kepe it in my feyth.

For on the same day that it was shewde, what tyme the syght was passyd, as a wrech I for soke[4] it, and opynly I seyde that I had ravyd. Than oure Lorde Jhesu of his mercy wolde nott lett it peryssch, but he shewde hyt all ageene within my soule, with more fullehed with the blessyd lyght of his precyous love, seyeng theyse wordes full myghtely and fulle mekely, *Wytt it now welle, it was no ravyng that thou saw this day*, as if he had seyde, *For the syghte was passyd fro the, thou lost it and cowth[5] or myght nott kepe it. But wytt it now*, that is to seye, *now thou seest it*. This was seyde nott onely for the same tyme, but also to sett there upon the grounde of my feyth, where he seyeth anone folowyng, *But take it, and lerne it, and kepe thee ther in, and comfort the ther with, and trust therto, and thou shalt nott be ovyr com*.

Chapter 71

In theyse vi wordes that folowyth wher he seyth, *Take it*, his menyng is to fasten it feytfully[6] in oure hert. For he wylle it dwelle with us in feyth in to oure lyfe's ende and after in fullehed of joye, wyllyng that we have evyr feythfulle trust of his blessydfulle promyses, knowyng his goodnesse. For oure feyth is contraryed in dyverse maner by oure owne blyndnesse and oure gostely enemys within and withoute.

2. Prime, the first hour of the day, around 6 A.M. or sunrise.
3. Revelation V, chapter 13.
4. Denied, forsook.
5. Could.
6. Faithfully.

And there fore oure precyous lover helpyth us with goostely lyghte and tru techyng on dyverse manner within and withoute, where by that we may know hym. And therfore in what manner that he techyth us, he wylle that we perceve him wysely, receyvyng hym swetly, and kepe us in hym feythfully.

For a bove the feyth is no goodnesse keppt in this lyffe as to my syght; and beneth the feyth is no helth of soule. But in the feyth, there wyll oure Lorde we kepe us, for we have by his goodnesse and his owne werkyng to kepe us in the feyth. And by his suffraunce throw goostely enmyte we are asayde in the fayth and made myghty.[7] For if oure feyth had nott enmyte, it shulde deserve no mede, as by the understandyng that I have in oure Lordes meynyng.

Glad and mery and swete is the blessydfulle, lovely chere of oure Lorde to oure soulys, for he behelde us evyr lyvyng in love longyng. And he wylle oure soule be in glad chere to hym to yelde hym his mede. And thus I hope with his grace he hayth and more shall drawe the utter chere[8] to the inner and make us all att one with hym and ech of us with other in tru, lastyng joye that is Jhesu.

I have menyng of thre manner of cherys of oure Lorde. The furst is chere of passion, as he shewde whyle he was with us in this lyfe dyeng. And though this beholdyng be mornyng and swemfulle,[9] yet it is glad and mery, for he is God. The seconde manner of chere, it is pitte and ruth and compassion, and this shewyth he to all his lovers with sekernesse of kepyng that hath nede to his mercy. The thyrde is the blessydfulle chere as it shalle be withoutyn ende, and this was oftenest shewyd and longeste contynuyd. And thus in the tyme of oure payne and oure woo he shewyth to us chere of his passion and his crosse, helpyng us to beer it by his owne blessyd vertu. And in tyme of oure synnyng he shewyth to us chere of reuth and pytte, myghtely kepyng us and defendyng agaynst all oure enmys. And theyse two be the comyn cherys whych he shewyth to us in this lyfe, therwith meddelyng[1] the thyrde, and that is his blessyd chere lyke in perty as it shalle be in hevyn, and that is by gracyous toucchyng of swete lyghtenyng of goostly lyfe, wher by that we ar kept in true feyth, hope, and charite, with contrycion and devotion and also with contemplacion and alle manner of tru joyes and swete comfortes. The blessydfull chere of oure Lorde God werkyth it in us by grace.

7. And by his permission through spiritual hatred we are tested in the faith and made powerful
8. Outer expression. "Hayth": has.
9. Sorrowful.
1. Mixing, combining. "Comyn cherys": common, public expressions.

Chapter 72[2]

But now me behovyth to telle in what manner that I saw synne deedly in the creatures whych shulde nott dye for synne, but lyve in the joye of God withoute ende. I saw that twoo contrares shulde not be to geder in one stede. The most contraryous that are is the hyghest blesse and the deppest payne.

The hyghest blesse that is is to have God in cleerte of endlesse lyght, hym verely seyng,[3] hym swetly felyng, hym all peasable havyng in fullhede of joye. And thus was the blessydfulle chere of oure Lorde God shewde in perty. In whych shewyng I saw that synne was the most contrary, so ferforth that as long as we be meddlyd with any part of synne we shall nevyr see cleerly the blessyd chere of God. And the horyblyer and the grevowser[4] that oure synnes be, the depper are we for that tyme fro this blessyd syghte.

And therfore it semyth to us oftyn tymes as we were in parelle[5] of deth and in a party of helle for the sorow and the payne that synne is to us, and thus we are deed for the tyme fro the very syght of oure blessydfulle lyffe. But in all this I saw feythfully that we be nott deed in the syght of God, ne he passyth nevyr from us. But he shall nevyr have his fulle blesse in us tylle we have oure full blesse in hym, verely seyng his feyer blessydfulle chere. For we are ordeyned therto in kynde and getyn therto by grace.

Thus I saw how synne is deedly for a short tyme to the blessyd creatures of endlesse lyffe. And evyr the more clerly that the soule seeyth the blyssefull chere by grace of lovyng, the mor it longyth to se it in fulhed, that is to sey, in his owne lycknes. For notwithstond-yng that oure Lorde God dwellyth now in us and is here with us and colleth us and beclosyth us[6] for tendyr love that he may nevyr leve us, and is more nere to us than tonge may telle or harte may thyngke, yet maye we nevyr stynte[7] of mornyng ne of wepyng nor of sekyng nor of longyng tyll whan we se hym clere in his blessydfulle chere. For in that precious syght ther may no woo abyde nor wele feyle.

And in this I saw mater of merth and mater of mornyng. Mater of myrth, that oure Lorde, oure maker, is so nere to us and in us, and we in hym, by feythfulnesse of kepyng of his great goodnes. Mater of mornyng, for oure gostly eye is so blynde, and we so boren downe with weyght of oure deedely flessch and darcknes of synne that we may nott see oure Lorde God clerly in his blessydfull chere. No, and

---

2. Corrected from S1; P has no chapter 72.
3. Clarity of endless light, truly seeing him.
4. More horrible and more grievous.
5. Peril.
6. Embraces us and encloses us.
7. Stop.

bycause of this darknesse, scarce we can beleve or trowe[8] his grete love and oure feythfulnes of kepyng. And therfore it is that I sey we may nevyr leve of mornyng ne of wepyng.

This wepyng menyth nott all in poryng out of teerys[9] by oure bodely eye, but also to more gostely understandyng. For the kyndly desyer of oure soule is so gret and so unmesurable that if it were yeve us to oure joy and oure comfort alle the nobley[1] that evyr God made in hevyn and in erth, and we saw nott the feyer, blessydfulle chere of him selfe, yett shuld we nevyr leve mornyng ne of gostely wepyng, that is to sey, of paynfull longyng tyll whan we se verely the feyer, blessedfull chere of oure maker. And if we were in all the payne that hart may thyngk or tong may telle, and we myght in that tyme se his blessydfull chere, alle this payne shule us nott greve. Thus is that blessydfull syght ende of alle manner of payne to lovyng soules and fulfyllyng of all manner joy and blysse. And that shewde he in the hye, mervelous wordes where he seyth, *I it am that is hyghest. I it am that thou lovyst. I it am that is alle.*[2]

It longyth to us to have thre manner of knowyng. The furst is that we know oure Lorde God. The seconde is that we know oure selfe, what we are by him in kinde and in grace. The thyrde is that we know mekely that oure selfe is a gaynst oure synne and agaynst oure febylnes. And for these thre was alle this shewyng made as to my understandyng.

Chapter 73

Alle this blessyd techyng of oure Lorde God was shewde by thre partys, that is to sey, by bodely syght, and by worde formyd in myne understondyng, and by gostely syghte. For the bodely syghte, I have seyde as I sawe as truly as I can. And for the words, I have seyde them ryght as oure Lorde shewde them me. And for the gostely syghte, I have seyde some dele, but I may nevyr fulle telle it. And therfore of this gostely syght I am steryd to sey more as God wylle geve me grace.

God shewde ii manner of sycknesse that we have. That one is unpacyens or slouth,[3] for we bere oure traveyle and oure payne hevyly. That other is dispeyer or doughtfulle drede,[4] as I shalle sey after. Generally he shewde synne, wher in alle is comprehendyd.[5] But in specyall he shewde noone but theyse ii, and theyse two are it that moste traveylyth and trobyllyth us, as by that oure Lorde shewde

8. Trust.
9. Pouring out of tears.
1. Nobility.
2. Revelation XII, chapter 26.
3. Impatience or sloth.
4. Despair or doubtful dread, anxiety.
5. Understood and included.

me, of whych he wylle we be amendyd. I speke of such men and women that for Goddes love hate synne and dyspose them to do Goddes wylle. Than by oure gostly blyndhed and bodely hevynesse we are most enclynyng to theyse. And therfore it is Goddys wylle that they be knowen, and than shulde we refuse them as we do other synnes.

And for helpe agaynst thys, full mekely oure Lorde shewd the pacyens that he had in his harde passion, and also the joy and the lykyng that he hayth of that passion for love. And this he shewde in example that we shulde gladly and esely bere oure paynes, for that is great plesyng to hym and endlesse profyte to us. And the cause why we are traveyled with them is for unknowyng of love. Though the thre Persons of the blessyd Trynyte be alle evyn in the selfe,[6] the soule toke most understandyng in love. Ye, and he wylle in alle thyng that we have oure beholdyng and oure enjoyeng in love. And of this knowyng are we most blynde. For some of us beleve that God is allmyghty and may do alle, and that he is alle wysdom and can do alle. But that he is alle love and will do alle, there we fayle.

And this unknowyng it is that most lettyth[7] Goddes lovers as to my syght. For whan we begynne to hate synne and amend us by the ordynaunce of holy chyrch, yett ther dwellyth a drede that lettyth us, by the beholldyng of oure selfe and of oure synne afore done, and some of us for oure every day synnes. For we holde nott oure promise nor kepe oure clennes[8] that oure Lorde settyth us in, but fall oftymes in to so moche wrechydnes that shame it is to say it. And the beholdyng of thys makyth us so sory and so hevy that unnethys[9] we can see ony comfort. And thys drede we take some tyme for a mekenes, but it is a foule blyndnes and a wyckydnesse. And we can nott dyspyse it as we do another synne that we know, whych comyth thorugh lack of true jugment, and it is agayne truth. For alle the propertees of the blessydfulle Trynyte, it is Goddys wyll that we have most feythfulnes and lykyng in love. For love makyth myght and wysdom fulle meke to us. For ryght as by the curtesy of God he forgetyth oure synne after the tyme that we repent us, so wylle he that we forgett oure synne as agaynst oure unskylfulle hevynesse[1] and oure doughtfulle dredes.

Chapter 74

For I understonde iiii manner of dredys. One is dreed of afray[2] that comyth to man sodeynly by freelte. This dreed doth good, for it

6. All equal in themselves.
7. Hinders.
8. Cleanness, purity.
9. Scarcely.
1. In protection against our unreasonable dejection.
2. Attack, assault.

helpyth to purge man as doth bodely sycknesse or such other payne
that is nott synne. For all such paynes helpe man if they be pacyently
taken. The seconde is drede of payne, wher by man is sterid[3] and
wakyd fro slepe of synne. For man that is harde of slepe of synne,
he is nott able for the tyme to receyve the softe comforte of the Holy
Goste tylle he hayth undertaken this drede of payne of bodely deth
and of gostly enemys. And this drede steryth us to seke comfort and
mercy of God, and thus this drede helpyth us as an entre and abyllyth
us[4] to have contrycion by the blessydfulle touchyng of the Holy Gost.
The thurde is doughtfull drede. Doughtfulle drede, in as moch as it
drawyth to dyspeyer, God wylle have it turnyd in us into love by tru
knowyng of love, that is to sey, that the bytternesse of doughte be
turned in to swetnes of kynde love by grace, for it may nevyr plese
oure Lorde that his servauntes doughte in his goodnesse. The iiii[th]
is reverent drede,[5] for ther is no drede that fully plesyth God in us
but reverent drede, and that is softe. For the more it is had, the lesse
it is felte for swetnesse of love.

Love and drede are bredryn,[6] and they are rotyd in us by the goodnesse of oure maker, and they shall nevyr be taken from us without
end. We have of kynd to love, and we have of grace to love, and we
have of kynd to drede, and we have of grace to drede. It longyth to
the lordeschyppe and to the faderhed to be dred, as it longyth to the
goodnes to be lovyd. And it longyth to us that are his servauntes and
his children to drede hym for lordshyppe and faderhed, as it longyth
to us to love hym for goodhed. And though this reverent drede and
love be nott both in oone, but it are two in properte and in wurkyng,
and neyther of them may be had without other. And therefore I am
suer he that lovyth, he dreedyth, though he feele it but lytylle.

Alle dredys other than reverent drede that are proferyd[7] to us,
though they come under coloure of holynesse, they are nott so tru.
And here by may they be knowen on sonder.[8] That dreed that makyth
us hastely to fle fro alle that is nott goode and falle in to oure Lordes
brest as the chlyde in to the moder's arme, with alle oure entent and
with alle oure mynde knowyng oure febylnes and oure greate nede,
knowyng his evyrlastyng goodnesse and his blessyd love, only sekyng
in to hym for salvation, clevyng to with feythfulle trust—that dreed
that bryngyth us in to this wurkyng, it is kynde and gracious and
good and true. And alle that is contraryous to this, eyther it is wrong
or it is medylde with wrong.

Than is this the remedy, to knowe them both and refuse the wrong.

3. Stirred.
4. Helps us as an entrance and enables us.
5. Respectful awe, dread.
6. Brethren, brothers.
7. Offered.
8. Told apart, distinguished.

For the kynde propyrte of drede whych we have in this lyfe by the gracious werkyng of the Holy Gost, the same shall be in hevyn afore God, gentylle, curteyse, fulle swete. And thus we shalle in love be homely and nere to God, and we in drede be gentylle and curtesse to God, and both in one manner lyke evyn.[9]

Desyer we than of oure Lorde God to drede hym reverently, and love hym mekly, and to trust in hym myghtly. For when we drede him reverently and love hym mekly, oure trust is nevyr in veyne. For the more that we trust and the myghtylyer that we trust, the more we plese and wurschyppe oure Lorde that we trust in. And if us feyle this reverent drede and meke love, as God forbyd we shuld, oure trust shalle sone be mysrulyd for that tyme. And therfore us nedyth moch to praye oure Lorde of grace that we may have this reverent drede and meke love of his gyfte in hart and in worke, for without this no man may plese God.

Chapter 75

I saw that God may do alle that us nedyth. And theyse thre that I shall seyen, neden: love, longyng, and pytte.[1] Pytte and love kepyth us in the tyme of oure nede, and longyng in the same love drawyth us in to hevyn. For the thurst of God[2] is to have the generalle man in to hym, in whych thurst he hath drawyn his holy soules that be now in blysse. And so gettyng his lyvely membris, evyr he drawyth and dryngkyth and yett hym thurstyth and longyth.[3]

I saw thre manner of longyng in God and alle to one ende. The furst is for that he longyth to lerne us to know hym and to love hym evyrmore and more, as it is convenyent and spedefulle to us. The seconde is that he longyth to have us uppe in to blysse, as soules are whan they be taken oute of payne in to hevyn. The thurde is to fulfylle us of blysse, and that shall be on the last day fulfylled evyr to last. For I saw, as it is knowyn in oure feyth, that than payne and sorow schall be endyd to alle that shalle be savyd. And nott only we shalle receyve the same blysse that soules afore have had in hevyn, but also we shall receyve a new, whych plentuously shalle flye oute of God in to us and fulfylle us. And thoo be the goodes whych he hayth ordeyned to geve us fro without begynnyng.

Theyse goods are tresowred[4] and hid in hym selfe, for in to that tyme creature is nott myghty ne worthy to receyve them. In this we shulde se verely the cause of alle the dedes that God hayth done,

9. Equally alike.
1. I shall say, we need. Corrected from S1; P has *say: nede, love, longyng*.
2. Thirst of God (see Revelation XIII, chapter 31).
3. And so getting his living members, ever he draws and drinks and yet he thirsts and longs. Julian uses the metaphor of Christ's spiritual thirst in reference to the figurative Mystical Body of Christ.
4. Treasured.

and ovyr more we shulde see the cause of alle thynges that he hayth sufferyd. And the blysse and the fulfyllyng shalle be so depe and so hygh that for wonder an merveyle all creatures shulde have to God so grett reverent drede, ovyr passyng that hath be sene and felte before, that the pyllours of hevyn shulle tremylle and quake.[5]

But this manner of tremelyng and drede shalle have no manner of payne, but it longyth to the worthy majeste of God thus to be beholde of his creatures dredfully tremelyng and quakyng for moch more of joy, endlesly merveylyng of the greatnesse of God, the maker, and of the lest parte of alle that is made. For the beholdyng of this makyth creature mervelous meke and mylde. Wherfore God wylle and also it longyth to us, boyth in kynde and in grace, to wylle have knowyng of this, desyeryng the syghte and the wurkyng. For it ledyth us in ryght wey, and kepyth us in tru lyfe, and onyth us to God.

And as good as God is, as grett he is. And as moch as it longyth to his Godhed to be lovyd, so moch it longyth to his grett hyghnesse to be drad. For this reverent dred is the feyerrer[6] curtesy that is in hevyn before Goddys face. And as moch as he shall be knowyn and lovyd, ovyr passyng that he is now, in so much he shall be drad, ovyr passyng that is now. Wherfore it behovyth nedys to be that alle hevyn, alle erth shall tremylle and quake whan the pillers shall tremylle and quake.

Chapter 76

I speke but lytylle of this reverent dred, for I hope it may be seen in this matter afore seyde. But wele I wott oure Lorde shewd me no soules but thoe that dred hym. For welle I wott the soule that truly takyth the techyng of the Holy Gost, it hatyth more synne for the vyelnesse and the horyblyte[7] than it doyth alle the payne that is in helle. For the soule that beholdeth the kyndnesse of oure Lorde Jhesu, it hatyth no helle but helle is synne[8] as to my syght. And therfore it is Goddys wylle that we know synne, and pray besyly, and traveyle wylfully, and seke techyng mekly that we falle nott blyndly there in; and yf we falle, that we reyse redely. For it is the most payne that the soule may have to turne fro God ony tyme by synne.

The soule that wylle be in rest, when other mennys synnes come to mynde, he shuld fle it as the payne of helle, sekyng in to God for helpe agayne that. For the beholding of other mennes synne, it makyth as it were a thyck myst afore the eye of the soule. And we may nott for the tyme se the feyerhede of God, but yf we may beholde

5. The pillars of heaven shall tremble and quake.
6. Fairer.
7. Vileness and horribleness.
8. It hates no hell except as hell is sin.

them with contrycion with him,[9] with compassion on hym, and with holy desyer to God for hym. For without this it noyeth and trobelyth and lettyth the soule that beholde them, for this I understande in the shewyng of the compassion.

In thys blessydfulle shewyng of oure Lorde I have understandyng of twoo contrarious. That one is the most wysdom that ony creature may do in this lyfe, that other is the most foly. The most wysdom is a creature to do after the wyll and the councelles of his hyghest sovereynn frende. This blessyde frend is Jesu, and it is his wylle and counceyle that we holde us with hym and fasten us homely to hym evyr more in what state so ever we been. For whether we be foule or clene, we are evyr one in his lovyng. For wele ne for woo he wylle nevyr we fle hym.

But for the chaungeablete that we are in oure selfe, we falle oftyn in to synne. Than have we this by the steryng of oure enemy and by oure owne foly and blyndnes. For they sey thus, "Thou wottest wele thou arte a wrech, a synner, and also untrew, for thou kepyst nott thy convaunt.[1] Thou promysse oftyn tymes oure Lorde that thou schallt do better, and anon thou fallest agayne in the same, namely, in slouth and in lesyng[2] of tyme." For that is the begynnyng of synne as to my syghte and, namely, to the creatures that have gevyn them selfe to serve oure Lorde with inwarde beholdyng of his blessydfulle goodnesse. And this makyth us a dred to appere afore oure curteyse Lorde. Than is it oure enmye that wylle put us aback with his false drede of oure wrechydnesse for payne that he thretyth us by.[3] For it is his menyng to make us so hevy and so sory in this that we schuld lett outt of mynde the blessydfull beholdyng of oure evyrlastyng frende.

Chapter 77

Owre good Lord shewde the enmyte of the fende, wherby I understode that alle that is contraryous to love and to peace, it is of the feende and of his perty. And we have of oure febylnesse and oure foly to falle, and we have of mercy and of grace of the Holy Gost to ryse to more joye. And yf our enmye owght wynnyth of us by oure fallyng (for it is his lycknes), he lesyth many tymes more in oure rysyng by charyte and mekenesse.[4] And this glorious rysyng, it is to hym so great sorow and payne for the hate that he hath to oure soule that he brynneth[5] contynually in envy. And alle this sorow that he

9. The sinner.
1. Covenant, agreement. "Wottest": know.
2. Losing, wasting.
3. Threatens us with.
4. And if our enemy wins anything from us by our falling (for it is his pretense), he loses many times more in our rising by charity and meekness.
5. Burns.

would make us to have, it shall turne in to hym selfe. And for this it was that oure Lorde skornyd hym and shewde that he shalle be skornyd, and this made me myghtely to lawgh.[6]

Than is this the remedy, that we be a knowyn of[7] oure wrechydnes and fle to oure Lorde. For evyr the more nedyr[8] that we be, the more spedfulle it is to us to touch hym. And sey we thus in oure meanyng, "I knowe wele I have deservyde payne, but oure Lorde is almyghty and may ponyssch[9] me myghtly. And he is all wysdom and can ponyssch me wisely. And he is alle goodnesse and lovyth me tendyrly." And in this beholdyng it is spedfulle to us to abyde. For it is a fulle lovely mekenes of a synnfulle soule, wrought by mercy and grace of the Holy Gost, whan we wyll wylfully and gladly take the skorgyng and the chastyssyng[1] that oure Lorde hym selfe wylle geve us. And it shalle be fulle tendyr and fulle esy yf we wylle onely holde us plesyd with hym and with alle his werkes.

For that pennance that man takyth uppon hym selfe, it was nott shewde me; that is to sey, it was not shewde me specyfyed.[2] But this was shewde specially and hyghly and with fulle lovely chere, that we shulde mekely and pacyently bere and suffer that pennawnce that God hym selfe gevyth us with mynde of hys blessyd passion. For whan we have mynde of his blessyd passion with pytte and love, then we suffer with hym lyke as his frendes dyd that saw it.

And this was shewd in the **thyrtene**, nere at the begynnyng where it spekyth of pytte.[3] For he seyeth, *Accuse not thy selfe that thy tryb-ulation and thy woo is alle thy defawght, for I wylle not that thou be hevy ne sorowfulle undiscretly.[4] For I telle thee, how so evyr thou do, thou shalle have woo. And therfore I wylle that thow wysely know thy pennaunce whych thou arte in contynually, and that thou mekely take it for thy pennaunce. And than shallt thou truly se that alle this lyvyng is pennaunce profytable.* This place is pryson. This lyfe is pennaunce, and in the remedy he wylle that we enjoy.

The remedy is that oure Lorde is with us, kepyng us and ledyng in to fulhed of joy. For this is an endlesse joy to us in oure Lordes menyng that he that shalle be oure blesse when we are there, he is oure keper whyle we are here, oure wey and oure hevyn in tru love and feythfulle trust. And of this he gave understandyng in alle and, namely, in shewyng of his passion where he made me myghtly to chose hym for my hevyn.[5] Flee we to oure Lorde, and we shall be

---

6. Revelation V, chapter 13.
7. Acknowledge.
8. More needy.
9. Punish.
1. Scourging, whipping and chastising, rebuking.
2. Specifically.
3. Chapter 28, but these words are not included among Christ's locutions.
4. Indiscreetly. "Defawght": fault.
5. Revelation VIII, chapter 19.

comfortyd. Touch we hym, and we shalle be made cleene. Cleve we to hym, and we shalle be suer and safe from alle manner of peryllys.

For oure curtese Lorde wylle that we be as homely with hym as hart may thyngke or soule may desyer. But be we ware that we take not so rechelously this homelyhed for to leve curtesye.⁶ For oure Lorde hym selfe is sovereyn homelyhed. And so homely as he is, as curtesse he is, for he is very curteyse. And the blessyd creatures that shalle be in hevyn with hym with out ende, he wylle have them lyke unto hym selfe in alle thyng. And to be lyke to oure Lorde perfetly, it is oure very salvacion and oure fulle blysse. And yf we wett⁷ nott how we shall do alle this, desyer we of oure Lorde, and he shalle lerne us. For it is his owne lykyng and his wurschyppe, blessyd mott he be.

Chapter 78

Owre Lorde of his mercy shewyth us oure synne and oure feblynesse by the swete gracious lyght of hym selfe, for oure synne is so foule and so horryble that he of his curtesy wylle not shewe it us but by the lyght of his mercy. Of iiii thynges it is his wylle that we have knowyng. The furst is that he is the grownde of whom we have alle oure lyfe and oure beyng. The seconde is that he kepyth us myghtly and mercyfully in the tyme that we are in oure synne among alle oure enmys that are fulle felle uppon us.⁸ And so moch we are in the more parell for we geve them occasyon therto and know not oure awne nede. The thyrde is howe curtesly he kepyth us and makyth us to know that we goo amysse. The iiii is how stedfastly he abydyth us and chaungyth no chere, for he wylle that we be turnyd and oonyd to hym in love as he is to us.

And thus by gracyous knowing we may se oure synne profytable without dyspeyer. For sothly us nedyth to see it, and by the syghte we shulde be made ashamyd of oure selfe and brekyng downe as agaynst oure pryde and oure presumpcion.⁹ For us behovyth verely to see that of oure selfe we are ryght nought but synne and wrechydnesse. And thus by the sygth of the lesse that oure Lorde shewyth us, the more is wastyd whych we se nott.¹ For he of his curtesy mesuryth the sygth to us, for it is so foule and so horryble that we shulde not endure to se it as it is. And thus by this meke knowyng, thorow contrycion and grace, we shall be broken from alle

---

6. But be we aware that we take not so carelessly this intimacy that we leave, forget courtesy.
7. Know.
8. Enemies who are very cruelly upon us.
9. We should be ashamed of ourselves and breaking down our pride and our presumption, overconfidence.
1. And thus by the sight of less (sin) that our Lord shows us, the more (sin) is destroyed that we see not.

thyng that is not oure Lorde. And than shalle oure blessyd Savyour perfetely cure us and oone us to hym.

This brekyng and this curyng oure Lorde menyth by the generall man. For he that is hyghest and nerest with God, he may se hym selfe synfull and nedy with me. And I that am the leste and the lowest of tho that shalle be savyd, I may be confortyd with hym that is hyghest. So hath oure Lorde oonyd us in charite. Whan he shewde me that I shuld synne and, for joy that I had in beholdyng hym, I entendyd nott redely to that shewyng,[2] oure curteyse Lorde restyd there and wolde no ferther tech me tylle whan that he gave me grace and wylle to entende. And herof was I lerned though that we be hyely lyftyd in to contemplacyon by the specialle gyfte of oure Lorde, yett us behovyth nydys therwith to have knowyng and syght of oure synne and of oure febylnes. For without this knowyng we may not have trew meknesse, and withoutyn this we may nott be safe.

And also I saw we may nott have thys knowyng of oure selfe nor of none of all oure gostly enmys, for they wylle nott us so moch goode. For if it were by ther wylle, we shoulde nevyr se it tylle oure endyng day. Than are we moch bounde to God that he wylle hym selfe for love shewe it us in tyme of mercy and of grace.

Chapter 79

Also I had in this more understandyng in that he shewde me that I shulde synne.[3] I toke it nakydly to myn owne synguler person, for I was no notherwyse steryd[4] in that tyme. But by the high, gracious comfort of oure Lorde that folowde aftyr, I saw that his menyng was for the generalle man, that is to sey, alle man whych is synfulle and shall be in to the last day, of whych man I am a membre, as I hope, by the mercy of God. For the blessyd comfort that I sawe, it is large inough for us alle. And ther was I lernyd that I shulde se my awne synne and nott other mennys, but if it may be for comfort or helpe of my evyn Crysten.

And also in the same shewyng ther I saw that I shuld synne, ther was I lernyd to be dradfull for unsykernesse of[5] my selfe. For I wot nott how I shalle falle, ne I know not the mesure ne the gretnesse of my synne. For that wolde I awyst dredfull,[6] and therto I had no answere. Also oure curteyse Lorde, in that same tyme he shewde fulle swetly and fulle myghtely the endleshed and the unchaunge-abylte of his love and also his grete goodnesse and his gracious inwardely kepyng that the love of hym and of oure sowlys shalle nevyr

2. Revelation XIII, chapter 37.
3. Revelation XIII, chapter 37.
4. I took it plainly to my own individual person, for I was not otherwise stirred.
5. Anxious for uncertainty about.
6. Would I learn full of dread.

be depertyd unto withouten ende. And thus in the dred I have matter
of mekenesse that savyth me fro presumpcoun, and in the blessyd
shewyng of love I have mater off true comforte and of joy that savyth
me fro dyspeyer.

Alle this homely shewynge of oure curteyse Lorde, it is a lovely
lesson and a swete, gracious techyng of hym selfe in comforthyng of
oure soule. For he wylle that we know by the swetnesse of the homely
love of hym that alle that we see or fele, within or withoute, whych
is contraryous to thys, that it is of the enmy and nott of God. As
thus, yf that we be steryd to be the more rechelesher of oure levyng
or of the kepyng of oure harte by cause that we have knowyng of this
plentuous love, than nedyth us gretely to beware of this steryng. If
it come, it is untrew and greatly we owe to hate it, for it hath noo
lycknes[7] of Goddys wylle. And whan we be fallen by freelte[8] or blyndnes, than oure curtesse Lord touchyng us, steryth us and kepyth us.
And than wylle he that we se oure wrechydnesse and mekely be it
aknowen.[9] But he wylle nott that we abyde therwith, ne he wylle nott
that we besy us gretly aboute oure accusyng, ne he wylle nott that
we be to wrechydfulle on oure selfe. But he wylle that we hastely
entende to hym, for he stondyth alle aloone and abydyth us contynually, monyng and mornyng tylle whan we come. And he hath haste
to have us to hym, for we are his joy and his delyght, and he is oure
salve[1] of oure lyfe. There I sey he stondyth alle aloone, I leeve the
spekyng of the blessyd company in hevyn and speke of his office and
his werkyng here in erth uppe the condicion of the shewyng.

Chapter 80

By thre thynges man stondyth in this lyfe, by whych iii God is
wurschyppyd and we be sped, kepte, and savyd. The furst is use of
mannes kyndly reson. The seconde is the comyn techyng of holy
chyrch. The iii is the inwarde gracious werkyng of the Holy Gost.
And theyse thre be alle of one God. God is grounde of oure kyndly
reson. And God is the techyng of holy chyrch. And God is the Holy
Gost. And alle be sondry gyftes to whych he wylle we have grete
regarde and accordyng us therto. For theyse wurke in us contynually
alle te geder, and thoo[2] be gret thinges, of whych gretnesse he wylle
we have knowyng here as it were in an A B C. That is to sey, that
we may have a lytylle knowyng where of we shulde have fulhed in
hevyn, and that is for to spede us.

We know in oure feyth that God aloone toke oure kynde and none

7. Likeness, conformity.
8. Frailty.
9. Acknowledged.
1. Healing ointment.
2. Those.

but he and, ferther more, that Crist aloone dyd alle the grett werkes that longyth to oure salvation and none but he. And ryghte so he aloone doth now in the last end. That is to sey, he dwellyth here in us, and rewlyth us, and gevyth us in this lyvyng, and brynggyth us to his blesse. And thus shalle he do as long as any soule is in erth that shalle come to hevyn. And so farforth that yf ther were none such soule in erth but one, he shulle be with that alle aloone tylle he had brought it uppe to his blesse.

I beleve and understonde the mynystracion of holy angelys, as clarkes telle,[3] but it was not shewde me. For hym selfe is nerest and mekest, hyghest and lowest, and doyth all. And not onely alle that us nedyth, but also he doyth alle that is wurschippefulle to oure joy in hevyn. And there I sey he abydyth us, monyng and mornyng, it menyth alle the trew felyng that we have in oure selfe, in contricion and in compassion, and alle monyng and mornyng for we are nott onyd with oure Lorde. And such as is spedfull, it is Crist in us. And though some of us feele it sylden,[4] it passyth nevyr fro Crist tylle what tyme he hath brought us oute of alle our woo. For love sufferyth hym nevyr to be without pytte.

And what tyme that we falle in to synne and leve the mynde of hym and the kepyng of oure owne soule, than beryth Cryst a loone alle the charge[5] of us. And thus stondyth he monyng and mornyng. Than longyth it to us for reverence and kyndnesse to turne us hastely to oure Lorde and lett hym nott aloone. He is here aloone with us alle; that is to sey, only for us he is here. And what tyme I be straunge[6] to hym by synne, dyspeyr, or slowth, then I lett my Lorde stonde aloone in as moch as he is in me. And thus it faryth with us all whych be synners. But though it be so that we do thus oftyn tymes, his goodnesse sufferyth us nevyr to be a loone. But lastyngly he is with us, and tendyrly he excusyth us and evyr kepyth us from blame in his syght.

Chapter 81

Owre good Lorde shewde hym to his creature in dyverse manner both in hevyn and in erth, but I saw hym take no place but in mannes soule. He shewde hym in erth in the swete incarnacoun and hys blessyd passion. And in other manner he shewde hym in erth where I seyde I saw God in a poynt.[7] And in other manner he shewde hym in erth thus, as it were a pylgrymage. That is to sey, he is here with

---

3. Ministration of holy angels, as clerks (clerics and scholars) tell.
4. Seldom.
5. Responsibility, burden. "Leve the mynde of": forget.
6. Unfriendly.
7. Revelation III, chapter 11.

us ledyng us and shalle be tylle whan he hath brought us alle to his blysse in hevyn.

He shewde hym dyverse tymes reignyng, as it is a fore sayde, but pryncypally in mannes soule. He hath take there his restyng place and his wurschypfulle cytte, oute of whych wurschypfulle see[8] he shalle nevyr ryse ne remeve withoute ende. Mervelous and solempne is the place where the Lorde dwellyth. And therfore he wylle that we redely intend to his gracious touchyng, more enjoyeng in his hole love than sorowyng in oure oftyn fallynges. For it is the most wurschyppe to hym of ony thyng that we may do that we leve[9] gladly and merely for his love in oure pennaunce. For he beholdyth us so tendyrly that he seth alle oure lyvyng here to be penaunce. For kynde longyng in us to hym is a lastyng penaunce in us, whych penaunce he werkyth in us, and mercyfully he helpyth us to bere it.

For his love makyth hym to long, his wysdom and his truth with his ryghfulhed makyth hym to suffer us here. And in this manner he wylle se it in us. For this is oure kyndly penaunce and the hyghest to my syght, for this penawnce comyth nevyr fro us tylle what tyme that we be fulfylled whan we shulde have hym to oure mede.[1] And therfore he wylle that we sett oure hartes in the ovyr passyng, that is to sey, fro the payne that we feele in to the blysse that we trust.

Chapter 82

But here shewde oure curteyse Lorde the monyng and the mornyng of oure soule, menyng thus, *I wott well thou wylt lyve for my love, merely and gladly sufferyng alle the penawnce that may come to the. But for as moch as thou lyvyst nott with out synne, therfore thou arte hevy and sorowfulle. And if thou myghtest lyve without synne, thou woldest suffer for my love alle the woo that myght come to the. And it is soyth. But be not to moch a grevyd[2] with synne that fallyth to the agaynste thy wylle.*

Ande here I understode that the Lorde behelde the servaunt with pytte and nott with blame, for this passyng lyfe askyth not to lyve alle without synne.[3] He lovyth us endlessly, and we synne customeably,[4] and he shewyth it us fulle myldely. And than we sorow and morne dyscretly, turnyng us in to the beholdyng of hys mercy, clevyng[5] to his love and to his goodnesse, seeyng that he is oure medy-

---

8. Seat (of dignity and authority).
9. Live.
1. Reward.
2. Distressed.
3. Does not require (us) to live all without sin. Julian is distinguishing venial sin, which is impossible to avoid, from mortal sin, which is much more serious and committed deliberately.
4. Habitually.
5. Clinging.

cyne, wyttyng that we do but synne. And thus by the mekenesse that we gett in the syght of oure synne, feythfully knowyng his evyrlastyng love, hym thangkyng and preysyng, we plese hym.

I love the and thou lovyst me, and oure love shall nevyr be depertyd on two. And for thy profyte I suffer. And all this was shewde in gostly understondyng, seyeng this blessyd worde, *I kepe the full sykerly.*[6] And be the grett desyer that I saw in oure blessyd Lorde that we sulle[7] lyve in this manner, that is to sey, in longyng and enjoyeng, as alle this lesson of love schewyth, ther by I understonde that alle that is contraryous to this is nott of hym, but it is of enmyte. And he wille that we know it by the swete, gracious lyght of hys kynde love.

Iff any such lyver be in erth whych is contynually kepte fro fallyng, I know it nott, for it was nott shewde me. But thys was shewde, that in fallyng and in rysyng we are evyr preciously kepte in oure love. For in the beholdyng of God we falle nott, and in the beholdyng of oure selfe we stonde nott. And boyth theyse be soth as to my syght, but the beholdyng of oure Lord God is the hygher sothnes.[8] Than are we moch bounde to hym that he wylle in this lyvyng shew us this hygh sothnes.

And I understode whyle we be in this lyfe, it is full spedfull to us that we se theyse boyth at onys. For the hygher beholdyng kepyth us in gostly joy and trew enjoyeng in God. That other that is the lower beholdyng kepyth us in drede and makyth us a shamyd of oure selfe. But oure good Lorde wylle evyr that we holde us moch more in the beholdyng of the hygher and nought leve the knowyng of the lower in to the tyme that we be broughte uppe above where we shalle have oure Lorde Jhesu to oure mede and be fulfyllyd of joy and blysse with oute ende.

Chapter 83

I had in party touchyng, syght, and feelyng in thre propertees of God, in whych the strenght and the effecte of alle the revelacoun stondyth. And it were seen in every shewyng and most properly in the **twelfe**, were it seyeth oftyn tymes, *I it am.* The propertees are theyse: lyfe, love, and lyght. In lyfe is mervelous homelyhed, in love is gentylle curtesse, and in lyght is endlesse kyndnesse.

Theyse iii propertees were seen in oone goodnesse, in to whych goodnesse my reson wolde be oonyd and clevyng to with alle the myghtes. I behelde with reverent drede and hyghly mervelyng in the syght and in feelyng of the swete accorde that oure reson is in God, understandyng that it is the hyghest gyfte that we have receyvyd and it is growndyd in kynd.

6. Revelation XIII, chapters 37 and 40.
7. Shall.
8. Truth.

Oure feyth is a lyght kyndly comyng of oure endlesse day that is oure Fader God, in whych lyght oure Moder Cryst and oure good Lorde the Holy Gost ledyth us in this passyng lyfe. This lyght is mesuryd dyscretly, nedfully stondyth to us in the nyght.[9] The lyghte is cause of oure lyfe, the nyght is cause of oure payne and alle oure woo, in whych woe we deserve endlesse mede and thanke of God. For we with mercy and grace wylfully know and beleve oure lyghte, goyng therin wysly and myghtely. And at the end of woe sodeynly oure eye shalle be opynyd, and in clernes of syght oure lyght shalle be fulle, whych lyght is God, oure maker, Fadyr and Holy Gost in Crist Jhesu oure Savyour. Thus I sawe and understode that oure feyth is oure lyght in oure nyght, whych lyght is God, oure endlesse day.

Chapter 84

Thys lyght is charite, and the mesuryng of this lyght is done to us profytably by the wysdom of God. For neyther the lyght is so large that we may se clerly oure blessydfulle day, ne it is all sperryd fro us.[1] But it is such a lyghte in whych we may lyve medfully with traveyle,[2] deservyng the wurschypfull thangke of God. And this was sene in the **syxte** shewyng, wher he seyth, *I thanke the of thy servyse and of thy traveyle.* Thus charite kepyth us in feyth and in hope. And feyth and hope ledyth us in charite, and at the ende alle shalle be charite.

I had iii manner of understondynges in this lyght of charite. The furst is charite unmade. The secounde is charyte made. The thyrde is charyte gevyn. Charyte unmade is God. Charyte made is oure soule in God. Charyte gevyn is vertu, and that is a gracious gyfte of wurkyng in which we love God for hym selfe and oure selfe in God, and alle that God lovyth for God.

Chapter 85

Ande in this syght I merveyled hyghly, for nott with stondyng oure sympylle lyvyng and oure blyndnesse heer, yett endlessly oure curtesse Lorde beholdyth us in this wurkyng, enjoyeng. And of alle thyng we may plese hym best, wysely and truly to beleve it and to enjoy with hym and in hym. For as veryly as we shulle be in blysse of God without end, hym praysyng and thankyng, as veryly we have been in the forsyght of God lovyd and knowyn in his endlys purpose fro with-

---

9. Necessarily enduring for us in the night.
1. For neither is the light so bright that we may see clearly our blessedful day nor is it all withheld from us.
2. Meritoriously with toil, hardship.

out begynnyng. In whych unbegonne[3] love he made us. In the same love he kepyth us and nevyr sufferyth us to be hurt, by whych oure blysse myght be lessyd.[4]

And therfore whan the dome is gevyn and we be alle brought uppe above, than shalle we clerely see in God the prevytees whych now be hyd to us. And then shalle none of us be steryd to sey in ony thyng, "Lorde, yf it had ben thus, it had ben wele." But we shalle alle sey with one voyce, "Lorde, blessyd mott thou be, for it is thus, it is wele. And now we see verely that alle thyng is done as it was thyn ordynawnce or[5] ony thyng was made."

Chapter 86

This boke is begonne by Goddys gyfte and his grace, but it is nott yett performyd[6] as to my syght. For charyte pray we alle to gedyr with Goddes wurkyng, thankyng, trustyng, enjoyeng, for this wylle oure good Lord be prayde by the understandyng that I toke in alle his owne menyng and in the swete wordes where he seyth fulle merely, *I am grownd of thy besechyng.*[7] For truly I saw and understode in oure Lordes menyng that he shewde it, for he wyll have it knowyn more than it is. In whych knowyng he wylle geve us grace to love hym and cleve to hym, for he beholde his hevynly tresure and solace in hevynly joye, in drawyng of oure hartes fro sorow and darknesse whych we are in.

And fro the tyme that it was shewde, I desyerde oftyn tymes to wytt in what was oure Lord's menyng. And xv yere after and mor I was answeryd in gostly understondyng, seyeng thus, "What, woldest thou wytt thy Lordes menyng in this thyng? Wytt it wele, love was his menyng. Who shewyth it the? Love. Wherfore shewyth he it the? For love. Holde the therin, thou shalt wytt more in the same. But thou schalt nevyr witt therin other withoutyn ende."

Thus was I lernyd that love is oure Lordes menyng. And I sawe fulle surely in this and in alle that or God made us he lovyd us, whych love was nevyr slekyd[8] ne nevyr shalle. And in this love he hath done alle his werkes. And in this love he hath made alle thynges profytable to us. And in this love oure lyfe is evyr lastyng. In oure makyng we had begynnyng, but the love wher in he made us was in hym fro

---

3. Never begun, ever existent.
4. Lessened.
5. Command before.
6. Completed, accomplished.
7. Revelation XIV, chapter 41.
8. Slackened, diminished. "Or": before.

without begynnyng, in whych love we have oure begynnyng. And alle this shalle we see in God with outyn ende.

Deo gracias.[9]

Explicit liber revelacionum Julyane anatorite Norwyche, cuius anime propicietur Deus.[1]

CONTEXTS

JULIAN OF NORWICH

From the Short Text of *The Showings*†

[Scholars speculate that Julian composed the short text sometime in the first two decades after 1373. This first version is extant only in British Library Additional Manuscript 37790, also known as the Amherst Manuscript after a previous owner, a mid-fifteenth-century reproduction of a copy made in 1413, while Julian was still living. Only one-sixth the length of the long text, the short text provides an account of Julian's visionary experience without articulating its more innovative implications. For example, this first version omits the showing about the great deed that God will perform at the end of time in Revelation XIII of the long text and all but the discussion of prayer in the first three chapters of Revelation XIV. Julian's voice is less authoritative in the short text than in the long. She is aware that she can be accused of violating St. Paul's prohibition against women preaching in 1 Corinthians 14:34–35. At the end of chapter 6 she disavows any special privilege at the same time that she claims the responsibility to convey God's message.]

[*A Woman as Teacher*]

* * *

Botte god for bede that ȝe schulde saye or take it so that I am a techere, for I meene nouȝt soo, no I mente nevere so; for I am a womann, leued, febille *and* freylle. Botte I wate wele, this that I saye, I hafe it of the schewynge of hym tha(t) es souerayne techare. Botte sothelye charyte styrres me to telle ȝowe it, for I wolde god ware knawenn, *and* mynn evynn crystene spede, as I wolde be my selfe to the mare hatynge of synne *and* lovynge of god. Botte for I am a womann, schulde I therfore leve that I schulde nouȝt tell ȝowe the goodenes of god, syne that I sawe in that same tyme that is his wille, that it be knawenn? And that schalle ȝe welle see in the same matere that folowes aftyr, if itte be welle and trewlye takynn. Thane schalle ȝe sone forgette me that am a wrecche, and dose so that I lette ȝowe nought, *and* behalde Jhesu that ys techare of alle. I speke of thame that schalle be safe, for in this tyme god schewyd me non othere; bot in alle thynge I lyeve as haly kyrke techis, for in alle thynge, this blyssede schewynge of oure lorde, I be helde it as ane in god syght, and I vndyrstode neuer nathynge þer yn that stoneȝ me ne lettes me of the trewe techynge of halye kyrke.

* * *

† From *A Book of Showings to the Anchoress Julian of Norwich*, ed. Edmund Colledge OSA and James Walsh SJ (Toronto: Pontifical Institute of Mediaeval Studies, 1978), I.22–23; translated by Denise Baker. Copyright © 1978 by Pontifical Institute of Mediaeval Studies.

But God forbid that you should say or take it that I am a teacher, for I mean not so, and I meant never so; for I am a woman, unlearned, feeble, and frail. But I know well this that I say, I have it of the showing of him who is sovereign teacher. But truly charity stirs me to tell you it, for I would God were known and my fellow Christians helped, as I would be myself, to greater hating of sin and loving of God. But because I am a woman should I therefore believe that I should not tell you the goodness of God, since I saw at the same time that it is his will that it be known? And that shall you well see in the same matter that follows after, if it be well and truly taken. Then shall you soon forget me who am a wretch (and do so that I hinder you not) and behold Jesus that is teacher of all. I speak of them that shall be safe, for at this time God showed me no others. But in all things I believe as holy church teaches, for in all things I beheld this blessed showing of our Lord as one in God's sight, and I never understood anything therein that bewildered me or kept me from the true teaching of holy church.

MARGERY KEMPE

From The Book of Margery Kempe†

[Margery Kempe recounts her visit to Julian of Norwich around 1413 in her *Book,* the second attributed to an English woman. An anchorite of local renown, Julian offers spiritual guidance to the younger holy woman from nearby King's Lynn. In chapter 80 Margery describes her meditation on the Passion of Christ during Holy Week. This devotion, popularized by the early fourteenth-century *Meditations on the Life of Christ* mistakenly attributed to St. Bonaventure, encouraged the visualization of events, both biblical and imagined, from Jesus' life to evoke compassion for his suffering and contrition in the sinner. Margery's meditation on the scenes from the Passion can be compared and contrasted to Julian's visions of the same scenes in Revelations I, II, IV, and VIII.]

[*A Visit with Julian of Norwich*]

* * * And then she was bidden by our Lord to go to an anchoress in the same city, who was called Dame Julian. And so she did and showed her the grace that God put in her soul of compunction, contrition, sweetness and devotion, compassion with holy meditation and high contemplation, and full many holy speeches and dalliances

† From *The Book of Margery Kempe, A Norton Critical Edition*, trans. and ed. Lynn Staley (New York: W. W. Norton, 2001), pp. 32–33, 139–42. Copyright © 2001 by W. W. Norton & Company, Inc. Reprinted by permission of W. W. Norton & Company, Inc.

that our Lord spoke to her soul, and many wonderful revelations which she showed to the anchoress to learn if there were any deceit in them, for the anchoress was expert in such things and good counsel could give.

The anchoress, hearing the marvelous goodness of our Lord, highly thanked God with all her heart for his visitation, counseling this creature to be obedient to the will of our Lord God and fulfill with all her mights whatever he put in her soul if it were not against the worship of God and profit of her fellow Christians, for, if it were, then it were not the moving of a good spirit but rather of an evil spirit.

"The Holy Ghost moves never a thing against charity, and, if he did, he would be contrary to his own self, for he is all charity. Also he moves a soul to all chasteness, for chaste livers are called the temple of the Holy Ghost, and the Holy Ghost makes a soul stable and steadfast in the right faith and the right belief. And a double man in soul is ever unstable and unsteadfast in all his ways. He that is evermore doubting is like the flood of the sea, which is moved and borne about with the wind, and that man is not likely to receive the gifts of God. What creature that has these tokens, he must steadfastly believe that the Holy Ghost dwells in his soul. And much more, when God visits a creature with tears of contrition, devotion, or compassion, he may and ought to believe that the Holy Ghost is in his soul. Saint Paul says that the Holy Ghost asks for us with unspeakable mournings and weepings, that is to say, he makes us ask and pray with mournings and weepings so plenteously that the tears may not be numbered. There may no evil spirit give these tokens, for Jerome says that tears torment more the devil than do the pains of hell. God and the devil are evermore contrary, and they shall never dwell together in one place, and the devil has no power in a man's soul. Holy Writ says that the soul of a righteous man is the seat of God, and so I trust, sister, that you are. I pray God grant you perseverance. Set all your trust in God and fear not the language of the world, for the more despite, shame, and reproof that you have in the world, the greater is your merit in the sight of God. Patience is necessary unto you for in that shall you keep your soul."

Much was the holy dalliance that the anchoress and this creature had by commoning in the love of our Lord Jesus Christ the many days that they were together.

* * *

[Meditation on the Passion]

80. Another time she saw in her contemplation our Lord Jesus Christ bound to a pillar, and his hands were bound above his head. And then she saw sixteen men with sixteen scourges, and each scourge had eight lead-tipped lashes on the end, and every metal tip was full of sharp prickles as if it had been the rowels[1] of a spur. And those men with the scourges made covenant that each of them should give our Lord forty strokes. When she saw this piteous sight, she wept and cried right loudly as if she should have burst for sorrow and pain. And, when our Lord was utterly beaten and scourged, the Jews unloosed him from the pillar and gave him his cross to bear on his shoulder.

And then she thought that she and our Lady went by another way in order to meet with him, and, when they met with him, they saw him bear the heavy cross with great pain; it was so heavy and so rough that hardly he might bear it. And then our Lady said unto him, "A, my sweet son, let me help to bear that heavy cross." And she was so weak that she might not but fell down and swooned and lay still as a dead woman.

Then the creature saw our Lord fall down by his mother and comfort her as he might with many sweet words. When she heard the words and saw the compassion that the mother had of the son and the son of his mother, then she wept, sobbed, and cried as though she should have died for the pity and compassion that she had of that piteous sight and the holy thoughts that she had in the meantime, which were so delicate and heavenly that she could never tell them afterward as she had them in feeling.

Afterward she went forth in contemplation through the mercy of our Lord Jesus Christ to the place where he was nailed to the cross. And then she saw the Jews with great violence rend from our Lord's precious body a cloth of silk, which had cleaved and hardened with his precious blood so completely and straightly to our Lord's body that it drew away all the hide and all the skin from his blessed body and renewed his precious wounds and made the blood to run down all about on every side. Then that precious body appeared to her sight as raw, as a thing that was newly flayed out of the skin, full piteous and rueful to behold. And so had she a new sorrow so that she wept and cried right sorely.

And anon after she beheld how the cruel Jews laid his precious body to the cross and afterward took a long nail, rough and huge, and set it to his one hand and with great violence and cruelness they drove it through his hand. His blissful mother and this creature beholding how his precious body shrank and drew together with all

---

1. The rowel is the part of a spur that is a small wheel with several rotating sharp points.

the sinews and veins in that precious body for the pain that it suffered and felt, they sorrowed and mourned and sighed full sorely. Then saw she with her ghostly eye how the Jews fastened ropes on the other hand, for the sinews and veins were so shrunken with pain that it might not come to the hole that they had marked for it, and drew thereon to make it meet with the hole. And so her pain and her sorrow ever increased. And afterward they drew his blissful feet in the same manner.

And then she thought in her soul she heard our Lady say to the Jews, "Alas, you cruel Jews, why fare you so with my sweet son and did he you never any harm? You fill my heart full of sorrow.[2]

And then she thought the Jews spoke again violently to our Lady and put her away from her son. Then the foresaid creature thought that she cried out on the Jews and said, "You cursed Jews, why slay you my Lord Jesus Christ? Slay me rather, and let him go."

And then she wept and cried passingly sore so that many of the people in the church wondered on her body. And anon she saw them take up the cross with our Lord's body hanging thereon and made a great noise and a great cry and lifted it up from the earth a certain distance and afterwards let the cross fall down into the hole. And then our Lord's body shook and shuddered, and all the joints of that blissful body burst and went asunder, and his precious wounds ran down with rivers of blood on every side. And so she had ever more cause of more weeping and sorrowing. And then she heard our Lord hanging on the cross say these words to his mother, "Woman, see your son, Saint John, the Evangelist."

Then she thought our Lady fell down and swooned, and Saint John took her up in his arms and comforted her with sweet words as well as he could or might.

The creature said then to our Lord, as it seemed to her, "Alas, Lord, you leave here a care-full mother. What shall we now do and how shall we bear this great sorrow that we shall have for your love?"

And then she heard the two thieves speak to our Lord, and our Lord said to the one thief, "This day you shall be with me in paradise."

Then was she glad of that answer and prayed our Lord, for his mercy, that he would be as gracious to her soul when she should pass out of this world as he was to the thief; for she was worse, she thought, than any thief.

And then she thought our Lord commended his spirit into his father's hands and therewith he died. Then she thought she saw our

2. The anti-Judaism of the *Book* should be compared to other Middle English treatments of the Passion, which are often more intensely expressed. For remarks about Kempe's use of contemporary anti-Judaism as a critique of Margery's fellow Christians, see Lynn Staley, *Margery Kempe's Dissenting Fictions* (University Park: Pennsylvania State University Press, 1994), 68–74.

Lady swoon and fall down and lie still as if she had been dead. Then the creature thought that she ran all about the place as if she had been a mad woman, crying and roaring. And afterward she came to our Lady and fell down on her knees before her, saying to her, "I pray you, Lady, cease from your sorrowing, for your son is dead and out of pain, for I think you have sorrowed enough. And, Lady, I will sorrow for you, for your sorrow is my sorrow."

Then she thought she saw Joseph of Arimethea take down our Lord's body from the cross and lay it before our Lady on a marble stone. Our Lady had then a manner of joy when her dear son was taken down from the cross and laid on the stone before her. And then our blissful Lady bowed down to her son's body and kissed his mouth and wept so plenteously over his blessed face that she washed away the blood from his face with the tears of her eyes. And then the creature thought she heard Mary Magdalene say to our Lady, "I pray you, Lady, give me leave to handle and kiss his feet, for at these get I grace."[3]

Anon our Lady gave leave to her and all those that were there about to do what worship and reverence they would to that precious body. And anon Mary Magdalene took our Lord's feet and our Lady's sisters took his hands, the one sister one hand and the other sister another hand, and wept full sorely while kissing those hands and those precious feet.

And the said creature thought that she ran ever to and fro as if she had been a woman without reason, greatly desiring to have had the precious body by herself alone so that she might have wept enough in the presence of that precious body, for she thought that she would have died with weeping and mourning in his death for the love that she had of him.

And immediately she saw Saint John the Evangelist, Joseph of Arimethea, and other friends of our Lord come and would bury our Lord's body and prayed our Lady that she would suffer them to bury that precious body. Our doleful Lady said to them, "Sirs, would you take away from me my Son's body? I might never look upon him enough while he live; I pray you, let me have him now he is dead, and part not my son and me asunder. And, if you will bury him anyway, I pray you bury me with him, for I may not live without him."

And the creature thought that they prayed our Lady so fair, till at the last our Lady let them bury her dear son with great worship and with great reverence as it belonged to them to do.

* * *

3. Mary asks to venerate the most humble aspect of the physical body of Jesus. She is traditionally pictured at the feet of Jesus. Later, in chapter 85, Margery, for whom the Magdalene is a powerful example of love and piety, venerates Jesus' toes.

AUGUSTINE

From The Trinity†

[St. Augustine, the most influential father of the church, composed *The Trinity* between 400 and 416 C.E. In its fifteen books he examines the mystery of three persons in one God from scriptural and psychological perspectives. Based on Genesis 1:26–27 ("And God said, Let us make man in our image, after our likeness. . . . So God created man in his own image, in the image of God created he him; male and female created he them"), he argues that the individual can better understand the divine Trinity by analyzing various psychic trinities within the mind. In Book XII, chapters 3 and 4, Augustine divides the mind into a higher and a lower reason. The higher part is directed toward the contemplation of eternal things, while the lower focuses on temporal and physical concerns. Although Augustine does not explicitly identify the higher reason as masculine and the lower as feminine, his comparison of these two functions to Adam and Eve is developed into a gendered model of the soul by later writers, like Walter Hilton. Augustine's discussion provides a context for Julian of Norwich's concept of the two parts of the soul, the substance and the sensuality.]

[*The Two Parts of the Mind*]

* * * For just as among all the beasts, a help like unto himself was not found for man, unless one were taken from himself and formed into his consort, so for our mind, by which we consult the superior and inner things, for such employment of corporeal things as the nature of man requires, no help like unto itself was found in the parts of the soul which we have in common with the beasts.

And, therefore, a certain part of our reason, not separated so as to sever unity, but diverted, as it were, so as to help fellowship, is set aside for the performing of its own proper work. * * *

* * * But we ought so to seek a trinity in the whole nature of the mind, that even if there be no action at all upon temporal things—help is needed to do this work and, therefore, a part of the mind is diverted to handle these inferior things—yet a trinity may still be found in the one mind that is nowhere divided; and that when this distribution has already been made, then in that part alone, to which belongs the contemplation of eternal things, there is not only a trinity but also an image of God; but in that which has been diverted to the action upon temporal things, even if a trinity can be found, yet it cannot be an image of God.

* * *

† From Saint Augustine, *The Trinity*, trans. Stephen McKenna, CSSR (Washington, D.C.: The Catholic University of America Press, 1963), pp. 345–46.

WALTER HILTON

From The Scale of Perfection†

[Born possibly in 1343, the same year as Julian, Walter Hilton was educated at Cambridge University and joined the Augustinian Canons in
1386. He wrote a number of letters and treatises about spirituality,
including *The Mixed Life*, a tract addressed to a layman who wished to
live as a contemplative but could not withdraw from his worldly duties.
Hilton's most famous work is *The Scale of Perfection*, a handbook on
how to prepare for mystical union with God composed at the request of
a nun who was about to become an anchorite. Although some scholars
have speculated that Julian knew *The Scale of Perfection*, its first book
was not completed until the mid-1380s and its second not until just
before Hilton's death in 1396. In Book II, chapter 13, Hilton identifies
the two parts of the soul, sensuality and reason, the latter divided into
a higher and a lower part. Hilton's analysis demonstrates the gendered
model of the soul that medieval theologians developed from Augustine's
discussion in *The Trinity* as well as the prevailing negative attitude
toward the body.]

[*The Two Parts of the Soul*]

* * *

For thou schalt undirstonde that a soule hath two parties.[1] The
toon is called the sensualité; that is the fleschli feelynge bi the fyve
outeward wittes,[2] the whiche is comoun to man and to beest. Up[3]
the whiche sensualité, whanne it is unskilfulli[4] and unordynateli
rulid, is maad the image of synne, as I have bifore seid, for than is
the sensualité synne, whanne it is not rulid aftir resoun. That tothir[5]
partie is callid reson, and that is departid on two—the overe[6] partie
and the nethere[7] partie. The overe is likned to a man, for it schulde
be maister and sovereyne, and that is propirli the ymage of God, for
bi that oonli the soule knoweth God and loveth God. And the nethere
is likned to a woman, for it schulde be buxum[8] to the overe partie of
resoun, as a woman is buxum to man. And that liyth in knowynge

---

† From Walter Hilton, *The Scale of Perfection*, ed. Thomas H. Bestul (Kalamazoo: TEAMS,
2000), p. 159. Copyright © 2000 by the Board of the Medieval Institute. All rights
reserved.
1. Parts. The definition of the soul that follows is based on Augustine, *The Trinity*, 12.3–14,
as elaborated by medieval theologians.
2. Senses.
3. Of.
4. Irrationally.
5. Other.
6. Upper.
7. Lower.
8. Obedient.

and rulynge of ertheli thinges, for to use hem discreteli aftir nede
and for to refuse hem whanne it is no nede; and for to have ai[9] with
it thyn iye[1] upward to the overe partie of resoun, with drede and with
reverence for to folwe it.

* * *

AELRED OF RIEVAULX[†]

From De Institutione Inclusarum

[The comparison of Jesus to a mother dates back to the Old Testament
and was prominent in twelfth-century writings on the humanity of
Christ. Two references to the maternity of Jesus occur in the first guide-
book for English anchorites, Aelred of Rievaulx's *De Institutione Inclusarum* (Concerning the Instruction of the Enclosed). Composed in Latin
around 1162 for his sister, *De Institutione* provides an early example of
affective spirituality, the range of medieval devotional attitudes, prac-
tices, and rhetoric that evokes an emotional response to the humanity
of Christ. The first selection printed here compares the image of the
crucified Christ on the anchorite's altar to a nursing mother. The second,
from the meditation on the Last Supper, envisions the Apostle John
asleep on Christ's chest as a nursing child. These selections are from a
translation of the last twenty sections of the *De Institutione Inclusarum*
into Middle English made no later than the end of the fourteenth century
and included in the Vernon manuscript, probably compiled between
1382 and 1400.]

[*Jesus as Mother*]

* * *

* * * And as touchyngge holy ymages, haue in þyn awter þe ymage
of þe crucifix hangynge on þe cros, which represente to þe þe pas-
sioun of Crist, which þu schalt folwe. Al-to-gydere he is ysprad
abrood to bykleppe þe in his armes, in which þu schalt haue gret
delectacioun; and hys tetys beþ al naked ischewd to þe to ȝyue þe
melk of spiritual delectacioun and confortacioun. * * *

Now, goode seynt Ihon, what swetnesse, what grace, what liȝt,
what deuocion, what goodnesse þu drawst vp of þat euere-wellyngge

9. Always.
1. Eye.
† From Aelred of Rievaulx, *De Institutione Inclusarum: Two English Versions*, trans. John
Ayto and Alexandra Barratt, Early English Text Society, OS 287 (London: Oxford Uni-
versity Press, 1984), pp. 35, 45–46; translated by Denise Baker. Copyright © The Early
English Text Society 1984.

welle Criste, I prey þe tel me, ȝif hit be þy wylle. Certayn, þer beþ
alle þe tresores off whit and of wysdom, þer is welle of mercy, hows
of pyte, hony of euere-lastyngge swetnesse. A, a, swete and diere
disciple, wher hast þu geten al þis? Art þu heȝȝere þan Petre; holiere
þan Andrew; more accepted þan alle þe apostles? Trewely, þe grete
pryuylegie of þy chastete haþ igete al þis dignite, for þu were ichose
a mayde of God, and þerfore among alle oþre þu art most iloued.
Now, suster, þu art clene mayde, be glad and reuerently go nyer and
chalange sum partye of alle þis swete wurþynesse. And ȝif þu darst
auntre þe no furþere, let þilke pryue disciple Ihon slepe stille at
Cristes brest, and let hym drynke þe precious wyn of ioye in know-
yngge of þe grete godheede; and ren þu, suster, to þe pappys of his
manhede, and þerof suk out melke, þat þu mowe gostly be fed in
þenkyngge what he dude for vs in vre flehs.

*   *   *

And regarding holy images, have on your altar the image of the
crucifix hanging on the cross, which represents to you the passion
of Christ that you shall follow. His limbs are spread wide apart in
every particular to embrace you in his arms, in which you shall have
great delectation; and his teats are shown to you all naked to give
you milk of spiritual delectation and comfort. *   *   *

Now, good Saint John, what sweetness, what grace, what light,
what devotion, what goodness you draw up from that abundant well-
spring Christ, I pray you tell me, if it be your will. Certainly, there
are all the treasures of wit and of wisdom, there is a well of mercy,
a house of pity, honey of everlasting sweetness. A, a, sweet and dear
disciple, where have you gotten all this? Are you higher than Peter,
holier than Andrew, more accepted than all the apostles? Truly, the
great privilege of your chastity has gained all this dignity, for you
were chosen a maiden of God, and therefore among all others you
are most loved. Now, sister, you are a pure maiden, be glad and
reverently go near and lay claim to some part of all this sweet worthiness. And if you dare enter no further, let this same secret disciple
John sleep still at Christ's breast, and let him drink the precious wine
of joy in knowing of the great Godhead; and run you, sister, to the
paps of his manhood, and thereof suck out milk, that you may spiritually be fed in thinking of what he did for us in our flesh.

*   *   *

ANONYMOUS

From Ancrene Wisse (A Guide for Anchoresses)†

[The *Ancrene Wisse,* one of the earliest prose texts in Middle English, was written during the first quarter of the thirteenth century for three sisters enclosed as anchorites in northern Herefordshire near the Welsh border. Following Aelred of Rievaulx's *De Institutione Inclusarum,* the anonymous author of the *Ancrene Wisse* divides his work into an outer rule concerned with external matters and bodily actions and an inner rule governing the heart. Like his predecessor, he compares Jesus to a mother in several passages. Because the thirteenth-century West Midlands dialect of the original text is so difficult, these selections are from a Modern English translation by Anne Savage and Nicholas Watson.]

[*Jesus as Mother*]

* * * Our Lord, when he allows us to be tempted, is playing with us as the mother with her young darling. She runs away from him and hides herself, and lets him sit alone and look eagerly about crying "Mother! Mother!" and crying for a while; and then with open arms she jumps out laughing, and hugs and kisses him and wipes his eyes. So our Lord sometimes lets us be alone and withdraws his grace, his comfort and his support, so that we find no sweetness in anything that we do well, nor savor in our hearts. And yet at the same moment our Lord loves us none the less, for he does it out of his great love. * * *

"So our beating fell on him" [Isaiah 53:5] because he put himself between us and his Father, who was threatening to strike us, as a compassionate mother puts herself between her child and the angry, stern father, when he is about to beat it. * * *

* * * If a child had such a disease that it needed a bath of blood before it could be healed, any mother who made this bath for it would love it greatly. Our Lord did this for us, we who were so sick with sin and so soiled with it that nothing could heal us or cleanse us except his blood alone. * * * That he loves us more than any mother her child, he says himself through Isaiah: * * * "Can a mother," he says, "forget her child? And even though she does, I cannot ever forget you" [Isaiah 49:15]. * * *

† From *Anchoritic Spirituality: Ancrene Wisse and Associated Works,* trans. Anne Savage and Nicholas Watson, Classics of Western Spirituality (Mahwah, N.J.: Paulist Press, 1991), pp. 132, 182, 193.

CRITICISM

GRACE M. JANTZEN

From The Life of an Anchoress†

At whatever stage of her life Julian entered the anchorhold, she had by that time come to believe that the best way for her to develop her life of prayer was in these enclosed circumstances. To us, this attitude may seem somewhat unusual. The vocation of an anchoress was one with which people of late medieval times were rather more familiar than we are today. It is therefore important for us to explore this lifestyle and its purpose in order to understand the theology and spirituality within which Julian developed.

The English word 'anchorite' is derived from the Greek verb meaning 'to retire': an anchorite (male) or anchoress (female) retired from the world to live strictly within the enclosure of their anchorhold. The impulse toward such solitary living had its roots in the tradition of the desert fathers of the fourth century, who retreated from the cities in which the Church was increasingly accommodating itself to the norms of society, and sought, through self-surrender and extreme austerity, to develop a profound relationship with God, conquering the demons which tempted them away from him.[1] This desire for solitude and immediacy of contact with God, having given up social intercourse and the pleasures and responsibilities it entails, was frequently emphasized in medieval spirituality.[2] In fact, however, there was also considerable suspicion of the solitary life, and pressure towards communal living in monasteries and convents, where the development of holiness could be facilitated by obedience to the Rule and the abbot or superior.[3]

In the eleventh century there was something of a revival of the

---

† From *Julian of Norwich: Mystic and Theologian* (New York/Mahwah, N.J.: Paulist Press, 2000), pp. 28–33, 48–49. Copyright © 1988, 2000 Paulist Press, Inc., New York/Mahwah, N.J. Used with permission of the publisher and the author.

1. For background to the desert fathers, see Rowan Williams, *The Wound of Knowledge* (Darton, Longman & Todd, London, 1979), Ch. 5; Derwas Chitty, *The Desert a City* (Blackwell, Oxford, 1966); Thomas M. Gannon and George Traub, *The Desert and the City: An Interpretation of the History of Christian Spirituality* (Collier-MacMillan, London, 1969), pp. 17–50.

2. Medieval hagiography often modelled itself on Athanasius' vastly influential *Life of St. Anthony*, the hero of the desert tradition; and spiritual giants caught up in political and ecclesiastical turmoil sighed for withdrawal and solitude: cf. Bernard of Clairvaux' letter to the Carthusians, Epistle 250, in *Patrologiae Latina*, ed. J.-P. Migne, 221 vols. (Paris, 1844–64), *CLXXXII*, col. 451. New monasteries, especially Cistercian and Carthusian, regularly referred to themselves as desert wildernesses and did, often, establish themselves in relatively remote areas. Cf. E. Margaret Thompson, *The Carthusian Order in England* (SPCK, London, 1930); Peter F. Anson, *The Call of the Desert* (SPCK, London, 1961).

3. Cf. Simon Tugwell, 'Monastic Rules in the West', in his *Ways of Imperfection*, Ch. 7 (Darton, Longman & Todd, London, 1984); Jean Leclercq, Part One in *The Spirituality of the Middle Ages* (volume II of *A History of Christian Spirituality*, by Louis Bouyer, Jean Leclercq and François Vandenbroucke (Seabury, New York, and Burns Oates, London, 1968).

eremitical ideal, but with an important difference: many of the hermits and anchorites did not remove themselves to solitary places away from all contact with humanity, but sought to develop their solitude in towns and villages: being in the world but not of it. As we shall see, this change had important implications for the contemporary understanding of the vocation of an anchoress or anchorite, who were thus in much closer contact with society than earlier recluses had been, and yet preserved strict enclosure in their anchorhold.

In this they were distinguished from hermits, who, though also living a solitary life, did not confine themselves to a single place or cut themselves off from social intercourse to the same extent: in the Middle Ages hermits often repaired bridges and roads, acted as ferrymen, or assisted travellers in other ways.[4] The anchorite, by contrast, had no such function. Their role was to be set apart for prayer and communion with God, to seek his presence and develop holiness of life. If their anchorhold was attached to a church, as was often the case, an anchorite might occasionally preach or assist at the Mass; one of the ancient guides for anchorites encourages this.[5] But this was unusual by the fourteenth century, and would in any case apply only to men, not to women. It was, however, taken for granted that their prayers would include intercession for the town in which they lived, and that they would be available to offer counsel to those who came to the anchorhold seeking it. They might in one sense be 'dead to the world', but they were not to be useless towards it, and their usefulness entailed clear-sighted awareness of its doings.[6]

Often their reputation for sanctity spread far and wide, so that even very important people would make a considerable effort to go to see them. The biographer of Wulfric of Haselbury tells us that

> he was above all a doctor of body and soul: crowds came to see him by day and he made it his business not to refuse them his help. Many came to consult him in their perplexities, some for advice about their vocation, others about their ailments. To those at a distance he sent holy water or blessed bread: on those who came to his window he laid his hands or healed them with the sign of the Cross.[7]

Whatever we make of these healings, it is clear both that Wulfric's withdrawal from the world, rigorous though it was, did not include

---

4. Cf. Rotha Mary Clay, *The Hermits and Anchorites of England* (Methuen, London, 1914; rpt. Singing Tree Press, Detroit, 1968), p. xvii.
5. Grimlaic, *Regulae Solitariorum* (PL 103 cols. 575–664); cited in Francis D. S. Darwin, *The English Medieval Recluse* (SPCK, London, 1944), p. 9.
6. Cf. Linda Georgianna, *The Solitary Self: Individuality in the Ancrene Wisse* (Harvard University Press, Cambridge, Mass., and London, 1981) esp. Ch. 2.
7. John, Abbott of Ford, *Wulfric of Haselbury*, ed. Maurice Bell, Somerset Record Society Library vol. 47 (Printed for subscribers only, London, 1933), p. 50.

withdrawal from compassionate ministry to those in need, and also that his contemporaries considered Wulfric a very holy man. This high regard was accorded him even by royalty: he was consulted on separate occasions by King Henry I, King Stephen, and Queen Matilda, whom he sternly rebuked for her arrogance and misrule, of which he was evidently well aware.[8]

Julian characteristically says nothing of herself as a counsellor, but we know that her reputation was similarly spreading because she is mentioned in the book of Margery Kempe of King's Lynn, who sought her out for her advice and spiritual guidance in about 1412 or 1413.[9] In any case, the function of counsellor and spiritual mentor of an anchoress was meant to be subservient to her dedication to a life of prayer, and was an outgrowth from it. The desert fathers to whom they looked back for inspiration had tried to escape human society altogether in their efforts towards a single-minded dedication to God: Aelred of Rievaulx, writing a Rule for his anchoress sister in about 1160, makes specific reference to them as her model:

> You must first understand the reasons that motivated the monks of old when they instituted and adopted this form of life . . . to avoid ruin, to escape injury, to enjoy greater freedom in express-ing their ardent longing for Christ's embrace.[1]

By the fourteenth century, when the escape from human society was of a different form from that desired by the desert fathers, the ancho-ress was perforce much more involved with human concerns; but like them, the sacrifice not only of possessions and reputation but also of human society was meant to facilitate above all their total devotion to God and availability to him. Julian of Norwich makes this her first priority, having from an early age the unqualified prayer that she might develop 'the wound of longing with my will for God'.[2]

The lifestyle of an anchoress was intended to serve the develop-ment of this ideal. There was no single rule of life for all recluses. Some anchorites and anchoresses would have come from a religious

---

8. Richard II also consulted with and made his confession to an anchorite at Westminster Abbey on 13 June, 1381 before setting out to confront Wat Tyler at Smithfield. Cf. Darwin, p. 40.
9. *The Book of Margery Kempe*, ed. W. Butler-Bowden (Oxford University Press, Oxford and New York, 1944), pp. 54–56; cf. Maureen Fries, 'Margery Kempe', in Paul Szarmach, ed., *An Introduction to the Medieval Mystics of Europe* (State University of New York Press, Albany, 1984), pp. 217–35.
1. Aelred of Rievaulx, *De vita eremitica ad sororem liber* (PL 32 cols. 1451–74), incorrectly placed among St Augustine's works; also called *Regula ad sororem, De institutione inclu-sarum*. English tr., 'A Rule of Life for a Recluse', I.1, in *Treatises and the Pastoral Prayer*, Cistercian Fathers Series: Number Two (Cistercian Publications, Kalamazoo, Michigan, 1971), hereafter RR. As Georgianna points out, however, Aelred somewhat loses sight of the positive final reason in the rest of his book (p. 44).
2. Edmund Colledge, OSA, and James Walsh, SJ, eds. and trans., *Julian of Norwich: Show-ings*, Classic of Western Spirituality (New York: Paulist Press, 1978), p. 179.

order and would therefore have a rule already, which they would continue to keep, perhaps with modifications necessary for the anchoritic situation. Laymen and laywomen could also enter an anchorhold, however, and the circumstances were too individual for there to be a single rule applicable in all cases. However, Aelred's Rule already referred to was influential, as also was an earlier document, the *Regula Solitariorum* written in about 891 by a monk named Grimlaic.[3]

Most significant, however, was the *Ancrene Riwle*, or rule of life for anchoresses, written early in the thirteenth century for three sisters who had become anchoresses, though the anonymous author clearly intended his book for a wider audience.[4] The anchoresses themselves had requested a Rule; but the author replies with what Linda Georgianna has called an 'antirule'.[5] Monastic Rules of the preceding period, including that of Grimlaic and Aelred, had concentrated on the external circumstances of life. There are instructions about when and what an anchoress was to eat, when she might sleep, what she ought to wear, and what prayers she was to say. The *Ancrene Riwle* does offer suggestions about these matters in the first and last chapters, which the author treats as the external wrappings of his book; but in his central chapters he insists that the primary concern is the inner life, which cannot be simply regulated with a set of external precepts.

It was this inner life which made the solitary vocation the highest and most demanding to which one could be called.[6] The gospel story of Mary who sat at Jesus' feet while Martha served him is regularly applied to the contemplative and the active life respectively, together with Jesus' words that Mary had chosen the 'better part'; and the anchoress was identified with the contemplative. Thus for instance the *Ancrene Riwle*, though cautioning the anchoresses not to scorn or meddle in 'Martha's business' since it is also a laudable calling, nevertheless says,

> Ye anchorites have taken to yourselves Mary's part, which our Lord himself commended . . . Housewifery is Martha's part, and Mary's part is quietness and rest from all the world's din, that nothing may hinder her from hearing the voice of God.[7]

And Aelred calls on his sister to do as Mary did and

3. PL 103 cols. 575–664.
4. For an account of the date and authorship of the *Ancrene Riwle*, sometimes called the *Ancrene Wisse*, see E. J. Dobson, *The Origins of the Ancrene Wisse* (Clarendon Press, Oxford, 1976).
5. For an illuminating account of the *Ancrene Riwle* as antirule, see 'Self and Religious Rules', in Georgianna, pp. 1–31.
6. For a typical example of its praise, cf. *The Cloud of Unknowing I*, Classics of Western Spirituality (Paulist Press, New York, with SPCK, London, 1981).
7. The *Ancrene Riwle* VIII, ed. James Morton (Chatto and Windus, London, and John W. Luce, Boston, 1907), pp. 314–15. Hereafter AR.

> Break the alabaster of your heart and whatever devotion you
> have, whatever love, whatever desire, whatever affection, pour
> it all out upon your Bridegroom's head, while you adore the man
> in God and God in the man.[8]

The life of the anchoress was meant to be an arduous one, but the
arduousness was not for its own sake but for the interior life which
it developed. Because of this they were unlike the desert fathers who
tested the extremes of asceticism. The rules we have for anchoresses,
especially the *Ancrene Riwle*, expressly prohibit ascetical heroics,
and suggest a moderate lifestyle when measured against the stan-
dards of living of the time.

The anchorhold itself would generally consist of a fair-sized room
or suite of rooms, and might well be less cramped than the homes
of the lower classes. Often, as in the case of St Julian's, it was built
against the side of a church, with a window or squint pierced through
the wall so that the anchoress could follow the daily service. The
Ancrene Riwle gives special instruction about this:

> To Priest's hours listen as well as you can, but you should nei-
> ther say the versicles with him nor sing so that he may hear it.[9]

The anchorhold would probably have an oratory with an altar; if the
anchorite were a priest, he might assist in celebration of the Mass,
but this would obviously not apply to women. In their case, the altar
was to be covered with a white linen cloth, symbolic of chastity and
simplicity; upon it was to be a crucifix and, if they wished, a picture
of Christ's Mother and his disciple on either side of it.[1] Apart from
those, they were not to have pictures or decoration in the anchorhold.

Besides the window to the church there would be a window to the
world, where people could come for counsel and guidance. It seems
that at least in some cases this window did not open directly to the
outdoors, but rather to a small parlour, so that visitors might sit in
it and speak to the anchoress through the window, away from prying
eyes and pouring rain.[2] * * *

From the main anchorhold, a door (or perhaps in some cases a
third window) would open into another room or rooms in which
stayed a servant or two, and which in turn opened to the outside
world. The servant was responsible for all the domestic necessities
of the anchoress—cooking, cleaning, shopping, and the like—the
'housewifery' in which the anchoress was not to allow herself to be
involved. It would clearly be very important to the anchoress that

---

8. RR 31, p. 85; cf. *Cloud* XVI–XXI.
9. AR I, p. 35.
1. RR 26, pp. 72–74.
2. cf. *Wulfric of Haselbury*.

her servant would be steady and responsible, and sympathetic to the aims of the anchoritic life; troubles with her domestic staff would be a perpetual source of distraction to an anchoress, and should be pre-empted by taking great care about the servant in the first place. If troubles did arise, they could result either from not getting along, or from getting along rather too well, so that the anchoress would be tempted to spend time chatting which she ought to spend in prayer. Aelred gives the following advice on the choice of the domestic:

> Choose for yourself some elderly woman, not someone who is quarrelsome or unsettled or given to idle gossip; a good woman with a well-established reputation for virtue. She is to keep the door of your cell, and, as she thinks right, to admit or refuse visitors; and to receive and look after whatever provisions are needed. She should have under her a strong girl capable of heavy work, to fetch wood and water, cook vegetables and, when ill-health demands it, to prepare more nourishing food. She must be kept under strict discipline, lest, by her frivolous behaviour she desecrate your holy dwelling-place and so bring God's name and your own vocation into contempt.[3]

The *Ancrene Riwle* lays down rules for the domestic when she goes out shopping or on any other business: 'by the way, as she goeth let her go singing her prayers', and be so dressed and deport herself in such a way that everyone recognizes her as the anchoress's servant and does not attempt to engage her in idle conversation. She is expected to say prayers of her own, not to desire a salary beyond her food and clothing (about which, however, the anchoress is to be liberal), and all in all, to live a life of very considerable devotion to the anchoress and to God. And 'let them by all means forbear to vex their mistress', but if, being human, they do, they are to accept the penance which the anchoress imposes upon them. Having imposed the penance, the anchoress in turn is not to nag at them or 'ever again thereafter upbraid her with the same fault'.[4]

The anchoress thus has a solemn responsibility before God for her domestics, and is to teach them with great diligence and care,

> in a gentle manner, however, and affectionately; for such ought the instructing of women to be—affectionate and gentle, and seldom stern. It is right that they should both fear and love you; but that there should always be more of love than of fear. Then it shall go well.[5]

3. RR 4.
4. AR VIII.
5. AR VIII, p. 324.

Prayer will go better in an atmosphere of affection and tranquillity than in an overly solemn and heavy-handed anchorhold. The joy and delicate touch Julian shows in her writings was no doubt also a part of her dealings with her domestics. As we have seen from the wills of the period, Julian had at least one servant who had a sufficiently high reputation to be given a bequest in her own right.[6] It is interesting to note that in her profound reflections on the relationship between God's transcendent greatness and his loving intimacy, Julian applies to our attitude to God this very mixture of love and fear which the domestic is to have toward the anchoress:

> And as good as God is, so great is he; and as much as it is proper to his divinity to be loved, so much is it proper to his great exaltedness to be feared. For this reverent fear is the fairer courtesy which is in heaven before God's face; and by as much as he will be known and loved, surpassing how he now is, by so much will he be feared, surpassing how he now is.[7]

The solitude of the anchoress, therefore, was not absolute, for besides giving counsel to those who consulted her she had a domestic or two in her care. Nevertheless, her special hallmark was her strict enclosure. She never left her cell, and was regularly referred to as dead to the world, shut up as with Christ in his tomb.[8] 'Cell' could be interpreted fairly broadly, to include a garden or perhaps the churchyard where she could take the air.[9] Beyond this, however, there was no release from the anchorhold until death, on pain of excommunication.[1]

The idea of the anchoress's death to the world was symbolized in the rite of enclosure, of which several forms survive. In the Sarum usage, to which others are similar, a requiem Mass was sung at the church. Then there was a solemn procession to the anchorhold. When they arrived, the officiant blessed the anchorhold, and led the anchoress inside. The anchoress was then given extreme unction, after which the bishop scattered dust on the anchoress and the anchorhold, which from henceforward was to be considered her grave. The bishop then left the anchoress inside, and bolted the door

6. ["A bequest in November 1415 by one John Plumpton, a citizen of Norwich, left forty pence to the 'ankeres in ecclesia sancti Juliani de Conesford in Norwice', as well as twelve pence each to her serving maid and to her former maid named Alice." See Norman P. Tanner, "Popular Religion in Norwich with Special Reference to the Evidence of Wills, 1370–1532" (Ph.D. diss., Oxford, 1973)].

7. LT 75. The phrase here translated, 'it is proper to his divinity to be loved', is 'it longyth to his godhed to be lovyd'. 'Godhed' could be translated 'goodness' (following S2), as Clifton Wolters does. This makes better sense of the passage and is an even closer parallel to AR.

8. RR 14, p. 62; cf. AR VI, p. 286.

9. Darwin, p. 10.

1. Though exceptions were sometimes made in cases of dire necessity, such as severe illness or extreme old age; cf. Dunn, in Frank D. Sayer, ed. *Julian and Her Norwich: Commemorative Essays and Handbook to the Exhibition "Revelations of Divine Love"* (Norwich, 1913), p. 23.

on the outside, after which the procession returned to the church. It was a dramatic ceremony; its psychological impact on the ancho- ress and on any observers was intended to reinforce the conception that she was now dead to the world, and was never again to emerge from her enclosure.[2]

* * *

LYNN STALEY JOHNSON

[The Trope of the Scribe and the Question of Literary Authority in the Texts of Julian of Norwich]†

The subject of medieval scribes is bound up with the question of textual authority. Scribes not only left their marks upon the manu- scripts they copied, they also functioned as interpreters, editing and consequently altering the meaning of texts. Writers, however, did not simply employ scribes as copyists; they elaborated upon the fig- urative language associated with the book as a symbol and incorpo- rated scribes into their texts as tropes.[1] Such "ghostly scribes" provided authors with figures through which they could project authorial personas, indicate what we would call generic categories, express a sense of community, or guide a reader's responses to a text. Though a writer like Chaucer employed scribal metaphors to signal his relative powerlessness, thereby indicating the outlines of a care- fully conceived and concealed persona, women writers such as Hil- degard of Bingen and Christine de Pisan exploited those same metaphors to signal both their sense of authority and their awareness of the social constraints placed upon it. The two most important English women writers of the late Middle Ages, Julian of Norwich and Margery Kempe, seem especially aware of the ways in which the deployment of a scribe could be used strategically, as a means of

2. Darwin, Ch. 6; cf. Clay, Appendix A, pp. 193–98; also pp. 94–96.
† From Lynn Staley Johnson, "The Trope of the Scribe and the Question of Literary Author- ity in the Works of Julian of Norwich and Margery Kempe" in *Speculum* 66 (1991), 820, 827–33. Reprinted by permission of the Medieval Academy of America. A shorter version of this essay was read at the 1991 meeting of the Medieval Academy of America in a session organized and chaired by Franz H. Bäuml. I appreciate the comments of Professor Bäuml and others who heard the paper. I also thank Prof. Russell A. Peck for reading and commenting on an earlier stage of this essay.
1. For a discussion of the book as a symbol throughout classical and medieval times, see Ernst Robert Curtius, *European Literature and the Latin Middle Ages*, trans. Willard R. Trask (New York, 1953, reissued 1963), pp. 302–47.

maintaining control over texts they profess neither to control nor to aspire to control.

* * *

Authorial efforts to control texts were * * * difficult for little-known figures or for women such as Julian of Norwich and Margery Kempe. Both of these women give evidence of seeking control over their texts and consequently deployed scribes in ways that illuminate their senses of themselves as authors. The image each projects is carefully designed to elicit certain responses in a reader. Unlike Hildegard of Bingen, Chaucer, and Christine de Pisan, Julian of Norwich and Margery Kempe were not authorized to speak as representatives of official culture. Hildegard, who was from a respected Benedictine house and was licensed to speak and write by the pope, rhetorically allied herself with the voice of the Old Testament prophets and thus spoke with a power and a directness she could ascribe to the force of the God who inspired her. Similarly, Christine de Pisan and Chaucer buttressed their works with the weight of traditional culture and evolved ways of speaking from within the confines and inevitable constrictions of that culture. In contrast, both Julian of Norwich and Margery Kempe inherited a different sort of tradition.

They inherited a tradition whereby the female text—whether that text was written word or the life of a holy woman—was mediated and thus verified by a male author or scribe. Thus the writings of Catherine of Siena and Catherine of Genoa were dictated to male confessors; the autobiography of Beatrice of Nazareth was translated from its original Flemish into Latin by an anonymous confessor; the revelations of Bridget of Sweden were transcribed into Latin by her confessor; and *The Mirror of Simple Souls* lost its female author and, desexed and anonymous, was treated as an orthodox and valuable work of mystical theology by its male translators and glossers.[2] In addition, the majority of late-medieval holy women had male biographers. Writers like Thomas of Cantimpré and Jacques de Vitry used the examples of holy women to shame their more secular contemporaries.[3] Officials of the church assumed positions of authority

2. See Caroline Walker Bynum, *Holy Feast and Holy Fast: The Religious Significance of Food to Medieval Women* (Berkeley, 1987), pp. 21–23; Edmund Colledge and Romana Guarnieri, "The Glosses by 'M.N.' and Richard Methley to 'The Mirror of Simple Souls,' " *Archivio italiano per la storia della pietà* 5 (1968), 357–82. Roger Ellis, *The Liber Celestis of St. Bridget of Sweden*, EETS 291 (London, 1987), p. 367; Richard Kieckhefer, *Unquiet Souls: Fourteenth-Century Saints and Their Religious Milieu* (Chicago, 1984), introduction; Wolfgang Riehle, *The Middle English Mystics* (London, 1981). Figures such as Gertrude the Great and Hadewijch are, of course, exceptions to this rule of female illiteracy.

3. See John W. Baldwin, *Masters, Princes and Merchants: The Social Views of Peter the Chanter and His Circle*, 2 vols. (Princeton, 1970), pp. 72 ff., 110; Bynum, *Holy Feast*, p. 229; Kieckhefer, *Unquiet Souls*, pp. 31–33. For a provocative discussion of the ways in which in the medieval West men told women's stories and women told their own, see Caroline W. Bynum, "Women's Stories, Women's Symbols: A Critique of Victor Turner's

over these women by serving as their confessors and by writing their lives, thereby using holy women such as Marie d'Oignies and Christine Mirabilis as goads to contemporaries presumably in need of such "texts." Behavior and views that might appear to subvert the official culture were organized by and integrated into it through the voice of the scribe, who testified, mediated, and verified.[4]

In addition, from the last part of the fourteenth century on, there were increasing constraints in England on theological writing.[5] Although it was not until the drafting of the constitutions of Archbishop Arundel in 1407 that those constraints became official, from 1378, when the pope censured John Wyclif for his views on temporalities, there was growing unease with heterodoxy.[6] That unease, of course, did not preclude the literature of dissent, but it is nonetheless important to recognize that, at the same time that literacy and the tendency toward private devotion were beginning to increase, an official distrust of both was also on the rise. This distrust finally became explicit in the Lollard trials of the early fifteenth century, when book ownership might well arouse suspicion of heterodox views. By that time Lollardy was also linked to political dissent, so the charge was more serious than it would have been in Chaucer's time. The very books that were seen as tokens of reverence and authority were also seen as potentially threatening to authorities.[7]

Theory of Liminality," in Frank Reynolds and Robert Moore, eds., *Anthropology and the Study of Religion* (Chicago, 1984), pp. 105–25.

4. For further thoughts on this tendency, see Bynum, *Holy Feast*, p. 230 ff., and "Women Mystics and Eucharistic Devotion in the Thirteenth Century," *Women's Studies* 11 (1984), 179–214; Michael Goodich, "The Contours of Female Piety in Later Medieval Hagiography," *Church History* 50 (1981), 20–32; Jeanne S. Martin, "Character as Emblem: Generic Transformations in the Middle English Saint's Life," *Mosaic* 8 (1975), 47–60.

5. On this subject, see James Simpson, "The Constraints of Satire in 'Piers Plowman' and 'Mum and the Sothsegger,'" in Helen Phillips, ed., *Langland, the Mystics and the Medieval English Religious Tradition*, (Cambridge, Eng., 1990), pp. 11–30; Andrew Wawn, "Truth-Telling and the Tradition of *Mum and the Sothsegger*," *Yearbook of English Studies* 13 (1983), 270–87.

6. For ecclesiastical legislation in this period, see David Wilkins, ed., *Concilia Magnae Britanniae et Hiberniae*, 4 vols. (London, 1737), vol. 3. For evidence of official concern with heterodoxy, see pp. 123, 157, 158–65, 159, 166–72, 176, 204, 208, 210, 211, 221–22, 225, 247–49, 252–54, 254–63, 265, 270, 282; for Arundel's constitutions, see pp. 314–19. For studies of this issue, see Janet Coleman, *Medieval Readers and Writers, 1350–1400* (New York, 1981), pp. 213 ff.; Anne Hudson, ed., *Selections from English Wycliffite Writings* (Cambridge, Eng., 1978), introduction; K. B. McFarlane, *John Wycliffe and the Beginnings of English Nonconformity* (London, 1952, and New York, 1953), pp. 89 ff.; May McKisack, *The Fourteenth Century, 1307–1399*, Oxford History of England 5 (Oxford, 1959), p. 290; Peter McNiven, *Heresy and Politics in the Reign of Henry IV* (Woodbridge, Suffolk, 1987), pp. 11 ff.; Russell A. Peck, "Social Conscience and the Poets," in Francis X. Newman, ed., *Social Unrest in the Late Middle Ages* (Binghamton, 1986), pp. 113–48; D. W. Robertson, Jr., *Chaucer's London* (New York, 1968), pp. 133–35.

7. See David Aers, *Community, Gender, and Individual Identity: English Writing, 1360–1430* (London, 1988), introduction; Margaret Aston, *England's Iconoclasts* (Oxford, 1988) and *Lollards and Reformers: Images and Literacy in Late Medieval Religion* (London, 1984); Anne Hudson, *The Premature Revolution: Wycliffite Texts and Lollard History* (Oxford, 1988); Jonathan Hughes, *Pastors and Visionaries: Religion and Secular Life in Late Medieval Yorkshire* (Wolfeboro, N.H., 1988); N. P. Tanner, *Heresy Trials in the Diocese of Norwich, 1428–31* (London, 1977).

The works of Julian of Norwich and Margery Kempe suggest that both women were aware of the possible constraints on a female devotional writer. However, their works also suggest that they nonetheless thought of themselves as authors and consequently sought to create texts that were not simply annals of spiritual experience but narratives intended to give a particular form or meaning to experience.[8] They thus found it necessary to evolve narrative strategies that establish a certain textual authority; for both, this authority is bound up with a scribal presence.[9]

In both the long and the short text of the *Showings* by Julian of Norwich we have evidence of a highly self-conscious author.[1] We owe our knowledge of her authorial care to her own precision about the dates of her vision and of her composition of the two accounts of her vision. On May 13, 1373, she experienced the series of visions that she soon thereafter recorded in what is known as the short text of the *Showings*. She says that she meditated on the meaning of these visions for fifteen or more years and then wrote a second text, which once seems to have existed in two versions. The second version of the long text, which contained the full exposition of her important allegory of the Lord and the Servant, was apparently composed around 1393; so we can surmise that she rewrote her original work from about 1388 to 1393. When considering Julian, it is important to keep in mind that she never had any more visions: all versions of the *Showings* are accounts of those she experienced in 1373, when, by her own account, she was thirty and a half years old. Thus, though she was certainly a recluse and a mystic, she was also a writer, one who sought to clarify and to represent experience, which she located in time, through a narrative, which she likewise anchored in time. Such references point to the process of composition, or to her sense of her own authority as a visionary and as a writer or interpreter. Like Chaucer, Gower, and Langland, Julian's acts of revision suggest that she was attentive to the ways in which her text was read and understood.[2]

8. On this distinction, see Hayden White, "The Value of Narrativity in the Representation of Reality," in *The Content of the Form: Narrative Discourse and Historical Representation* (Baltimore, 1987), pp. 1–25.

9. For thoughtful considerations of the functions of literacy, see Franz H. Bäuml, "Varieties and Consequences of Medieval Literacy and Illiteracy," *Speculum* 55 (1980), 237–65, and "Medieval Texts and the Two Theories of Oral Formulaic Composition: A Proposal for a Third Theory," *New Literary History* 16 (1984), 31–50.

1. For important studies of Julian's artistry see the introduction to Edmund Colledge and James Walsh's edition, *A Book of Showings to the Anchoress Julian of Norwich*, 2 vols., Studies and Texts 35 (Toronto, 1978), and Barry Windeatt's article "Julian of Norwich and Her Audience," *Review of English Studies* 28 (1977), 1–17. All quotations from the *Showings* refer to the above edition and will be cited by page number in the text.

2. For a stimulating discussion of Langland's manipulation of authorial "inscription," see Anne Middleton, "William Langland's 'Kynde Name': Authorial Signature and Social Identity in Late Fourteenth-Century England," in *Literary Practice and Social Change in Britain, 1380–1530*, ed. Lee W. Patterson (Berkeley, 1990), pp. 15–82.

The types of revisions she made hint at her desire to control the meaning of her text by projecting a persona whose shifting relationship to a scribal presence underlines her growing understanding of the art of narrative and, perhaps, of her ability to "constitute" the public whom she addresses in her text.[3] The short text of the *Showings* is, for the most part, a record of the visions themselves and reads like the testimony of a singular experience. It seems designed to locate its authority as a devotional text in the fact that it bears witness to an extraordinary experience. Thus its authorial voice seems less authoritative than the one we encounter in the long text. The opening sentence of the short text presents Julian through the eyes of another, presumably a scribe: "Here es a visionn schewed be the goodenes of god to a deuoute womann, and hir name es Julyan, that is recluse atte Norwyche and ʒitt ys onn lyfe, anno domini millesimo CCCC xiij; in the whilke visyonn er fulle many comfortabylle wordes and gretly styrrande to alle thaye that desires to be Crystes looverse." This opening frames Julian in a highly specific way. It identifies her by gender, by vocation, by geographic location, and by chronology. The final clause designates the way in which we are to take this vision: it will stir up devotion in those who desire to be Christ's lovers. Julian is thereby insinuated into the circle of Richard Rolle and others who were linked to the fervent and mystical love of Christ. Julian's short text, which was clearly still circulating in 1413, was not only assimilated into an emotive or affective framework; it was also assigned a genre.

Later, in chapter 6, Julian pauses to focus on the problems of authority inherent in her gender. After emphasizing that love and vision shall teach and comfort the person who needs comfort (p. 221), she says: "Botte god for bede that ʒe schulde saye or take it so that I am a techere, for I meene nouʒt soo, no I mente nevere so; for I am a womann, leued, febille and freylle. Botte I wate wele, this that I saye, I hafe it of the schewynge of hym tha(t) es souerayne techare. . . . Botte for I am a womann, schulde I therfore leve that I schulde nouʒt telle ʒowe the goodenes of god, syne that I sawe in that same tyme that is his wille, that it be knawenn?" (p. 222). Julian here draws a distinction between teaching and telling. She certainly is not teaching (and thereby possibly incurring ecclesiastical censure) *because* she is a woman, but should she condemn herself to silence simply because she *is* a woman? She defines her authority as issuing from God, or from the visions she has experienced. However, lest she be accused of too much "singularity," she ends the chapter by stressing her allegiance to the teachings of the church: "bot in alle thynge I lyeve as haly kyrke techis, for in alle thynge, this blys-

---

3. The phrase is Bäuml's. See "Varieties," p. 253.

sede schewynge of oure lorde, I be helde it as ane in god syght, and I vndyrstode neuer nathynge þer yn that stoneʒ me ne lettes me of the trewe techynge of halye kyrke" (p. 223). Julian's strategy here suggests her own awareness of the tension between her identity as a daughter of the church and as a recluse and author of private visions. She uses the weakness implicit in her gender to a particular end, since only the writings of holy women, whose holiness had been verified by others, circulated with such authority.

Near the end of the short text, in the twenty-third chapter, Julian seems to project such an image by conjuring up the presence of a scribe who listens to and thus verifies her account of her visions: "Alle the blissede techynge of oure lorde god was schewed to me be thre partyes, as I hafe sayde before, that es to saye be the bodely sight, and be worde formed in mynn vndyrstandynge, and by gastelye syght. For the bodely sight, I haffe sayde as I sawe, als trewlye as I cann. And for the wordes fourmed, I hafe sayde thamm ryght as oure lorde schewed me thame" (pp. 272–73). Her language in this passage is designed to depict a specific scene in which the visionary dictates what she has seen through "bodily" and "ghostly" sight. The fact that these "sayings" now appear in the form of a book bears witness to the authoritative nature of the visions and hence of the book in which they now appear. Julian thus sketches in a familiar triune relationship, in which the seer (in this case a female visionary) is authenticated by God, who inscribes teachings upon the spiritual eye of the visionary, and by the scribe, who inscribes that vision (or the visionary) upon parchment.

In the long text Julian seems to be striving for a different type of authority. The long text opens merely with "Here begynneth the first chapter. This is a reuelation of loue that Jhesu Christ our endles blisse made in xvi shewynges" (p. 281). Not only are the specifics of the first sentence of the short text omitted, but what follows is a summary of the content of each vision recorded in the book. Such tables of contents emerged from the university world of the thirteenth century and the new attitude towards books as objects meant for private study and use. Although such tables tended to be added onto texts by the scribes, Edmund Colledge and James Walsh feel that this one was the work of Julian herself.[4] If so, she clearly foresaw a particular type of reader for her book, which she sought to inscribe with an opening that at once enhanced its usefulness as a spiritual guide and suggested its authority as a book designed for serious thought. This first chapter also prepares us for a representation of

---

4. Paul Saenger, "Silent Reading: Its Impact on Late Medieval Script and Society," *Viator* 13 (1982), 367–414; Colledge and Walsh, *Showings*, p. 284, n. 51. In the prologue to his life of Mary of Oignies, Jacques de Vitry explains that he has provided chapter headings for the reader's convenience; he thus indicates his own expectations that a reading of the life might well be a private devotional experience.

visionary experience, containing not only accounts of the visions themselves but the author's glosses upon that experience. To this end, the long text, which is indeed much longer, is more concerned to explain the meaning of the visions and is thus more theologically inclined than the short text.

In the long text Julian is also interested in projecting a different type of persona. First, she omitted the references to her gender that occur in the short text.[5] Since by drawing on the "unlearned, feeble, and frail woman" topos Julian had earlier categorized her work as experiential, emotive, and perhaps prophetic, she may have perceived the inherent constrictions that topos imposed on her as a writer. She spoke neither as a prophet nor as a saint but as a person who had had a series of revelations, the meaning of which had continued to preoccupy her for a number of years. Thus her life was not the text that authorized her written text; she spoke as a thoughtful, intelligent Christian. Second, she may have felt that her authority as a theological writer was implicitly compromised by her gender and therefore chose a persona that linked her to countless other authors whose employment of the modesty topos was quickly belied by the rhetorical polish of their works. After the first chapter, a summary of the content of each vision, chapter 2 begins: "This reuelation was made to a symple creature vnlettyrde leving in deadly flesh, the yer of our lord a thousannde and three hundered and lxxiij, the xiij daie of May, which creature desyred before thre gyftes by the grace of god" (p. 285). The ironies of this sentence would have been apparent to any alert and educated reader, for the *Showings* demonstrates Julian's mastery of rhetorical figures, of the Latin of the Vulgate, and of what Colledge and Walsh refer to as "the Western monastic traditions of *lectio divina*."[6] In fact, one of the differences between the two texts of the *Showings* is the rhetorical sophistication of the long text, suggesting that Julian spent the fifteen years not only thinking about her visions but also mastering the conventions of classical rhetoric.

Despite the subtlety of the long text, it appears at once less individualistic and more authoritative than the short. In omitting details that are not central to her point, she trims some things that make the short text a more personal work.[7] In the short text, for example, she says her desire for three spiritual wounds was inspired by a reading in church of the story of St. Cecilia (pp. 204–6). That personal and immediate reference, which links her desire to her own experi-

5. See also Bynum, *Holy Feast*, p. 418, n. 49; Colledge and Walsh, *Showings*, p. 222, n. 40.
6. See Colledge and Walsh, *Showings*, pp. 45–47, and their appendix to the *Showings*, "Rhetorical Figures Employed by Julian," pp. 735–48. For a discussion of humility formulas to be found in Latin prefaces, see Tore Janson, *Latin Prose Prefaces: Studies in Literary Conventions*, Studia Latina Stockholmiensia 13 (Stockholm, 1964), pp. 120 ff.
7. In "Julian of Norwich and Her Audience," Windeatt also makes this point.

ence, is transformed in the long text to a more generally accessible statement: "by the grace of god and teeching of holie church I con-ceiued a mightie desyre to receive thre woundes in my life" (p. 288). Just as the "teaching of Holy Church" replaces an account of per-sonal experience, so, as Colledge and Walsh remark, Julian tends to replace the singular pronouns of the short text with the plural pro-nouns of the long text.[8] The unlearned and feeble woman has become a voice aligned with the community of the church (as the often-repeated phrase "my evyn cristen" implies) and speaking with the authority of the seer and the teacher. Although Julian retained the passage in which she describes herself as dictating her visions, its position in the long text (p. 666) mitigates its force. Rather than appearing two short chapters from the end, as it does in the short text, it occurs in chapter 73 of a book of eighty-six chapters. In fact, in the final chapter of the long text, she emphasizes the number of years she has devoted to trying to understand "oure lords menyng" (p. 732). The answer she offers is worthy of quoting in full:

> Wytt it wele, loue was his menyng. Who shewyth it the? Loue. (What shewid he the? Love.) Wherfore shewyth he it the? For loue. Holde the therin, thou shalt wytt more in the same. But thou schalt nevyr witt therin other withoutyn ende.
>
> Thus was I lernyd, that loue is oure lordes menyng. And I sawe fulle surely in this and in alle that or god made vs he lovyd vs, whych loue was nevyr slekyd ne nevyr shalle. And in this loue he hath done alle his werkes, and in this loue he hath made alle thynges profytable to vs, and in this loue oure lyfe is evyr lastyng. In oure makyng we had begynnyng, but the loue wher in he made vs was in hym fro with out begynnyng. In whych loue we haue oure begynnyng, and alle this shalle we see in god with outyn ende. (Pp. 733–34)

This statement issues from no frail figure; it is magisterial and full-voiced. That Julian's assumption of authority may well have troubled a scribe is borne out by a scribal epilogue that appears in two of the manuscripts of the long text warning the reader not to take only the part of the work that seems pleasing ("after thy affection"), "for that is the condition of an heretique."[9]

The long text is the work of a writer, not a seer. It presents expe-rience mediated by time, literary craft, intelligence, and study. I do not deny that Julian was and saw herself as a visionary, but the long text testifies to her growing understanding of her role as a writer. In effect, she became her own secretary or scribe. She apparently pro-vided the text with its introductory apparatus. She depersonalized

8. Colledge and Walsh, *Showings*, p. 285, n. 11.
9. Colledge and Walsh, *Showings*, p. 734, n. 29.

the text and thus did not need to explain why she, a woman, was
writing a book like this. She made every attempt to link herself with
the community of Christ, seeking to avoid the charge of "singularity"
and of presumption. She derived her authority in the long text not
only from her visionary experience but from her years of meditation
and study. Finally, in the opening sentence of the last chapter, she
affirmed her book as a text for a life: "This boke is begonne by goddys
gyfte and his grace, but it is nott yett performyd, as to my syght"
(p. 731).[1] The book's "performance" will be the life lived in the
knowledge and love of God. The book, then, stands as a text whose
authority is derived from God and manifested in the life of prayer. Its
author has become our mediator and our guide for this still-
unfinished text. She thus suggests, not that we should read her book
because she is a holy woman, but that her book might be used as a
guide to the holy. She thereby adopted the persona of the author who
inscribes a text, not of the saint whose life is inscribed upon a text.

*   *   *

<h1 style="text-align:center">DAVID AERS</h1>

From The Humanity of Christ: Reflections on Julian
of Norwich's Revelation of Love†

> I beheld with reverent drede, and hyghly mervelyng in the syght and
> in feelyng of the swete accorde that oure reson is in god, under-
> standyng that it is þe hyghest gyfte that we haue receyvyd, and it is
> growndyd in kynd.
>
> —Julian of Norwich

In many respects it might seem reasonable to read Julian of Norwich
as a contemplative whose visions of Christ belong unequivocally to
the conventional and dominant late medieval representation of
Christ's humanity as a tortured, bleeding, and dying body. It might
also seem reasonable to treat her work as part of the traditions of
women's mysticism so copiously illustrated by Caroline Bynum in
Holy Feast and Holy Fast. After all, Julian's "reuelacion of loue"
begins with a move that is part of the dominant late medieval tradition of representing and meditating on Christ's humanity, the one
decisively shaped by the pseudo-Bonaventuran *Meditationes Vitae*

---

1. In "Julian of Norwich and Her Audience," Windeatt also considers this sentence.

† From David Aers and Lynn Staley *The Powers of the Holy: Religion, Politics, and Gender
in Late Medieval English Culture* (University Park: Pennsylvania State UP, 1996), pp. 77–
78, 81–87. Copyright © 1996 The Pennsylvania State University. Reprinted by permission
of the publisher and the author.

Christi.[1] She recalls her initial desire to have "mynd of the passion," and to experience it as if she had been "that tyme with Magdaleyne and with other that were Christus louers, that I might have seen bodilie the passion that our lord suffered for me" (2/285). This seems bound up with thoroughly conventional versions of imitation and affective response. She reports the wish to have "suffered with him," reflecting the familiar form of identification fostered by the *Meditationes Vitae Christi* and its traditions. And she stresses how she assumed that her wish entailed a focus on the tortured body. This assumption too is one she would have assimilated from a culture of discourse dominated by the tortured body on the cross and she herself emphasizes the focus of her desire on this body: "And therefore I desyred a bodely sight, wher in I might have more knowledge of the bodily paynes of our sauior, and of the compassion of our lady" (2/286). On top of these apparent convergences there is her work's currently well known and widely celebrated representation of Christ as "mother," a representation that might seem precisely the kind of "feminization" of Christ which Caroline Bynum has illustrated so thoroughly and which has stimulated much interest among feminist medievalists working on English writings.[2]

* * *

Julian is reproducing a conventional version of Christ's humanity, figured through the tortured, wounded, bleeding body on the cross. But only *seems*. For while Julian does undoubtedly set out from the dominant commonplace of late medieval devotion with which this part of our book began, her distinctive rhetorical strategies actually resist it, unravel it, estrange us from it and, gradually but decisively, supersede it.

How she achieves this I will now illustrate, an illustration that demands rather longer quotations than are normally required. We can begin * * * with the opening of the first revelation:

> And in this sodenly I saw the reed bloud rynnyng downe from vnder the garlande, hote and freyshely, plentuously and liuely,

1. The edition of Julian used here is Edmund Colledge and James Walsh, eds., *A Book of Showings to the Anchoress Julian of Norwich*, 2 vols. (Toronto: Pontifical Institute of Mediaeval Studies, 1978); references in my text are to chapter followed by page: all references are to the revised long text unless preceded by "Sh"; here quotation is on 281. The traditions represented and shaped by the *Meditationes Vitae Christi* were discussed in Chapter 1; their relevance here is noted by Marion Glasscoe, *English Medieval Mystics: Games of Faith* (London: Longmans, 1993), 215–16.
2. Caroline Walker Bynum, *Holy Feast and Holy Fast* (Berkeley: University of California Press, 1987) discussed in Chapter 1; Bynum, *Jesus as Mother: Studies in the Spirituality of the High Middle Ages* (Berkeley: University of California Press, 1982) is also relevant. It seems that the earlier book emphasizes the masculine engenderment of such language and iconography while this is much diminished in *Holy Feast and Holy Fast;* see Bynum (1982), 111–46, 161–62, 185, 246, and especially the comments on 111–12, 143–45. As the previous chapters have suggested, I think the earlier emphasis more astute about the effects of power than the later.

right as it was in the tyme that the garland of thornes was
pressed on his blessed head. (4/294)

Here we meet the most familiar icon of late medieval devotion, complete with concentration on physical details, the "bodely sight" and
"knowledge of the bodily paynes of our sauiour" that she had prayed
for. But instead of elaborating these images, she adds a section to
the Short Text that does not fulfill such conventional expectations:

> And in the same shewing sodeinly the trinitie fulfilled my hart
> most of ioy, and so I vnderstode it shall be in heauen without
> end to all that shall come ther. For the trinitie is god, god is the
> trinitie. The trinitie is our maker, the trinitie is our keper, the
> trinitie is our everlasting louer, the trinitie is our endlesse ioy
> and our bleisse, by our Lord Jesu Christ, and in our Lord Jesu
> Christ. And this was shewed in the first syght and in all, for
> wher Jhesu appireth the blessed trinitie is vnderstand, as to my
> sight. And I sayd: Benedicite dominus. (4/294–96)

What happens here is that the kind of elaborations encouraged by
the dominant forms of devotion of Christ's humanity and passion
are not delivered. Indeed, they are positively blocked off as the familiar images are turned into theological reflections on the Trinity—
already, at the beginning of the text's first revelation. Furthermore,
the reflections are in a language that is ratiocinative and abstract, a
language that resists the kind of physicality we had been encouraged
to expect.[3] Similarly, the next chapter emphasizes that even as she
saw the bleeding head she had "a gostly sight of his homely louyng"
(5/299). What then did she see? She tells us that she "saw that he
is to vs all thing that is good and comfortable to our helpe. He is
oure clothing, that for loue wrappeth vs and wyndeth vs, halseth vs,
and all becloseth vs, hangeth about vs for tender loue" (5/299). Once
more this is neither an attempt to visualize the physical particularities of the crucified body nor even to encourage us to compose the
crucifixion scene. We are being directed to move away from the literal, a movement maintained by the ensuing image in which Christ,
from the cross, "shewed" her "a little thing, the quantitie of an hazel-
nott" in the palm of her hand, "as me semide" (5/299). Not, we note,
that she saw a hazelnut, or anything else particularized, but "a little
thing" whose "quantitie" is her focus. As she looks at this "little
thing," she writes, "I looked theran with the eye of my vnderstanding"
(5/300). Marion Glasscoe is surely right to remark that "far from

3. There is an excellent analysis of this passage and its "progression towards abstraction and
generalization" by Nicholas Watson in "The Trinitarian Hermeneutic in Julian of Norwich's *Revelation of Love*," in *The Medieval Mystical Tradition in England*, Exeter Symposium V, ed. Marion Glasscoe (Cambridge: Brewer, 1992), 79–100; see also Vincent
Gillespie, "Strange Images of Death: The Passion in Later Medieval English Devotional
and Mystical Writing," *Analecta Cartusiana* 117 (1987): 154–55 n. 62.

being a visual image of the world as a hazel-nut held safely in the palm of her hand, this is a 'gostly sight.' "[4] As with her writing on the Trinity in the previous chapter, Julian's language here is analytic, rationally curious, abstract:

> I marvayled how it might laste, for me thought it might sodenly haue fallen to nawght for littlenes. And I was answered in my vnderstanding: It lasteth and ever shall, for god loueth it; and so hath all thing being by the loue of god. (5/300)

There is no incitement here for affective identification, for concentration on the body, whether "feminized" or not. Nor do the next sentences change this mode:

> In this little thing I saw iii propreties. The first is þat god made it, the secund that god loueth it, the thirde that god kepyth it. But what behyld I ther in? Verely, the maker, the keper, the louer. For till I am substantially vnyted to him I may never haue full reste ne verie bliss; þat is to say that I be so fastned to him that ther be right nought that is made betweene my god and me.
>
> This little thing that is made, me thought it might haue fallen to nought for littlenes. (5/300–301)

This extensive quotation shows how Julian sustains a language that is a vernacular version of a scholastic discourse, a reasoning inquiry with carefully articulated questions and answers deploying pointedly abstract terms such as "properties" and "substantially vnyted." We can see how the image of the bleeding head from which the first revelation started has actually been a provocation to explore metaphysical questions with her "vnderstanding, and thought."[5] We are, in fact, receiving lessons in spiritual reading. The image of the "little thing" is used to stimulate further reflections on our mistaken attempts to find stability, plenitude, completion in a realm of pervasive impermanence and necessary lack:

> For this is the cause why we be not all in ease of hart and of sowle, for we seeke heer rest in this thing that is so little, wher no reste is in, and we know not our god, that is almightie, all wise and all good, for he is verie reste. God will be knowen, and him lyketh that we rest vs in him; for all that is beneth him suffsyeth not to vs. And this is the cause why that no sowle is in reste till it is noughted of all thinges that is made. When she is wilfully noughted four loue, to haue him that is all, then is she able to receive ghostly reste. (5/301)

---

4. Glasscoe (1993), 224.
5. On such use of imagery in Julian, see Gillespie (1987), 131–43.

Thus the fragility of a little thing, its propensity to have suddenly "fallen to nawght for littlenes" is assimilated to theological reflections on the nature of desire in a language that is, again, strikingly abstract. As for the "feminine," we note that it is placed in the pronoun "she," the human "sowle," in fact, which cannot be "in reste till it is noughted of all thinges that is made," till "she is wilfully noughted for loue." Far from being the "feminine" as physicality, as flesh, the feminine here is the human "anima" in a discourse which encourages "the eye of my vnderstanding" to consider some extremely paradoxical and metaphysical reflections. For instance, the passage asks its readers to consider how the created universe is a "quantitie" that could be contained in the palm of Julian's hand, so tiny that it seems "it might sodenly haue fallen to nawght" were it not continually sustained by God's love; and yet, also, that unless the soul herself is "noughted of all thinges that is made," "wilfully noughted," she will never find peace, happiness. In this quest for "knowledge" Julian has superseded her culture's ideologies of gender and sexual differentiation even as she blocks out the imagery from which she begins in a strategy that would not be out of place in *The Cloud of Unknowing*.

Not that there is any inclination to suggest images must or can be decisively "noughted." For while her strategy has been to supersede the conventional image from which she started, she then goes on to observe that even as her reflections developed in her "vnderstanding," "in gostely syght," she simultaneously held "the bodely syght" that her own text has so subtly set aside (5/300, 7/311). In chapter 7 she returns to this "bodely syght":

> The grett droppes of blode felle downe fro vnder the garlonde lyke pelottes, semyng as it had comynn ouȝte of the veynes. And in the comyng ouȝte they were browne rede, for the blode was full thycke; and in the spredyng abrode they were bryght rede. (7/311)

This addition to the Short Text seems to return us to the normative figurations of devotion to Christ, to the *Meditationes Vitae Christi* and its successors. * * * And yet, if we continue the quotation, if we do not isolate this passage from its context, something far less straightforward seems to be happening:

> And whan it camme at the browes, ther they vanysschyd; and not wythstonding the bledyng continued tylle many thynges were sene and vnderstondyd. Nevertheles the feyerhede and the lyuelyhede continued in the same bewty and lyuelynes. (7/311–12)

First, it is less straightforward because we are told that copious bleeding both "vanysschyd" and "contynued." Second, her attention involves a spectatorially detached and strikingly aesthetic sense of the image's "bewty and lyuelynes." Third, Julian comments that this bleeding image was part of a design whose end was to encourage understanding ("tylle many thynges were sene and vnderstondyd"). Together these features make striking qualifications to a mode that was traditionally organized to produce intense affective and emotional responses followed by a redirection of the will in a manner that circumvented the analytic processes of rational exploration. Julian's continuation of this passage develops some well-known and exceptionally memorable images:

> The plentuoushede is lyke to the droppes of water that falle of the evesyng of an howse after a grete shower of reyne, that falle so thycke that no man may nomber them with no bodely wyt. And for the roundnesse they were lyke to the scale of heryng in the spredyng of the forhede. (7/312)

How do these images work and what is Julian doing with them? Important to acknowledge is that *they draw attention to themselves*. In making them do this, Julian shows that her aim is not to evoke Christ's pain on Calvary, not to induce the affective responses we might have expected in a conventional meditation on the Crucifixion, and not to move us to any affective imitation of a suffering, tortured body as an "imitation of Christ" we should want to follow. On the contrary, the reader is placed in a rather detached, speculative relationship to images which have been designed to emphasize their constructedness, their rhetorical composition. Attention is thus directed away from the particularities of the Crucifixion and its familiar meditational elaborations even as it is directed toward house eaves after abundant rain and to the pattern, and texture, of herrings' scales. That this is her purpose Julian emphasizes by reiterating the images in the following lines (7/312, lines 27–30) and then offering this comment:

> Thys shewyng was quyck and lyuely and hidows and dredfulle and swete and louely; and of all the syght that I saw this was most comfort to me, that oure good lorde, that is so reverent and dredfulle, is so homely and so curteyse, and this most fulfylld me with lykyng and syckernes in soule. (7/313)

The vision may be "dredfulle" but its beholder is detached enough to include in her responses what can only be described as an aesthetic dimension, one also displayed in the striking images she had just written. And now, instead of elaborating instruments of torture, wounds, torturers, mockers, and sympathizers, she turns away from the bodily scene to reflect on what she calls the "homely" and "curteyse" aspect of God, reflections unfolded in an "open example" of

"a solempne kyng or a gret lorde" and "a pore seruante" (7/313–14).
The lord's gracious willingness to show the servant "a fulle true menyng" inspires joy and love, faith and solace (7/314–15). So what had
seemed to be an elaboration of commonplace late medieval figurations of Christ turns out to be nothing of the sort. Instead, the inter-
actions of image, exegesis, and reflection discourage any affective
identifications with the crucified body, discourage any attempt to
compose an "imitatio Christi" as an imitation of a suffering,
wounded, and bleeding body.

* * *

SANDRA J. McENTIRE

From The Likeness of God and the Restoration of Humanity in Julian of Norwich's *Showings*†

The *Showings* of Julian of Norwich depicts the ways, directly and
indirectly, that she negotiates both the conformity of and the distance between her personal mystical experience and its subsequent
insights and that which is deemed acceptable within the parameters
of traditional patriarchal and theological authority. In an age fraught
with intense scrutiny from political and ecclesiastial authority,[1] Julian needed to balance her own assertions and the authority of the
heresy-sensitive church. Indeed, any text written by a woman in the
medieval period necessarily reflects not only an assertion of her own
authority but also an awareness of the limits of the discourse she
relies on to make her assertion. While subject to the intellectual,
cultural, and social frames of reference that contextualize her and
her text, her subjective experience coaxes her to embrace new positions vis-a-vis her self, her text, and authority.

The tradition that Julian interiorizes and examines asserts views of
the human and the divine identities that are at variance with Julian's
post-revelatory experience. How she moves from the traditional discourse to a position of dissent constitutes the topic of this essay.
While remaining subject and indeed loyal to the primary tradition,
she nonetheless is liberated from it, but only after long and conscien-
tious inner negotiation, particularly in the intervening years between

---

† From *Julian of Norwich: A Book of Essays*, ed. Sandra J. McEntire (New York: Garland,
    1998), pp. 1–7, 9, 11–19. Copyright © 1998 Sandra McEntire. Reprinted by permission
    of the author.
1. For the most thorough examination to date of the political and social world informing
    Julian and her text, see Lynn Staley and David Aers, *The Powers of the Holy* (University
    Park, PA: Pennsylvania State UP, 1996).

the Short and Long Texts of her book. Indeed, as Lynn Staley observes, the Long Text is "an extended dialogue between her spiritual understanding and her belief in the teachings of Holy Church" (PH 141).[2] Whereas Staley and David Aers probe the politics of Julian's *Showings*, I would like to interrogate further the ways in which Julian and her text negotiate the interior tension between the complex authority she inherits and the original insights of her theology.

This negotiation assumes a dialogue, however unconscious it may be, between the individual and what Mikhail Bakhtin calls "authoritative discourse," that is, the word that has come down as tradition, as established, as resistant to change. Although feminist criticism has been proficient at producing evidence of a body of mysogynist literature, I would like to reference briefly a single source of the powerful discourse that in the course of patriarchal history takes on nearly absolute authority, the exegesis on the Book of Genesis, Chapters 1 through 3.

I. "Authoritative Discourse": Woman as Eve

Although autobiographical texts seem at first glance to be univalent in presentation of voice, a closer look reveals the numerous dialogues that undergird the apparent monologue. Besides recreating actual conversations and dialogue with others, particularly the divine being, mystical revelation is also inherently dialogical, negotiating an internal conversation about the events and experiences taking place. The two loquators of that internal conversation include the inherited word, or in Bakhtin's phrase, the "authoritative discourse," and "one's own," that is, populated with intention and accent, and adapted to a particular "semantic and expressive intention."[3] Explaining further Bakhtin says: "Within the arena of almost every utterance an intense interaction and struggle between one's own and another's word is being waged, a process in which they oppose or dialogically interanimate each other" (354). What is particularly novel about late medieval, often vernacular mystical texts, according to Bernard McGinn, is their dialogue with the older tradition, that is, the Latin "monologic triumph of the authoritative male voice of ecclesiastical authority."[4] Julian's word, her *Showings*, represents

2. Barbara Newman, in referencing Nicholas Watson, makes a similar observation: "the entire Long Text is constructed as a dialogue not so much between God and Julian as between Julian-the-inspired-visionary (who received the showings) and Julian-the-questing-believer (who struggles to understand them)." See *From Virile Woman to WomanChrist* (Philadelphia: U of Pennsylvania P, 1995), 131.

3. M. M. Bakhtin, *The Dialogic Imagination* (Austin: U of Texas P, 1981), 293.

4. "The Changing Shape of Late Medieval Mysticism," *Church History* 65 (1996): 204. Laurie Finke makes the same observation in her analysis of the way this discourse regulated the female body in *Feminist Theory, Women's Writing* (Ithaca, NY: Cornell UP, 1992), especially 78ff. See also Nicholas Watson's " 'Yf wommen be double naturelly': Remaking 'Woman' in Julian of Norwich's Revelation of Love," *Exemplaria* 8 (1996): 1–34.

both her critique of this misogynous tradition and her interaction and struggle with the inevitably gendered nature of the discourse.

Authoritative discourse shapes behavior and the bases of ideological interrelations with the world. It becomes internally persuasive. Bakhtin says:

> The authoritative word demands that we acknowledge it, that we make it our own; it binds us, quite independently of any power it might have to persuade us internally; we encounter it with its authority already fused to it. The authoritative word is located in a distanced zone, organically connected with a past that is felt to be hierarchically higher. It is, so to speak, the word of the fathers. Its authority was already *acknowledged* in the past. It is a *prior* discourse. It is therefore not a question of choosing it from among other possible discourses that are its equal. . . .
>
> It is not a free appropriation and assimilation of the word itself that authoritative discourse seeks to elicit from us; rather, it demands our unconditional allegiance. (342–43)

Hard-edged, calcified, inert, authoritative discourse "cannot be represented—it is only transmitted" (344).

One place to look for an example of an authoritative discourse and to situate a discussion of Julian's *Showings* within that discourse can be found in the Biblical exegetical tradition.[5] The primary and symbolic locus for the marginalizing of women and the valorizing of a dominant male voice is embedded in the writings on the creation stories of Genesis 1–3, but especially Genesis 2 and 3. This central text defines what it means to be human, what the relationship between men and women, husbands and wives, authority and subordinate should be.

Although a considerable portion of the exegetical literature on Genesis asserts positivist and essentialist theories about the importance of women in the scheme of the created universe, an equally considerable body of misogynistic literature, both more pervasive and thus in some ways more influential, permeates the theological, intellectual, and cultural world view. Augustine, for example, cannot imagine why God created the prelapsarian Eve in the first place. Even as a helper he finds her wanting, thinking it much more agreeable for two male friends to provide each other company and conversation (Clark 29). Other commentators also saw Eve's position as

5. Thorough research on this topic has been summarized in: Alcuin Blamires, ed., *Woman Defamed and Woman Defended* (Oxford: Clarendon, 1992); Elizabeth A. Clark, *Women in the Early Church.*, Message of the Fathers of the Church. Vol 13 (Wilmington, DE: Glazier, 1983; rpt. 1987), Julia O'Faolain and Lauro Martines, eds. *Not in God's Image* (New York: Harper, 1973), and Elaine Pagels, *Adam, Eve, and the Serpent* (New York: Random, 1988). See also Howard Bloch, *Medieval Misogyny and the Invention of Western Romantic Love* (Chicago: U of Chicago P, 1991).

inferior. That Eve was created from the physical body of Adam and not from the earthly dust as he was comes to signify a fundamental inferiority, physical, moral, and intellectual. Only connected with the man can she reflect the image of God; even in that relation she has no authority or autonomy.

If the pre-lapsarian Eve is gendered and suspect, the discussions of the post-lapsarian Eve reveal the definitions of woman which most deeply inform the discourse of authority. Indeed, in these writings, not only does Eve cause the fall of man, but it is precisely because she fails to obey Adam, that is, to maintain the divinely ordained and appropriate order of the man as the head of the women, that sin enters and disrupts the world. Asserting that man fell because of woman, commentators such as Ambrose indicate that woman is the originator of man's wrongdoing (Clark 41). Chrysostom ups the ante by putting into the mouth of God a judgement that extends to all women:

> You did not use your authority well, so consign yourself to a state of subordination. You have not borne your liberty, so accept servitude. Since you do not know how to rule—as you showed in your experiment with the business of life—henceforth be among the governed and acknowledge your husband as lord. (Clark 43)

The conclusion which the fathers draw about Eve's and woman's place in the world is absolute and determined. In a passage which, as Howard Bloch indicates, "shifts the ethical burden of sexuality toward women, making her the passive agent . . . of the seduction of males" (39), Tertullian says in this widely cited text:

> God's judgement on this sex lives on in our age; the guilt necessarily lives on as well. *You* are the devil's gateway; *you* are the unsealer of that tree; *you* are the first foresaker of the divine law; *you* are the one who persuaded him whom the devil was not brave enough to approach; *you* so lightly crushed the image of God, the man Adam; because of your punishment, that is, death, even the Son of God had to die. (Clark 39; also Bloch 40 and O'Faolain 132)

Against this exegetical backdrop, and with a "deep distrust of the body and materiality" (Bloch 45), the ambivalence about sexual values is found. Sexual desire and sexual knowledge followed the fall. The knowledge of good and evil eventuated sexual awareness. Clement and Irenaeus put forth arguments that would influence later generations of apologists and the subsequent ambivalence about sexuality. While confirming the blessedness of marriage, sexual passion had to be purged, thereby dichotomizing the desires of the flesh and the higher functions of will and reason.

Even better, however, than chaste marital relations is virginity. Only then might a woman "become the equal of man" (Bloch 93). The loathing of the flesh, a loathing that overflows in revulsion against the female body, is best found in Augustine and in Jerome, particularly the latter's diatribes against Jovinian, who counsels a more sensible, balanced view. As a result of woman's role in bringing man down to his baser instincts, she must suffer the consequences of childbirth pain.

From this highly summarized overview, a few conclusions might be drawn. As creature woman is conceived in bodily inferiority and intellectual insufficiency. As such she possesses no authority or autonomy of her own. As Howard Bloch points out, "she is, in a sense, as powerfully entangled as the story of the Fall itself, entrapped by the logic of a cultural ideal that, internalized, makes her always already in a state of weakness, lack, guilt, inadequacy, vulnerability" (91). These assumptions constitute the "authoritative discourse" which women struggled with.

* * *

II. Julian's Discourse: The Theology of Likeness

Although the source of Julian of Norwich's learning cannot be known, her *Showings* attests to a learned author, one familiar with some of the most important patristic texts and commentaries.[6] Further, she would have known the *Ancrene Wisse*. She most certainly heard and read the principal teachings of the fathers about women's inferiority and flawed nature. But only exceptionally does this frame of reference intrude in her text. * * *

* * * It is my contention that this absence reflects not that such assumptions failed to impress upon her their weight and import but that she carefully and consciously resists them as a result of her own experience and revelation. Indeed, as the editorial practice of the Long Text demonstrates, Julian explicitly altered and excised material which she found unacceptable. While she could not directly oppose the teachings of the church, her own spiritual journey led her, particularly during the twenty or more years between the short and long versions of her text, to a set of internally persuasive truths profoundly liberated "from the authority of the other's discourse" (Bakhtin 348).

6. See, for example, the discussion of Julian's intellectual formation in Edmund Colledge and James Walsh, eds., *A Book of Showings to the Anchoress Julian of Norwich*, 2 vols. (Toronto: Pontifical Institute of Mediaeval Studies, 1978), 1:43–59. Denise N. Baker, *Julian of Norwich's Showings: From Vision to Book* (Princeton: Princeton UP, 1994), notes that by 1393, the time of the final version of her text, "she had acquired an understanding of moral and mystical theology that enabled her to use this discipline's terminology and adapt its concepts with subtle creativity" (12–13).

If authoritative discourse is hard, concrete, and binding, "internally persuasive discourse," according to Bakhtin, is "tightly interwoven with 'one's own word' ";

> its creativity and productiveness consist precisely in the fact that such a word awakens new and independent words, that it organizes masses of our words from within, and does not remain in an isolated and static condition. . . . The semantic structure of an internally persuasive discourse is *not finite*, it is *open*; in each of the new contexts that dialogize it, this discourse is able to reveal ever newer *ways to mean*. (345).

By struggling with the prior discourse, indeed stimulated by it, individuals "will sooner or later begin to liberate themselves from the authority of the other's discourse" and come "to ideological consciousness" (348). The *Showings* of Julian of Norwich, particularly the Long Text, testifies to her ideological consciousness and liberation from the patriarchal discourse.

The interior dialogue that Julian undertakes with the dominant discourse encompasses far more, however, than the semantics of self-representation. The structure of resistance and revision is most evident in Julian's exegesis of Genesis. Even though she omits any direct disputation about the Fall, the role of woman in it, or its implications for the body, her text strategizes a dissenting theology from the assumptions previously established and most particularly expressed in the exegesis of Augustine which directly implicates divine and human nature. Augustine, who returns to this Biblical narrative five times in the course of his lifetime,[7] figures as a source Julian both knows and ultimately rewrites. In order to do so, she, like her near contemporary Margery Kempe, needed to disguise her "strongly original and in some cases, destabilizing, insights into systems of theology."[8] The resulting narrative points to a theology that is at once double-gendered and inclusive, divine and human, substantial and sensual.

In the parable of the Servant, Julian provides a reading of Genesis which not only "revises the prevailing Augustinian reading of Genesis 3" (Baker 86), but also expresses disagreement with Augustine's premises about the nature of humankind's likeness to the divinity. Diverging from Augustine's gendered, dualistic interpretation about Adam and Eve as made in the image and likeness of God, Julian adopts an approach at once more relational and more inclusive. It is instructive that she never mentions Eve or her role in the Fall, nor

---

7. *On Genesis against the Manichees, On the Literal Interpretation of Genesis, Confessions, On the Trinity*, and *City of God*. See Roland Teske, *St. Augustine. On Genesis* (Washington, DC: Catholic U of America P, 1991), 3.

8. Lynn Staley, *Margery Kempe's Dissenting Fictions* (University Park, PA: Pennsylvania State UP, 1994), 3.

does she assign blame to either party. This omission or gap in the text silences or blocks the authoritative discourse of male privilege and substitutes new meaning. The post-lapsarian Adam has a dual identity of substance and sensuality. And in the new Adam, the sensual is redeemed.

Julian's understanding of the Fall undergoes a significant process of sophistication in the years between the Short and the Long text.[9] Her earlier revelation consists in the simple assertion "that Adammes synne was the maste harme that euer was done or ever schalle to the warldes ende" ["that Adam's sin was the greatest harm ever done or ever to be done until the end of the world"]. Further, she is taught the atonement "is mare plesande to the blissede godhede and mare wyrschipfulle to mannes saluacionn with owten comparysonn than euer was the synne of Adam harmfulle" ["is more pleasing to the blessed divinity and more honourable for man's salvation, without comparison, than ever Adam's sin was harmful."][1] But the intervening years of contemplation of this revelation led to her explication of the Servant parable whereby the focus is less on the fall than on the hurt and injury that the servant suffered on the one hand and the compassion and mercy of the lord, on the other. Augustine, in contrast, is preoccupied with the sin and the dispensing of blame as well as the means by which original sin is transmitted to the human race. For Augustine, Adam is the transmitter of original sin through his active seed, for which woman is the passive receptor.[2] But the sin itself was a result, first of Eve's seduction by Satan, and second, of Adam's persuasion by Eve (Børresen 53). Although Adam remains responsible for the Fall, Augustine asserts that the sin began with the woman ("a muliere initium factum est peccati" [Børresen 65]), and it is this latter notion that takes on nearly incantatory force in the tradition. Julian, however, "offers an alternative to the doctrine of original sin crucial to Augustine's juridical theodicy," disagrees with "the Augustinian premises about the nature of sin and the character of God's response to it," and "epitomizes her opposition to retributive theodicy" (Baker 86). Julian finds no cause for blame and "refuses to attribute disobedience to Adam or wrath to God. She

9. Nicholas Watson suggests that the intervening time between revisions may well exceed the usually accepted twenty years, "perhaps as many as forty," in "The Composition of Julian of Norwich's *Revelation of Divine Love*," *Speculum* 68 (1993): 82.

1. Colledge and Walsh, *A Book of Showings*, 14.247; *Julian of Norwich: Showings*, trans. Edmund Colledge and James Walsh. Classics of Western Spirituality (New York: Paulist, 1978), 149–50. Subsequent references will be provided parenthetically within the text. Baker notes the difficulty Julian must have experienced resolving this vision with the teachings of the Church. She seems to solve these difficulties only at the end of her many years of reflection. "Her failure to mention either the parable or the idea of Jesus as Mother suggests that most of this revelation was composed during the second revision of the short text" (85).

2. Kari Elisabeth Børresen, *Subordination and Equivalence. The Nature and Role of Woman in Augustine and Thomas Aquinas* (Washington, DC: University P of America, 1981), 42.

presents the original transgression as an inadvertant separation from God rather than a deliberate act of rebellion" (Baker 88). Observing the servant falling, she says: "I behelde with avysement to wytt yf I culde perceyve in hym ony defauȝte, or yf the lorde shuld assigne in hym ony maner of blame; and verely there was none seen, for oonly hys good wyll and his grett desyer was cause of his fallyng" (51.516) ["I looked carefully to know if I could detect any fault in him, or if the lord would impute to him any kind of blame; and truly none was seen, for the only cause of his falling was his good will and his great desire" (268)]. Not only is blame eliminated but he is "rewardyd withoute end" (51.518) that is, above what he would have had he not fallen.

The servant is initially identified as Adam, but by "Adam" Julian does not mean a single individual. She provides a thorough exegesis of the term, allegorizing the identifier: "For in the servannt, that was shewed for Adam as I shall sey, I sawe many dyverse properteys that myght by no manner be derecte to syngell Adam" (519) ["For in the servant, who was shown in Adam, as I shall say, I saw many different characteristics which could in no way be attributed to Adam, that one man" (269)]. Indeed, Adam represents all humanity, "For in the syghte of god alle man is oone man, and oone man is alle man" (522) ["For in the sight of God all men are one man, and one man is all men" (270)]. Here Julian seems to follow Augustine's anthropology whereby "through all seminal creation, *informatio,* Eve is a human being like Adam, *homo*" (Børresen 18). Her soul, like that of man, says Augustine, is created and derived directly from God and is rational, that is, made in God's image.

What is particularly telling about this inclusiveness is Julian's veiled intention to exonerate Eve from blame as well. Her non-gendered understanding of Adam is made clear when she applies her insights, using such pronouns as "we," "us," and "our," that is, all men and women.[3] Not only is Adam found blameless, but Eve, too, must be included in the compassion and pity of God. Adam, God's "most lovyd creature" (524), includes all, Adam, Eve, and all humanity. The judgement of weakness, deception, subjection, subordination, servitude is not only lacking but also completely and thoroughly dismissed. Julian's disagreement with the traditional interpretation of Genesis 3, while veiled in visionary metaphor, nevertheless dem-

---

3. For example, "And this was a begynnyng of techyng whych I saw in the same tyme, wherby I myght come to knowyng in what manner he beholdeth *vs* in *oure* synne. And then I saw that oonly payne blamyth and ponyschyth, and *our* curteyse lorde comfortyth and socurryth, and evyr he is to the soule in glad chere, lovyng and longyng to bryng *vs* to his blysse" (51.522–23) ["And this was a beginning of the teaching which I saw at the same time, whereby I might come to know in what manner he looks on *us* in our sin. And then I saw that only pain blames and punishes, and *our* courteous Lord comforts and succours, and always he is kindly disposed to the soul, loving and longing to bring *us* to his bliss" (271)]. Emphasis added.

onstrates both her theological sophistication and her resistance to the tradition.

When Julian's revelation moves on to the interpretation of the servant as the new Adam, we find an even more complex set of images. As Denise Baker has demonstrated, Julian is familiar with the notion of the fall as a fall into the "*regio dissimilitudinis*, or land of unlikeness" (88).[4] But Julian goes further. She adds that the new Adam, Christ, fell into humankind and restored likeness: "And what tyme that he of hys goodnesse wyll shew hym to man, he shewyth hym homely *as* man" (51.525) ["And when he of his goodness wishes to show himself to man, he shows himself familiar, *like* a man" (272)] [emphasis added]. The Fall of Adam is complemented by the Fall of Christ:

> When Adam felle godes sonne fell; for the ryght onyng whych was made in hevyn, goddys sonne myght nott be seperath from Adam, for by Adam I vnderstond all man. Adam fell fro lyfe to deth, in to the slade of this wrechyd worlde, and aftyr that in to hell. Goddys son fell with Adam in to the slade of the meydens wombe, whych was the feyerest doughter of Adam, and that for to excuse Adam from blame in hevyn and in erth. (51.533–34)

> [When Adam fell, God's son fell; because of the true union which was made in heaven, God's Son could not be separated from Adam, for by Adam I understand all mankind. Adam fell from life to death, into the valley of this wretched world, and after that into hell. God's Son fell with Adam, into the valley of the womb of the maiden who was the fairest daughter of Adam, and that was to excuse Adam from blame in heaven and on earth. (274–5)]

Julian's exegesis of the servant parable establishes a distinct complementary relationship between the fall whereby humankind became unlike God, and the Incarnation where the new Adam, and God, became like humanity. This likeness is not a similitude, but real. For Augustine, the materiality of the first couple radically differentiates their relationship. Eve, dependent on Adam for her material creation is thus subordinate to him; "she is a woman, *femina*" (Børresen 18). And it is precisely her sexual body (*femina*), that creates the duality not only between the two persons, but within the person of the woman. Since the divine resides in the *homo*, "the inferiority of *femina* prevents woman from showing in her body the superiority of her

---

4. Also 94–95 and 97–98 where she provides the traditional texts which centerpiece this notion.

rational soul" (Børresen 27). Man, however, is not dual; he reflects God's image in both his soul (*homo*), and in his body (*vir*). The feminine is thus subordinate to the masculine.

Julian rejects Augustine's gendered anthropology of redeemed corporal humanity. For Augustine, because of the dualism of his anthropology, woman must wait for the restoration of her full humanity until the resurrection of the flesh (Børresen 82). Julian, extending the servant allegory, says: "The wyth kyrtyll is his fleshe; the singlehede is that ther was ryght noght betwen the godhede and the manhede" (51.535–36) ["The white tunic is his flesh, the scantiness signifies that there was nothing at all separating the divinity from the humanity" (275)]. Adam's "kyrtyll," corporeal humanity, is hereby dignified, not rejected, not gendered, not split. The Incarnation, according to Julian, is a restoration of the dwelling place of God within humanity—"I saw hym heyly enjoye for the worschypfull restoryng that he wyll and shall bryng hys servannt to by hys plentuous grace" (527) ["I saw him greatly rejoice over the honourable restoration to which he wants to bring and will bring his servant by his great and plentiful grace" (272)]—the establishment of a *regio similitudinis*, as it were.

The fall of the second person of the Trinity is not without price: "for the godhed sterte fro þe fader in to þe maydyns wombe, fallyng in to the takyng of oure kynde, and in this fallyng he toke grete soore. The soore that he toke was oure flessche, in whych as sone he had felyng of dedely paynes" (51.540) ["for the divinity rushed from the Father into the maiden's womb, falling to accept our nature, and in this falling he took great hurt. The hurt that he took was our flesh, in which at once he experienced mortal pains" (277)]. While Augustine compares the formation of Christ in the womb of Mary to the formation of Eve from the side of Adam (Børresen 19), he fails to recognize the implications of this detail either in his soteriology or his anthropology. But Julian imparts the significance precisely. The price the Servant pays is the original punishment, labour. Indeed, the Servant is a "laborer," winning peace "with hys hard travayle"; the Father permits the Son to "suffer all mans payne without sparyng of him" (51.540–41). According to Julian, this labour encompasses all human labor, not only of Adam, but also of Eve even to the birthing labor which will bring humankind to its renewed relationship with God. In language distinctly evocative of childbirth, the language Julian uses to encode the death and life struggle of the new Adam is inclusive:

And by the walowyng and wrythyng, gronyng and monyng, is vnderstonde that he myght nevyr ryse all myghtyly fro that tyme þat he was fallyn in to the maydyns wombe, tyll his body was sleyne and dede, he yeldyng the soule to the fadyrs hand with alle mankynde for whome he was sent. (51.541–42)

[And by the tossing about and writhing, the groaning and moaning, is understood that he could never with almighty power rise from the time that he fell into the maiden's womb until his body was slain and dead, and he had yielded his soul into the Father's hand, with all mankind for whom he had been sent. (277)]

The transmutation of the Servant Adam into a woman giving birth to humanity transforms the meaning of humanity itself. As Nicholas Watson puts it:

The servant, who is both Adam and Christ, God and human, in effect . . . becomes a woman at the event which is at once Fall and Incarnation, and is thus occasion at once of humanity's greatest grief and greatest glory. For to be "woman" in this sense is, for Julian, simply to be human; it is the inevitable, the proper metaphor for all life that is lived in the flesh. (" 'Yf wommen,' " 25)

The birthpains, the suffering and death, result in the reunification of the human with the divine and the transformation of the flesh not awaiting the resurrection of the body but in a realized eschatology, that is, already in the resurrected body of Christ:

And oure foule dedely flessch, that goddes son toke vppon hym, whych was Adams olde kyrtyll, streyte, bare and shorte, then by oure savyoure was made feyer, new, whyt and bryght, and of endlesse clennesse, wyde and seyde, feyer and rychar than was the clothing whych I saw on the fader. (51.543)

[And our foul mortal flesh, which God's Son took upon him, which was Adam's old tunic, tight-fitting, threadbare and short, was then made lovely by our saviour, new, white and bright and forever clean, wide and ample, fairer and richer that the clothing which I saw on the Father. (278).]

Julian appropriates the inferior female body for an image of humanity and its salvation and hereby reverses Augustine's anthropology.

The significance of this reversal might best be uncovered through Bakhtin's explication of the bodily hierarchy of upper and lower strata. The upper stratum localizes bodily reality in the head and the word, that is, in thought and speech. The surface of the body remains closed, smooth, and impenetrable and "limits the body as a separate and completed phenomenon."[5] In Augustinian terms, the upper stratum of the body is notably masculine. The lower stratum of Bakh-

5. *Rabelais and His World* (Bloomington, IN: Indiana UP, 1984) 318.

tin's   analysis replicates the Augustinian limits of the female body without undermining its importance. Bahktin calls it the grotesque body. "The gaping mouth, the protruding eyes, sweat, trembling, suffocation, the swollen face—all of these are typical symptoms of the grotesque life of the body" (308). In contrast to the idealized body, "the grotesque body . . . is a body in the act of becoming. It is never finished, never completed; it is continually being built, created, and builds and creates another body" (317). In the lower stratum of the grotesque body, "the entire mechanism of the word is transferred from the apparatus of speech to the abdomen. . . . It is a miniature satyrical drama of the word, of its material birth, or the drama of the body giving birth to the word" (309). Finally, "in grotesque realism" Bakhtin says, "the bodily element is deeply positive. . . . It makes no pretense to renunciation of the earthly, or independence of the earth and the body" (19). Coinciding as it does with birth, "in the grotesque body . . . death brings nothing to an end" (322).[6]

Not only does Julian appropriate female bodily imagery in her pietistic practice by embracing extreme physical suffering in her own body, but she also goes much further than other female mystics by representing the divinity as having a female body that groans and moans, endures wounding and torture. Translating her own grotesque body onto that of the divine, she sees the divinity assume the grotesque female body. If Augustine sees female humanity as ineluctably dual and that therefore "woman is nearer to the devil and further removed from God" (Børresen 53), Julian envisions a God who exploits the duality of human spirit and physicality. Humanity, as it were, reveals divinity. If the [female] human being is dual, so is God. Thus where traditional theological discussion had been preoccupied with how man is made in the image and likeness of God and woman's inability to reflect that image,[7] Julian articulates an internally persuasive discourse that distinctly revises that prior view and embraces imagery that opposes Augustine's view of the body as limitation. Engaging as it were with the tradition, she adopts not only a more inclusive point of view but also adapts distinctly female imagery to articulate her theology of inclusion. She both appropriates the discourse of gender and, setting it alongside the equally

6. Essential reading on this topic include Laurie Finke's two essays: "Mystical Bodies and the Dialogics of Vision," in *Maps of Flesh and Light*, ed. Ulrike Wiethaus (Syracuse: Syracuse UP, 1993), 28–44; and the chapter "The Grotesque Mystical Body: Representing the Woman Writer," in *Feminist Theory, Women's Writing*, 75–107.

7. Only in relationship with the man can the woman reflect the image of God, asserts Augustine. ". . . Not the woman but the man is the image of God. . . . When she is referred separately in her quality of helpmate, which regards the woman herself alone, then she is not the image of God; but as regards the man alone, he is the image of God as fully and completely as when the woman too is joined with him" (O'Faolain 130).

gendered discourse of tradition, decodes the metaphors which comprise the discourse.[8]

* * *

JOAN M. NUTH

[Human Nature: The Image of God]†

Julian's anthropology is the most difficult part of her theology to understand. Her descriptions of the "substance and sensuality" of the human soul, their dual creation, and their relationship to Christ are not without ambiguity. I have found it necessary to move behind her statements to what I consider to be their source, the Augustinian notion of the image of God. Within the interpretative framework provided by the notion of image, some of Julian's most puzzling statements about the human being begin to gain clarity.

The *imago Dei* was one of the dominant themes of medieval anthropology in the Western Church. Based upon Gen 1:26–27, it is the idea that the human being, specifically the human soul, was created in the image and likeness of God. The theme was first developed by the Eastern patristic writers and creatively modified by Augustine.[1] Countless medieval theologians reflected upon it in a variety of ways, especially on its meaning for the spiritual life.[2] Julian was influenced by this theme, especially as it developed in the West under Augustine's influence, and it forms the background to her own anthropology.

Certain aspects of the *imago Dei* tradition considered women, because of their closer ties to physicality, as less perfect or deficient images of God. While Julian was probably aware of this, she chose to ignore it.[3] In doing so, she exhibits a consistency with most medi-

---

8. Grace M. Jantzen, *Power, Gender and Christian Mysticism* (Cambridge: Cambridge UP, 1995), esp. 301–303.

† From *Wisdom's Daughter: the Theology of Julian of Norwich* (New York: Crossroad Publishing, 1991), pp. 104–16, 194–97. Copyright © 1991 Joan M. Nuth. Reprinted by permission of the publisher and of the author.

1. For the Greeks, see Gerhard Ladner, *The Idea of Reform: Its Impact on Christian Thought and Action in the Age of the Fathers* (Cambridge: Harvard University Press, 1959), 83–107, and John Edward Sullivan, O.P., *The Image of God: The Doctrine of St. Augustine and Its Influence* (Dubuque: Priory Press, 1963), 163–95. For Augustine, see Sullivan, 3–162, and Ladner, 185–203. The differences between Augustine and those who preceded him are summarized in Sullivan, 194–95.

2. For some examples, see Sullivan, 204–16 and 288–94. Julian is mentioned on 293. In addition, Sullivan's extensive treatment of the theme in Aquinas is found on 216–72.

3. For example, if Julian knew Augustine's *De trinitate*, as I think highly likely, she surely would have been aware of the fact that Augustine considered women to be deficient images of God: "The woman, together with her own husband, is the image of God, so that the whole substance may be one image, but when she is referred to separately in her quality

eval women, who were generally less self-conscious about gender distinctions and roles than men were. Creation in and restoration to God's image were prominent themes in their spirituality.[4] Thus Julian drew heavily upon the Augustinian notion of image, assuming it to be inclusive of all humanity.

Julian follows Augustine in seeing the human soul as an image of the trinity: "the blessed trinity made [humankind] in their image and their likeness."[5] More specifically, "God is endless supreme truth, endless supreme wisdom, endless supreme love uncreated; and a [human] soul is a creature in God which has the same properties created" (44:256). God's image resides in the human intellectual faculties: in the mind or memory, which reflects God's truth or might; in the reason or understanding which reflects God's wisdom; in the will which reflects God's love. In her own development of this pattern, Julian most often uses the triad of human might, wisdom, and love. By might she means the inner strength and ability to accomplish what one desires;[6] by wisdom, true sight or knowledge of what one desires, and by love, the desire for God.

This image is humanity's true nature and substance, a sharing in the nature and substance of God. It is more than simply participating in God's being, which all creatures do. It means that there is nothing more like God than the human soul in the hierarchy of being. This point is essential to the Augustinian notion of image,[7] and in her search for a way to express this truth, Julian makes statements like the following:

---

as a helpmeet, which regards the woman alone, then she is not the image of God, but as regards the male alone, he is the image of God as fully and completely as when the woman too is joined with him in one" (7.7.10; trans. in Ruether, 95). See Ruether's further discussion of this misogynist strain in the *imago Dei* tradition, 93–99, in *Sexism and God-Talk: Toward a Feminist Theology* (Boston: Beacon Press, 1983).

4. Caroline Walker Bynum, " ' . . . And Woman His Humanity': Female Imagery in the Religious Writing of the Later Middle Ages," in *Gender and Religion: On the Complexity of Symbols*, ed. Caroline Walker Bynum, Steven Harrell, and Paula Richman (Boston: Beacon Press, 1986), 260–62.

5. Julian of Norwich, *Showings*, trans. Edmund Colledge and James Walsh, Classics of Western Spirituality (New York: Paulist Press, 1978), 10:194. All subsequent quotations are from this source and will be identified parenthetically in the text by chapter and page numbers.

6. Although Julian usually refers to this as human might, at times she calls it truth, mind, or memory, using the terms interchangeably. Augustine's concept of mind or memory designates the foundation or inner essence of human intellectual creation which expresses itself through the operations of understanding and will (Sullivan, 44–49). It was common from the twelfth century on to substitute "power" for "truth, mind or memory." It would be interesting to explore exactly how this change occurred, and how it altered the meaning of the concept expressed. Julian clearly uses "might," the Middle English equivalent of "potentia," to mean the ability to accomplish what one desires.

7. "Not every thing which is in some way like God in creatures is also to be called his image, but only that to which he alone is superior; namely, that which has been expressed from him, and between which thing and himself no other nature has been interposed" (*De trinitate* 11.5.8, translated and discussed in Sullivan, 16).

Our soul, which is created, dwells in God in substance, of which substance, through God, we are what we are. And I saw no difference between God and our substance, but, as it were, all God; and still my understanding accepted that our substance, is in God, that is to say that God is God, and our substance is a creature in God (54:285).[8]

Being image of God means that there is nothing between the human soul and God on the ladder of creation and that the human soul mirrors God's might, wisdom, and love in its own faculties. But it also means that there is an eternal union of love between the image and the creator so close that nothing can destroy it:

For before [God] made us he loved us, and when we were made we loved him; and this [love] is made only of the natural substantial goodness of the Holy Spirit, mighty by reason of the might of the Father, wise in mind of the wisdom of the Son. And so is [the human] soul made by God, and in the same moment joined to God (53:283–84).

And again:

Our soul is united to [God] who is unchangeable goodness. And between God and our soul there is neither wrath not forgiveness in God's sight. For our soul is so wholly united to God, through his own goodness, that between God and our soul *nothing can interpose* (46:259; emphasis mine).

Julian's stress upon God as Love is all important here. The fact that the human soul is next to God in the chain of being designates not only a static ontological reality, but also a relational one; it means being united to God in love: "And in this endless love [the human] soul is kept whole" (53:284).

Again Julian follows Augustine who saw the image as related to its exemplar not only in origin and likeness, but also in a dynamic tendency to return to it. This last is based upon Augustine's theology of creation, which, for the spiritual creature, involves an immediate recall and conversion to God, simultaneous with the act of creation, both of which take place before time.[9] When Julian says that the substance of the human soul is eternally united to or grounded in God's love "from without beginning" she is expressing this Augustin-

---

8. The beginning of this passage could be subject to a pantheistic interpretation, something Julian seems to be aware of, since she immediately adds a qualification. A striking parallel is found in *The Spirit and the Soul*, 24: "The soul is a spiritual substance. . . . We should not believe it to be a part of God nor of the same substance as God, nor yet made out of some elemental matter. Rather it is a creature of God, created out of nothing." See *Three Treatises on Man: A Cistercian Anthropology*, ed. Bernard McGinn (Kalamazoo: Cistercian Publications, 1977), 217.

9. For Augustine's theology of creation, see Ladner, 167–85, in which the most relevant texts are cited. For a shorter discussion, see Sullivan, 17–21.

ian concept in her own words.[1] The soul, by virtue of being God's image, is drawn back to God and held in a unity of love that transcends time.[2] The term Julian uses to designate this notion of image, "substance of the soul," includes an ontological understanding, but it primarily designates a relation, the eternal union of the soul to God through love.

Julian makes this point repeatedly: "God judges us in our natural substance, which is always kept one in [God], whole and safe, without end" (45:256); "Our natural substance is now full of blessedness in God, and has been since it was made, and will be without end" (45:258); "In our creating [God] joined and united us to himself and through this union we are kept as pure and as noble as we were created" (58: 293). This union is not due to any effort on the part of human nature, but to the eternal love of God which is ever active in the preservation of God's image in the human soul: "Just as we were to be without end, so we were treasured and hidden in God, known and loved from without beginning" (53:284).[3] Because this union is eternal, it is permanent and unchanging. It is the source of God's promise that, in spite of what seem to us to be the endless fluctuations and confusions of human life in time, all will be well.

What does Julian mean, precisely, by statements like these? Does she mean that the essence of the soul literally exists united to God from all eternity and descends to earth at a point in time? Or does she mean that the soul exists as an idea in the mind or intention of God, eventually to come into actual existence? My sense is that Julian continues to speak here, as she does with respect to evil, from God's eternal perspective as opposed to our temporal one. God sees things as already accomplished. The distinction between what is in God's mind as an intention or idea and what actually has existence is a useless one in such a perspective. Furthermore, Julian is convinced that God's loving will is strong to effect what it desires. To be an idea in God's mind or intention is, in effect, to be.

Another part of the *imago Dei* tradition stressed the place of

1. "For I saw that God never began to love humankind; for just as humankind will be in endless bliss, fulfilling God's joy with regard to his works, just so has that same humankind been known and loved in God's prescience *from without beginning* in his righteous intent" (53:283); we find in Christ, the mediator "our full heaven in everlasting joy by the prescient purpose of all the blessed trinity *from without beginning*" (53:283); "In our creation we had beginning, but the love in which he created us was in him *from without beginning*" (86:342–43; emphasis mine).

2. Note how well this idea captures the thought of Augustine: "the concept of image used by Augustine demands the presence of God, not simply as a principle of origin . . . but requires the enduring presence of the exemplar as the term of the dynamic activity found in an image" (Sullivan, 21).

3. Note the conflation of several scriptural texts here: the author of Colossians wishes his readers the knowledge of Christ, "in whom are hid all the treasures of wisdom and knowledge" (Col 2:2–3) and later says: "your life is hid with Christ in God" (Col 3:3). Julian combines these with the idea that God "chose us in him [Christ] before the foundation of the world" (Eph 1:4).

Christ. Here the primary and only perfect image of God is the Logos, the second person of the trinity, in whose image the human soul is made image of God.[4] Julian draws upon this tradition when she says that our true natural substance (God's image in us) is preserved eternally in God by being united to the human soul of Christ. This union has its origins in the eternal purpose of God:

> God the blessed trinity, who is everlasting being, just as he is eternal from without beginning, just so was it in his eternal purpose to create human nature, which fair nature was first prepared for his own Son, the second person; and when he wished, by full agreement of the whole trinity he created us all at once (58:293).

The specific role of Christ is described as follows:

> By the endless intent and assent and the full accord of all the trinity, the mediator wanted to be the foundation and the head of this fair nature, out of whom we have all come, in whom we are all enclosed, into whom we shall all go (53:283).[5]

Thus Christ is the beginning and end of the human soul, its efficient, exemplary and final cause.[6]

The parable of the lord and the servant clarified humanity's relation to Christ for Julian: "our good Lord showed his own Son and Adam as only one" (51:275); "because of the true union which was made in heaven, God's Son could not be separated from Adam" (51:274). Therefore,

> [God] makes no distinction in love between the blessed soul of Christ and the least soul that will be saved. . . . Where the blessed soul of Christ is, there is the substance of all the souls which will be saved by Christ (54:285).

Where is the blessed soul of Christ? It is eternally with God through its union with the second person of the trinity. There it is eternally loved by God; there too, the person of the Son eternally loves the Father, which love is the Holy Spirit. Humanity's eternal union with God in love is thus mediated by the love God has for Christ, and it is also through Christ that humanity can be said to love God eternally. This is why God loves us; when God sees us, God sees Christ. And Christ's human soul includes not only the individual soul of Jesus of Nazareth, but all humanity: "Christ, having joined in himself [everyone] who will be saved, is perfect [humanity]" (57:292).

---

4. For the roots of this idea in the Pauline corpus, see Ladner, 54–59; for the idea in Augustine, see Sullivan, 13–14, 21–22; in Bernard, see Etienne Gilson, *The Mystical Theology of St. Bernard*, translated by A. H. C. Downes (New York: Sheed & Ward, 1940), 52.
5. This is the theme of Col 1:15–20.
6. "I am the Alpha and the Omega" (Rev 1:8) and "I am the first and the last, and the living one" (Rev 1:17–18). Cf. Sullivan, 21.

So far we have spoken only of the substance of the human soul, wherein alone lies the image of God.[7] What of the body? How is it united to the soul? Julian shared the difficulty of all Western theology in coming to a satisfactory answer to this question.[8] The Christian doctrines of incarnation and bodily resurrection were not readily compatible with the neoplatonic notion of a spiritual, immutable, and eternal soul, free from bodily influences. Augustine himself always asserted the unity of the human body and spirit, and, although he struggled to give this a satisfactory philosophical solution, his efforts were never free from ambiguity.[9] While in general the problem of the unity between soul and body could lead to a devaluation of the body, important qualifications to this tendency were introduced. This is certainly true of Augustine himself, in spite of the fact that he is grossly misunderstood today in this area.[1] Among the twelfth century Cistercians, efforts to reconcile the unity of soul and body resulted in a concentration on medicine and physiology as important to human self-knowledge, the theme of the human as microcosm of the universe, and the use of analogies between body and soul as a way of mediating the dichotomy between the two.[2] Of all the theologians before Julian's time, Aquinas probably achieved the most favorable solution to the unity between body and soul available to the Middle Ages.[3] However, Julian exhibits no indebtedness to Aquinas in this area.

Though Julian does not consider the body as such in any systematic way, she is generally free from statements which devalue the body. In fact, her only description of the body finds God directing even the lowliest bodily function of the elimination of waste:

> A man walks upright, and the food in his body is shut in as if in a well-made purse. When the time of his necessity comes, the purse is opened and then shut again, in most seemly fashion. And it is God who does this, as it is shown when he says that he comes down to us in our humblest needs. For [God] does not despise what he has made, nor does he disdain to serve us

7. The human body as such is not the image of God. Again, this is a basic Augustinian insight, followed by virtually all medieval thinkers (Sullivan, 44–52).
8. Etienne Gilson, *The Spirit of Philosophy*, translated by A. H. C. Downs (New York: Charles Scribner's Sons, 1936), 168–75.
9. Margaret R. Miles, *Augustine on the Body* (Missoula: Scholars Press, 1979); Sullivan, 48–49; McGinn, *Three Treatises*, 5–10.
1. Miles, 1–8, 127–31.
2. McGinn, *Three Treatises*, 87.
3. For a discussion of the effects of Aristotelian philosophy upon the problem of the unity of soul and body and for Aquinas' solution, see Anton C. Pegis, *At the Origins of the Thomistic Notion of Man* (New York: Macmillan, 1963), and, more briefly, Gilson, *The Spirit of Philosophy*, 175–88; Caroline Walker Bynum, *Holy Feast and Holy Fast: The Religious Significance of Food to Medieval Women* (Berkeley: University of California Press, 1987), 254.

> in the simplest natural functions of our body, for love of the
> soul which he created in his own likeness. For as the body is
> clad in the cloth, and the flesh in the skin, and the bones in the
> flesh, and the heart in the trunk, so are we, soul and body, clad
> and enclosed in the goodness of God (6:186).

The value of human bodiliness in God's eyes was made even more
explicit by God's actually assuming human flesh in the incarnation.
Julian exhibits a comfort with human bodiliness consistent with a
truly incarnational spirituality.[4]

One of the ways classical and medieval authors maintained the
unity between soul and body was through the tradition of the bi-
partite soul. Augustine used the term "mens" to designate the spiritual, intellectual soul, untouched and unaffected by the body, and
the inferior "spiritus" to designate the soul in its contact with the
body and with external material reality. The lower faculty of the soul
acted as a mediator between the purely intellectual soul and the
physical body.[5] This tradition was dominant throughout the Middle
Ages, and various terms were introduced to designate the dual soul:
higher and lower, internal and external, spirit and soul.[6] One strand
of the tradition even distinguished the two as animus and amina,
identifying the higher faculty as male and the lower as female, but
Julian makes no use of this distinction.

The terms Julian uses for the dual soul are "substance," indicating
the higher power of the soul that is always united to God, and "sensuality," indicating the lower power of the soul united directly to the
body. And, insofar as the "sensual soul" is linked to the body, Julian's
use of the term "sensuality" can at times be interpreted to include
the body itself. It is important to remember that there is only one
soul, and that these words designate the soul as related to God and
to the body, and are not disjointed "parts" as such (56:289; 55:288).

As far as I can tell, the pairing of the words "substance and sensuality" in this context is unique to Julian. It is not hard to speculate
where she may have acquired the term "substance" because the soul
was generally called a "spiritual substance." What Julian means by
"substance" sounds very like what is described in the anonymous
twelfth century Cistercian treatise, The Spirit and the Soul: "The
intellectual soul is a certain substance. . . . God is its proper element
and dwelling place, deriving from the fact that it was made in God's

---

4. See Bynum's discussion of medieval women's attitudes toward the body (Holy Feast, 212–
28) and of the medieval view of physicality (245–59).

5. Miles, 22–28.

6. See, for example, The Spirit and the Soul 9: "The life of the soul is twofold, for it lives in
the flesh and in God. There are consequently two kinds of sense knowledge in man, an
interior and an exterior one, each one having its own proper object which is its means of
being renewed. The interior faculty is renewed in the contemplation of divine things and
the exterior in the contemplation of things human. God became man, then, in order that
the total man might find happiness in him" (McGinn, Three Treatises, 191).

likeness."[7] Later in the same treatise, we find: "Sensuality is the power of the soul which makes the body grow, and by the bodily senses it knows and discerns what is outside itself."[8] However, the terms this treatise generally uses for the dual soul are "spirit and soul," not "substance and sensuality."

In Julian's theology, unlike the soul's substance which is eternally united to God, sensuality is changeable, seeming to be "now one thing and now another, as it derives from parts and presents an external appearance" (45:256). It is affected by the changeableness of this "passing life" which can confuse us; we often do not know "in our sensuality what our self is," and need faith to help us see this (46:258). While we are full and complete in our substance, "in our sensuality we are lacking," unfinished, incomplete (57:291). We need God's mercy and grace to bring our sensuality to completion.

Julian separates the creation of the substance of the soul and its becoming sensual. Human substance was created "all at once" when the human soul of Christ was created (58:293). The body, on the other hand, came from "the slime of the earth" (53:284). When the substance of the soul "is breathed into our body" then "we are made sensual" (55:286). Again Julian is indebted to Augustine, for whom the sequence of creation as described in the six-day cycle of Genesis 1, although causal, was not a temporal succession, but occurred before time in its entirety.[9] The human soul, as image and likeness of God, was created *actually* within this atemporal work, but the body was created then only in its "seminal reasons" and would make its actual appearance, corresponding to its formation from the earth, only in time.[1] Thus, what Julian calls the "substance" of the human

---

7. McGinn, *Three Treatises*, 182–83. This treatise, composed almost completely of verbatim quotations from various sources, was very popular (there are 60 manuscripts of it in the British Museum alone) and was cited by many thirteenth-century theologians, probably because it was thought to be of Augustinian origin. I think it highly likely that Julian knew its contents, for there are several instances, besides this one, where her thought is remarkably similar. For information on its origins and influence, see ibid., 63–74.

8. Ibid., 242. Cf. also "the sensuality, or animality of the soul is its lower energy which draws with it the sensuality of the flesh as an obedient servant" (244). Both quotations are taken from sections 37 and 38, which are transcriptions of Hugh of St. Victor's *Didascalion*.

9. My source here is Ladner, 177–83, who includes the relevant Augustinian texts in his notes. Augustine's chief source for the idea of the simultaneity of creation, which he cites repeatedly, is the Vulgate's rendering of Ecclesiasticus 18:1: "Qui vivit in aeternum, creavit omnia simul."

1. This explanation allowed Augustine to reconcile the account of Genesis 2 with that of Genesis 1 (Ladner, 183). *The Spirit and the Soul*, 41, has an interesting interpretation of this part of Augustine's doctrine: "After the first act of creation, no new bodily materials were created, but all created at one time, bodies are propagated by formation in time. Souls were not essentially all made together in this way, but they were made in a like nature, in the image and likeness of God. Thus they are thought to have been made together but judged not to have been sent out together for the sake of the essence, but made together for the sake of the form that is like to the image and likeness of God. Flesh is passed on to flesh in the act of procreation, but the spirit is in no way begotten by the spirit" (McGinn, *Three Treatises*, 247).

soul exists with God before time, while its "sensuality" begins only with its insertion into the body in the course of time.

Julian solves the problem of the union between substance and sensuality by situating it in God, "the mean which keeps the substance and the sensuality together" (56:289). More specifically, this union is due to the incarnation of the Wisdom of God in human history:

> In the same time that God joined himself to our body in the maiden's womb, he took our soul, which is sensual, and in taking it, having enclosed us all in himself, he united it to our substance. In this union he was perfect [humanity] (57:292).[2]

"Perfect humanity" means that the whole human race is the full human nature of Christ. But it also means the union of human sensuality with the image of God that is the substance of the soul. This is what Julian calls the "increase" of human nature which is effected by the incarnation, and it is something permanent: substance and sensuality "will never separate" (56:289).

This solution, as stated by Julian, is not without ambiguity. Let me interpret what I think she means. The substance of the human soul of Christ, the created reality most like the Logos, the one true image of God, was the highest being created before time and eternally joined to the Logos. The substance of all human souls was created at the same time and made one with the substance of Christ's human soul, thereby eternally united with God. The sensuality of human souls appears only in time as their bodies gradually develop from the seminal reasons. In the human being, the same soul, whose substance is eternally united to God, becomes related to corporeal nature, but the unity between substance and sensuality is a fragile one, incomplete, partial. Full unity between human substance and sensuality was not achieved until the substance of Christ's soul united itself to a human body in time. Thus the incarnation, God's work of mercy in time, completes human nature by bringing sensuality into complete union with the soul's substance.

* * * There is an incipient "evolutionary" perspective to Julian's thought here. She cannot speak of human nature in its entirety except in light of the incarnation. As a result of the incarnation, humanity's increase, that is, the assumption of human sensuality into union with its substance, is made possible by Christ. But it is

---

2. For a similar idea in Augustine, see Miles, 95–96. See also *The Spirit and the Soul* 9: "God became man, then, in order that the total man might find happiness in him" (McGinn, *Three Treatises*, 191).

only by a gradual process of growth in the life of grace, through the presence of the Holy Spirit, that this increase occurs:

> All the gifts which God can give to the creature he has given to his Son Jesus for us, which gifts he, dwelling in us, has enclosed in him until the time that we are fully grown, our soul together with our body and our body together with our soul. Let either of them take help from the other, until we have grown to full stature as creative nature brings about; and then in the foundation of creative nature with the operation of mercy, the Holy Spirit by grace breathes into us gifts leading to endless life (55: 287).[3]

Here we see again the growth of the soul as imaging the trinity's acts in human history. As the first person of the trinity is the principle and foundation of the others, so is substantial human nature, which is always held in God, the foundation upon which the works of mercy and grace build in order to bring human sensuality into union with its substance:

> Our faith comes from the natural love of our soul, and from the clear light of our reason, and from the steadfast memory which we have from God in our first creation. And when our soul is breathed into our body, at which time we are made sensual, at once mercy and grace begin to work, having care of us and protecting us with pity and love, in which operation the Holy Spirit forms in our faith the hope that we shall return up above to our substance, into the power of Christ, increased and fulfilled through the Holy Spirit (55:286).

By substance or nature, humanity is created in the image of the trinity's might, wisdom, and love, a task appropriated to the Father's creative power. But that image is meant to be increased by the action of God's Wisdom and perfected by the action of God's Spirit in human history, through the union of human sensuality and substance. Thus it is true to say that human sensuality, too, though not the image of God as such, "is founded in nature, in mercy and in grace, and this foundation enables us to receive gifts which lead us to endless life" (55:287).

Sensual human life, fleshly existence in the world of time, is, from a human perspective, gradually lifted up and included in the eternity of God. In the process the image of God's might, wisdom, and love in the human being is increased and fulfilled. Made in God's image,

---

3. Note the similarity of this passage to the thought of Eph 4:4–13: "There is one body and one Spirit, just as you were called to the one hope that belongs to your call. . . . Grace was given to each of us according to the measure of Christ's gift. . . . And his gifts were . . . for building up the body of Christ, until we all attain to the unity of the faith and of the knowledge of the Son of God, to mature manhood, to the measure of the stature of the fulness of Christ" (Colledge and Walsh, 567.31).

the human is meant to become even more like God through earthly existence. The neoplatonic *exitus et reditus* theme is here, to be sure, but without the denigration of earthly existence that can often accompany it. We are meant to be with God in eternity, and cannot be entirely happy until we are there, but when we do arrive there, we bring our sensuality with us, increased and fulfilled by our earthly sojourn. Again, the root of Julian's thought is Augustinian: "that reform of the inner man which was made possible by Incarnation and Redemption was not a return only to the spiritual aspect of creation, but the completion and elevation of a spiritual-corporeal compound."[4] According to Gerhard Ladner, the Western tradition differs essentially from the East in its emphasis upon the corporeality of what is brought back to God and upon the eternal value of time and history. Julian is squarely in the Western tradition here.[5]

Human sensuality is something very precious; in fact, Julian calls it the city of God, "that honorable city in which our Lord Jesus sits." He is enclosed therein, together with human substance which is enclosed in Christ (56:289). This has been true from the moment the soul entered the body:

> In the same instant and place in which our soul is made sensual, in that same instant and place exists the city of God, ordained for [God] from without beginning. He comes into this city and will never depart from it, for God is never out of the soul, in which he will dwell blessedly without end (55:287).

The phrase "city of God" is loaded with allusions, first of all to the church, sign of the kingdom of God on earth, obviously dependent upon Augustine's classical work in which the church's historical and corporeal character is developed. Further, calling the individual soul the "city of God" was common among medieval spiritual writers.[6] While Julian sometimes calls the soul without qualification the city of God, the fact that she often specifically designates sensuality as God's city shows that she was conscious of the historical and bodily implications of the term as employed by Augustine. For Julian, human bodiliness is important to both humans and to God. It is not to be dismissed as useless or detrimental to human spiritual growth. In fact, its development over the course of human life in time contributes to that increase of God's image in the human which God predestined "from before beginning" and in which humanity and God will eternally rejoice in heaven.

4. Ladner, 184.
5. This difference is marked in a comparison between Augustine and Gregory of Nyssa (ibid., 71–75, 175–77, 184–85).
6. To cite only one example, Hugh of St. Victor developed the theme elaborately; see Ford Lewis Battles, "Hugo of Saint-Victor as a Moral Allegorist," *Church History* 18 (1949): 220–40, esp. 231–39.

It is clear that Julian knows nothing of a human nature that is untouched by God's grace. Yet she is precise in distinguishing between God's "natural goodness," which is "uncreated nature" from which mercy and grace flow (63:303), and human "natural goodness" which is able to receive mercy and grace:

> In our substance we are full and in our sensuality we are lacking, and this lack God will restore and fill by the operation of mercy and grace, plentifully flowing into us from God's own natural goodness. And so this natural goodness makes mercy and grace to work in us, and the natural goodness that we have from [God] enables us to receive the operation of mercy and grace (57:291).

Nonetheless, the presence of God's grace to that created natural goodness is constant. Julian would agree with Karl Rahner that there is no such thing, practically speaking, as "pure nature" untouched and unaffected by God's grace, although it is necessary to distinguish the two conceptually.[7]

With such an optimistic picture of human nature united eternally to God through the bond of love, it is no wonder that Julian asked the question, "What is sin?" For Julian, God's image is not lost by sin, but damaged.[8] Retained in the soul's eternal substance, God's image is distorted in human sensuality: "though the soul may be always like God in nature and in substance . . . , it is often unlike [God] in condition, through sin" (43:253).[9] Of the three faculties by which the sensual soul images God, might and wisdom are hurt by sin, but the will seems to be relatively unaffected. As a result of his fall, the servant of the parable "was injured in his powers and made most feeble, and in his understanding he was amazed, because he was diverted from looking on his lord, but his will was preserved in God's sight" (51:270).

Julian could be indebted for the root of this idea to Bernard's treatise *On Grace and Free Choice*, where the image of God which remains constant in the human being after sin is situated in the will, in the power of free choice, mirroring God's freedom. As originally created, the human being also had two "likenesses" to God: free pleasure which mirrored God's might, and free counsel which mirrored God's wisdom. These two were completely lost as a result of sin.[1] Julian does not distinguish image from likeness as Bernard does.

7. See, for example, "Concerning the Relationship between Nature and Grace," *Theological Investigations* I, 297–317, esp. 311–15.
8. Again Julian follows the mature Augustine, who saw that the divine image remains in its roots in humanity in spite of sin, since it belongs to the very nature of the intellectual soul to be the image of God (Sullivan, 42–44).
9. I have deleted the words "restored by grace" here, following the suggestion that this phrase is a scribal addition (Colledge and Walsh, 475.3n). If one understands Julian's idea of the image of God, this is a superfluous addition.
1. See Bernard McGinn's introduction to *On Grace and Free Choice in Treatises III: The*

For her the image of God resides in all three faculties and remains constant in the substance of the soul which is always held united to God. But in sensual human life, what mirrors God's might and wisdom is weakened and blinded, while the desire of the will to love God remains constant. For both Bernard and Julian, the ability to mirror God's might and wisdom, that is, the ability to effect and understand what one wills, is damaged by sin, while the image remains in the will, although Julian means something more by this than mere free choice.

For Julian, the damage done by sin to the soul's might and wisdom prevents the realization in sensual existence of who one truly is in God's sight. This damage also prevents a knowledge of the will to some extent, but the will continues to assert itself: "Our natural will is to have God, and God's good will is to have us, and we can never stop willing or loving until we possess [God] in the fulness of joy" (6:186). The way the image is discernible in the will is in its desire for God, which remains so strong that it can never fully assent to sin:

> In each soul which will be saved there is a godly will which never assented to sin nor ever will, which will is so good that it cannot ever will evil, but always constantly it wills good and it does good in the sight of God (53:283).[2]

Hatred of sin is natural to the human: "our self is opposed to our sin and to our weakness" (72:321). When humans sin, they paradoxically go against their own deepest desire.

This constancy of will is the result of God's love, which is so strong that it draws the soul like a magnet, holding it always in union with God. Because "we are they whom [God] loves . . . eternally we do what [God] delights in" (37:242). The bond of love which unites the soul to God is so strong that it can never be broken, and the soul is always aware of this on some level, though that awareness be dimmed. It is felt in the longing "to be filled with endless joy and bliss" (45:258), which remains in spite of the weakness and blindness that cause one to be distracted by other desires:

Works of Bernard of Clairvaux, ed. and trans. by Daniel O'Donovan, O.C.S.O., and Conrad Greenia, O.C.S.O. (Kalamazoo: Cistercian Publications, 1972), 28–29, and Gilson, *Mystical Theology*, 46–59. For another parallel to Julian's idea see *The Spirit and the Soul*, 48, where the author writes: "Free will was committed to man. After Eve was seduced by the serpent and fell, man lost the goodness of his nature and the vigor of his judgment but not the power of choice, lest he not have the means to emend his sin. It remained to him to seek salvation by free will, that is by rational choice; but first he had to be helped and inspired by God to seek salvation. That we accept the inspiration to salvation is within our power; that we attain what we desire to attain is a divine gift" (McGinn, *Three Treatises*, 256).

2. These words are an exact repetition of 37:241.

For the natural desire of our soul is so great and so immeasurable that if all the nobility which God ever created in heaven and on earth were given to us for our joy and our comfort, if we did not see [God's] own fair blessed face, still we should never cease to mourn and to weep in the spirit, because, that is, of our painful longing, until we might see our creator's fair blessed face (72:321).

The deepest need of the human soul is to have God; thus "in our intention we wait for God" (52:279). This is Julian's way of expressing what Augustine called the human restless search for God and what we might today call the constant drive of human transcendence toward what lies beyond the world of space and time. The image cannot refrain from seeking full and complete union with the Love that created it. This is the central theme of Julian's anthropology.

One might well ask at this point what part freedom plays in the life and destiny of the human being. Being eternally united to God in a bond of love that nothing, not even sin, can destroy seems deterministic. Unfortunately, Julian does not treat the question of human freedom formally. We can only draw implications from her discussion of other issues to speculate about how she understood the role of human freedom in the Christian life.

An important clue is found in the parable of the lord and the servant, where the servant stood eager to do the lord's will. * * * Christ "voluntarily" went to his death because he wanted the same thing the Father did, the salvation of those he loved. But the servant also represents all humanity, and we can come to a similar conclusion about the relationship of God's will to human free will.

Humans are made in such a way that they freely desire union with God. The more the human will becomes conformed to what God wills, the more free human beings are to become who they truly desire to be.[3] God's will for humanity and humanity's own deepest desire are the same: ultimate union with God. It is when humans resist God and the desire of their true self (human "substance") that they experience a lack of freedom. Thus, Julian says that "reluctance and deliberate choice are in opposition" within the human self (19:212). The reluctance to move in the direction of God, which humans experience within the self as a result of sin, prevents them on occasion from freely and fully choosing what they most deeply desire. Freedom is hindered, not increased, by choosing other than what God wills. The fact that God holds human beings in an eternal bond of love thus enables the exercise of human freedom, allowing the

3. See Karl Rahner's discussion on this in "On the Theology of the Incarnation," *TI* V, 177; cf. Anne E. Carr, *Transforming Grace: Christian Tradition and Women's Experience* (San Francisco: Harper & Row, 1988), 150.

"deliberate choice" of God and God's will, which is also consistent
with the deepest desire of the human heart.

Thus it is logical to Julian that God should reward those who have
"voluntarily served God" (14:203), especially those who have "voluntarily and freely" offered their youth to God (14:204). Humans
are not automatons mechanically doing what God wills, but "part-
ners in [God's] good will and work" (43:253), exercising free will in
cooperation with God. Christ is working in us, but "we are by grace
according with him" (54:286). Christ "wants us to be his helpers,
giving all our intention to him" (57:292) and "[keeping] ourselves
faithfully in him" (71:318). All of these sayings indicate Julian's
belief in the free cooperation of the human will with God's grace.

CAROLINE WALKER BYNUM

[Jesus as Mother]†

Biblical and Patristic Background

Any explanation of the medieval theme of God as mother must
begin by noting that it is not an invention of twelfth-century devotional writers. In the Old Testament, God frequently speaks of himself as mother, bearing the Israelites in his bosom, conceiving them
in his womb (e.g., Isa. 49:1, 49:15, and 66:11–13).[1] The wisdom of
God is a feminine principle; in Ecclesiasticus she says: "I am the
mother of fair love, and of fear, and of knowledge, and of holy hope.
. . . Come over to me, all ye that desire me: and be filled with my
fruits" (Ecclus. 24:24–26).[2] In the New Testament such imagery is
nonexistent. The gospel of John does apply to Christ some of the
titles of the Old Testament wisdom literature (e.g., John 14:6)[3] but
it uses no feminine language. Christ is, however, described as a hen
gathering her chicks under her wings in Matt. 23:37.[4] And the contrast drawn in the Epistles between milk and meat as symbols of
types of instruction (1 Cor. 3:1–2; Heb. 5:12; 1 Pet. 2:2) seems to

---

† From *Jesus as Mother: Studies in the Spirituality of the High Middle Ages* (Berkeley: U of
   California P, 1982), pp. 125–26, 129–34. Copyright © 1982 the Regents of the University
   of California. Reprinted by permission of the publisher.
1. See Phyllis Trible, "God, Nature of, in the Old Testament," *Interpreter's Dictionary of the
   Bible*, supplementary vol. (Nashville, 1976), pp. 368–69; and André Cabassut, "Une dévotion médiévale peu connue; la dévotion à 'Jésus Notre Mère,' " *Mélanges Marcel Viller,
   Revue d'ascétique et de mystique* 25 (1949): 236–37.
2. Edmund Colledge and James Walsh, eds., *A Book of Showings to the Anchoress Julian of
   Norwich*, 2 vols. (Toronto, 1978), 1:154.
3. Ibid.
4. Mark 3:35, where Christ refers to any faithful follower as his mother or brother, is a very
   different use of mother as symbol.

have suggested to later writers that the apostles responsible for the
Epistles, Peter and Paul, themselves provided the milk for beginners
and should therefore be seen as mothers. The possibly gnostic *Odes*
of Solomon, the apocryphal third-century Acts of Peter, and the writings of Clement, Origen, Irenaeus, John Chrysostom, Ambrose, and
Augustine all describe Christ as mother.[5] In general the Greek
fathers, particularly those influenced by gnosticism, seem to have
been more at home with maternal metaphors.[6] The Latin translator
of the Acts of Peter suppressed "mother" in his list of titles for
Christ,[7] and the passing references to Christ's maternal love in
Augustine and Ambrose in no way compare to the elaborate and
lengthy passages that Clement of Alexandria devotes to the nursing
Christ.[8] With the exception of Bede's references to God's wisdom as
feminine,[9] the theme is unimportant in the early Middle Ages. * * *

The Theme of "Mother Jesus" as a Reflection of Affective Spirituality

Several of the scholars who have noticed the use of maternal
imagery in medieval authors from Anselm of Canterbury to Julian of
Norwich have associated this particular image with the rise, from the
eleventh century on, of a lyrical, emotional piety that focuses
increasingly on the humanity of Christ.[1] Descriptions of God as a
woman nursing the soul at her breasts, drying its tears, punishing its
petty mischief-making, giving birth to it in agony and travail, are part
of a growing tendency to speak of the divine in homey images and
to emphasize its approachability. If Christ presents himself to us as

5. See Cabassut, "Une dévotion peu connue"; Eleanor C. McLaughlin, " 'Christ My Mother':
   Feminine Naming and Metaphor in Medieval Spirituality," *Nashota Review* 15 (1975):
   228–48; Ritamary Bradley, "The Motherhood Theme in Julian of Norwich,"
   Fourteenth-Century English Mystics Newsletter 2.4 (1976):25–30; Elaine H. Pagels, "What
   Became of God the Mother? Conflicting Images of God in Early Christianity," *Signs:
   Journal of Women in Culture and Society* 2 (1976): 293–303; idem, *The Gnostic Gospels*
   (New York, 1979); Eleanor McLaughlin, "God's Body and Ours: Possibilities for Refor-
   mation in Medieval Spirituality," unpublished lecture, Vanderbilt Theological School,
   October 1976; Colledge and Walsh, *A Book of Showings*. To their references, I add: Irenaeus, *Adversus haereses*, bk. 3, chap. 24, par. 1, *Patrologia graeca*, ed. J.-P. Migne, 7: cols.
   966–67; and Augustine, *In Johannis Evangelium Tractatus CXXIV*, chap. 15, par. 7, chap.
   16, par. 2, chap. 18, par. 1, and chap. 21, par. 1, Corpus christianorum 36 (Turnhout,
   1954), pp. 153, 165, 179, and 212.
6. Pagels, "God the Mother," and *Gnostic Gospels*.
7. Cabassut, "Une dévotion peu connue," p. 237.
8. Compare, for example, Ambrose, *De virginibus*, bk. 1, chap. 5, PL 16: col. 205, with
   Clement of Alexandria, *Paedagogus*, bk. 1, chap. 6, *Clemens Alexandrinus*, 2 vols., ed. Otto
   Stählin, Die griechischen christlichen Schriftsteller der ersten drei Jahrhunderte 12 and
   15 (Leipzig, 1936–39) 1:104–21.
9. Colledge and Walsh, *A Book of Showings* 1:154.
1. Cabassut, "Une dévotion peu connue"; Giles Constable, "Twelfth-Century Spirituality and
   the Late Middle Ages," *Medieval and Renaissance Studies* 5 (1971): 45–47; E. McLaughlin,
   " 'Christ My Mother' "; idem, "Women, Power and the Pursuit of Holiness in Medieval
   Christianity," *Women of Spirit: Female Leadership in the Jewish and Christian Traditions*, ed.
   Rosemary Ruether and Eleanor C. McLaughlin (New York, 1979), pp. 122–27.

a child playing in a carpenter's shop or a young man stopping, dusty and tired, for a meal with friends, what can possibly be wrong with earthy metaphors that associate his love with that of female as well as male parents, his sustenance with milk as well as meat? Seeing Christ or God or the Holy Spirit as female is thus part of a later medieval devotional tradition that is characterized by increasing preference for analogies taken from human relationships,[2] a growing sense of God as loving and accessible, a general tendency toward fulsome language, and a more accepting reaction to all natural things, including the physical human body.[3] But the idea of mother Jesus is not merely an aspect of increasing attention to the human Christ. It also expresses quite specifically certain of the emphases that underlay the affective spirituality of the twelfth to the fourteenth centuries.[4]

The affective piety of the high Middle Ages is based on an increasing sense of, first, humankind's creation "in the image and likeness" of God and, second, the humanity of Christ as guarantee that what we are is inextricably joined with divinity. Creation and incarnation are stressed more than atonement and judgment. Christ is seen as the mediator who joins our substance to divinity and as the object of a profound experiential union; God is emphasized as creating and creative; the cooperation of the Trinity in the work of creation is stressed. The dominant note of piety is optimism and a sense of momentum toward a loving God. Concentration on the eucharist and on Christ's suffering in the Passion, which increases in thirteenth- and fourteenth-century devotions, is not primarily a stress on the sacrifice needed to bridge the enormous gap between us in our sin and God in his glory; it is rather an identification with the fact that Christ is what we are. Moreover, both the imaginative identification with Christ's humanity, which is so stressed by late medieval preachers and devotional writers, and the increased theological emphasis on creation and incarnation are answers to the major heresies of the twelfth to fourteenth centuries. Affirmation of

2. This has been pointed out by R. Javelet, *Image et ressemblance au douzième siècle de saint Anselme à Alain de Lille*, 2 vols. (Paris, 1967).

3. This latter point is stressed by E. McLaughlin, " 'Christ My Mother'," and "Women, Power. . . ." It should not, however, be misunderstood. From the twelfth century on, negative attitudes toward sexuality, at least among the religious, probably increased; see John Boswell, *Christianity, Social Tolerance, and Homosexuality: Gay People in Western Europe from the Beginning of the Christian Era to the Fourteenth Century* (Chicago, 1980).

4. Of those scholars who have written on maternal imagery, Ritamary Bradley, "The Motherhood Theme in Julian of Norwich,"; idem, "Patristic Background of the Motherhood Similitude in Julian of Norwich," *Christian Scholar's Review* 8 (1978): 101–13; Kari Elizabeth Børresen, "Christ notre mère, la théologie de Julienne de Norwich," *Mitteilungen und Forschungsbeiträge der Cusanus-Gesellschaft* 13 (Mainz, 1978): 320–29; and Colledge and Walsh, *A Book of Showings*, have been concerned with the theological tradition more than the devotional; all three treat this through a search for the sources of Julian of Norwich's Trinitarian theology, which is expressed through the motherhood metaphor.

God's creation of all things and of the joining of physicality to divinity countered Cathar dualism; affirmation of the centrality of the eucharist countered the neglect or abandonment of the church's rituals that was implicit in various antisacerdotal movements and in Free Spirit antinomianism. In addition to expressing and evoking the emotional response so highly valued in the twelfth and thirteenth centuries, the devotion to mother Jesus conveyed the specific emphases of this piety on mystical union and the eucharist.

In spiritual writers from Anselm to Julian, we find three basic stereotypes of the female or the mother: the female is generative (the foetus is made of her very matter) and sacrificial in her generation (birth pangs);[5] the female is loving and tender (a mother cannot help loving her own child);[6] the female is nurturing (she feeds the child with her own bodily fluid).[7] This threefold concept of the female

5. Anselm, prayer 10, *Opera omnia*, ed. F. S. Schmitt, 6 vols. (Edinburgh, 1940–1961), 3: 33 and 39–41; Marguerite of Oingt, *Pagina meditationum*, chaps. 30, 32–33, 36–37 and 39, *Les oeuvres de Marguerite d'Oingt*, ed. and trans. Antonin Duraffour, P. Gardette and P. Durdilly, Publications de l'Institut de Linguistique Romane de Lyon 21 (Paris, 1965), pp. 77–79; and Julian of Norwich, *A Book of Showings*, the long text, passim and especially chaps. 58–60, 2:582–600. On the complex problems of the text of Julian's revelations, see also E. Colledge and J. Walsh, "Editing Julian of Norwich's Revelations: A Progress Report," *Mediaeval Studies* 38 (1976): 404–27. The theme of God as mother is developed in the later, longer version.

6. *Ancrene Riwle: The English Text of the Cotton Nero A. XIV*, ed. Mabel Day, Early English Text Society 225 (London 1952), p. 103 (and see also p. 180); Hugh Lacerta, *Liber de doctrina vel liber sententiarum seu rationum beati viri Stephani primi patris religionis Grandmontis*, chap. 10, CCCM 8 (Turnhout, 1968), p. 14; Bernard of Clairvaux, sermon 12, par. 4, *Sancti Bernardi opera* (hereafter OB), ed. J. Leclercq, C. H. Talbot, and H. M. Rochais (Rome, 1957–), 1:62–63; sermon 23, par. 2, 1:139–40; sermon 26, par. 6, 1:173; letter 258, PL 182: cols 466A-67A; and *De diligendo Deo*, chap. 7, par. 17, OB 3:134; Julian, *A Book of Showings*, the long text, especially chaps. 61 and 63, 2:601–9 and 614–18; Gertrude the Great, *Revelationes Gertrudianae ac Mechtildianae 1: Sanctae Gertrudis magnae virginis ordinis sancti Benedicti Legatus divinae pietatis . . .* ed. the monks of Solesmes [Dom Paquelin] (Paris, 1875), bk. 4, chap. 5, p. 314; and bk. 5, chap. 28, p. 546; Mechtild of Hackeborn, *Revelationes Gertrudianae ac Mechtildianae 2: Sanctae Mechtildis virginis ordinis sancti Benedicti Liber specialis gratiae*, ed. the monks of Solesmes (Paris, 1877), bk. 2, chap. 16, pp. 149–50; bk 3, chap. 9, p. 208; bk. 4, chap. 7, p. 264; and bk. 4, chap. 59, p. 311.

7. See the following by Bernard of Clairvaux: Letter 1, in *Epistolae*, ed. J. Mabillon, PL 182, cols. 72 and 76A–C, trans. Bruno Scott James, *The Letters of St. Bd of Clairvaux* (London, 1953), letter 1, pp. 3 and 7; Sermon 10, par. 3, OB 1:49–50, trans. Kiliam Walsh, *On the Song of Songs* 1, The Works of Bernard of Clairvaux 2, Cistercian Fathers Series 4 (Spencer, Mass., 1971): 62–63; Sermon 23, par. 2, OB 1:139–40, trans. Walsh, *Song* 2:27. Guerric abbot of Igny, Second sermon for SS. Peter and Paul, chap. 2, *Sermons*, 2 vols., ed. J. Morson and H. Costello, Sources chrétiennes 166 and 202, Série des texts monastiques d'Occident 31 and 43 (Paris, 1970 and 1973), 2:384–86, trans. the monks of Mount St. Bernard Abbey, *Liturgical Sermons*, 2 vols., Cistercian Fathers Series 8 and 32 (Spencer, Mass., 1970–71), 2:155. Aelred of Rievaulx, *De institutione inclusarum*, chap. 31, in *Opera omnia*, ed. A. Hoste and C. H. Talbot, CCCM 1 (Turnhout, 1971), 1:671, trans. M. P. McPherson in *The Works of Aelred of Rievaulx 1: Treatises and Pastoral Prayer*, Cistercian Fathers Series 2 (Spencer, Mass., 1971): 90–91. Thomas of Cantimpré, *Vita S. Lutgardis*, in J. Bollandus and G. Henschenius, *Acta sanctorum . . . editio novissima*, ed. J. Carnandet et al., June, vol. 4 (Paris, 1867): 189–210, especially bk. 1, chap. 1, sec. 2, pp. 191F–92A, and bk. 1., chap. 1, sec. 13, pp. 193C-E. See also Ursmer Berlière, *La devotion au sacré-coeur dans l'Ordre de St. Benôit*, Collection Pax 10 (Paris, 1923), pp. 20–23. The monk of Farne, *Meditations*, chaps. 40 and 50–51, "The Meditations of the Monk of Farne," ed. Hugh Farmer, *Studia Anselmiana* 41–42, *Analecta monastica* 4 (1957), pp. 182–83 and 189–90, trans. a Benedictine nun of Stanbrook, *The Monk of Farne: The*

parent seems to have been particularly appropriate to convey the new theological concerns, more appropriate in fact than the image of the male parent if we understand certain details of medieval theories of physiology.

People in the high Middle Ages argued that the ideal child-rearing pattern was for the mother to nurse her own child; in medieval medical theory breast milk is processed blood.[8] According to medieval understanding of physiology, the loving mother, like the pelican who is also a symbol for Christ, feeds her child with her own blood. Thus, the connection of blood and milk in many medieval texts is based on more than merely the parallelism of two bodily fluids. Clement of Alexandria as early as the second century makes explicit the connection between breast milk and the blood supplied to the foetus in order to use the nursing Christ as an image of the eucharist.[9] In medieval legends like the lactation of St. Bernard[1] and in medieval devotions like the sacred heart,[2] milk and blood are often interchangeable, as are Christ's breasts and the wound in his side.[3] What writers in the high Middle Ages wished to say about Christ the savior who feeds the individual soul with his own blood was precisely and concisely said in the image of the nursing mother whose milk *is* her blood, offered to the child.

Meditations of a Fourteenth-Century Monk, ed. Hugh Farmer, *The Benedictine Studies* (Baltimore, 1961), pp. 64 and 73–74; Gertrude the Great, *Oeuvres spirituelles*, vols. 2 and 3: *Le Héraut*, Sources Chrétiennes 139 and 143, Série des textes monastiques d'Occident 25 and 27 (Paris, 1968), bk. 3, chap. 4, 3:24; Richard Rolle, "Richard Rolle's Comment on the Canticles, Edited from MS Trinity College, Dublin, 153," ed. Elizabeth M. Murray (Ph.D. Dissertation, Fordham, 1958), pp. 29–30 and 33; and Julian, *A Book of Showings*, the long text, chap. 60, 2:596–97.

8. Mary M. McLaughlin, "Survivors and Surrogates: Children and Parents from the Ninth to the Thirteenth Centuries," *The History of Childhood*, ed. L. DeMause (New York, 1974), pp. 115–18; Michael Goodich, "Bartholomaeus Anglicus on Child-rearing," *History of Childhood Quarterly: The Journal of Psychohistory* 3 (1975): 80.

9. Clement, *Paedagogus*, bk. 1, chap. 6, *Clemens Alexandrinus* 1: 104–21.

1. See Léon Dewez and Albert van Iterson, "La lactation de saint Bernard: Legende et iconographie," *Cîteaux in de Nederlanden* 7 (1956): 165–89. We should also note in this connection the legend, found in a work attributed to John Chrysostom and repeated by Guerric, that the apostle Paul bled milk rather than blood when he was beheaded (see Guerric of Igny, *Liturgical Sermons* 2: 154, n.7). St. Catherine of Alexandria is also supposed to have bled milk when decapitated: see G. Bardy, "Catherine d'Alexandrie," *Dictionnaire d'histoire et de géographie ecclésiastiques* 11 (Paris, 1949): cols. 1503–5. Moreover lactation as an act of filial piety (an adult female offering the breast to a parent or an adult in a desperate situation) was a solemn theme in the literature and religion of pagan antiquity; Adolphe de Ceuleneer, "La Charité romaine dans la littérature et dans l'art," *Annales de l'Académie Royale d'archéologie de Belgique* 67 (Antwerp, 1919): 175–206. On medieval devotion to the Virgin's milk, see P. V. Bétérous, "A propos d'une des légendes mariales les plus répandues: le 'lait de la Vierge,' " *Bullétin de l'association Guillaume Budé* 4 (1975): 403–11.

2. See Jean Leclercq, "Le sacré-coeur dans la tradition bénédictine au moyen âge," *Cor Jesu: Commentationes in litteras encyclicas Pii PP. XII 'Haurietis aquas'*, 2 vols. (Rome, 1959), 2:3–28; see also Cyprien Vagaggini, "La dévotion au sacré-coeur chez sainte Mechtilde et sainte Gertrude," ibid., pp. 31–48.

3. For examples of this interchangeability, see Guerric of Igny, second sermon for SS. Peter and Paul, chap. 2, *Sermons* 2:384–86; Aelred, *De institutione*, chap. 31, *Opera omnia* 1: 671; the monk of Farne, *Meditations*, chap. 40, "The Meditations of the Monk of Farne," ed. Hugh Farmer, 182–83.

Medieval images of the maternal also stressed mother-love as instinctive and fundamental: the mother is tender and loving, sometimes dying to give the child life; she tempts or disciplines only with the welfare of the child in mind. Such imagery could, of course, be highly sentimental and was apt to bring affective response. It was peculiarly appropriate to a theological emphasis on an accessible and tender God, a God who bleeds and suffers less as a sacrifice or restoration of cosmic order than as a stimulus to human love.

Moreover, in medieval physiological theories—however confused they may be on the subject—the female in some sense provides the matter of the foetus, the male the life or spirit.[4] Medieval theologians sometimes stressed that, as Eve came from the matter of Adam, so Christ came from the matter of Mary.[5] Thus, the mother was, to medieval people, especially associated with the procreation of the physicality, the flesh, of the child. Here again, the emphases of physiological theory were particularly useful, given the devotional concerns of the later Middle Ages. For a theology that stressed the humanity of Christ as a taking up into divinity of humankind's fleshliness, female generativity could be an important symbol. For a theology that maintained—over against Cathar dualism—the goodness of creation in all its physicality, a God who is mother and womb as well as father and animator could be a more sweeping and convincing image of creation than a father God alone. (It could also, of course, be dangerous, with implications of pantheism or antinomianism.) Thus, the growth of maternal names for God in the later Middle Ages reflects the general tendency to see God as "accessible" and "like man," to apply to him homey metaphors and anthropomorphic analogies; it also reflects the fact that what medieval authors assume the female to be coincided with what they increasingly wished to emphasize about God the creator and about the Incarnation.

*   *   *

4. Vern Bullough, "Medieval Medical and Scientific Views of Women," *Viator* 4 (1973): 483–501. See also John F. Benton, "Clio and Venus: An Historical View of Medieval Love," *The Meaning of Courtly Love*, ed. F. X. Newman (Albany, 1969), p. 32, and Charles T. Wood, "Menstruation in the Middle Ages," *Speculum*, to appear.
5. M.-T. d'Alverny, "Comment les théologiens . . . voient la femme?" *Cahiers de civilisation médiévale* 20 (1977): 115–24. See also Basile Studer, "Consubstantialis Patri, consubstantialis Matri: Une antithèse christologique chez Léon le Grand," *Revue des études Augustiniennes* 18 (1972): 87–115; and Karl F. Morrison, " 'Unum ex multis': Hincmar of Rheims' Medical and Aesthetic Rationales for Unification," *Nascita dell'Europa ed Europa carolingia: un'equazione da verificare*, Settimana di Studio del Centro Italiano di Studi sull' Alto Medioevo 27 (Spoleto, 1980), to appear.

B. A. WINDEATT

The Art of Mystical Loving: Julian of Norwich†

Why do mystics *write?* To praise God? To make a record of their experience? To instruct others? For one thing, mystical writers are unlikely to be interested in conveying that which probably attracts to them many of their modern readers. Mystics know that the mystical life cannot be experienced vicariously by their readers in the act of reading through the literary effects of artistic creation. To read a mystical work cannot properly be a mystical experience in itself. For the mystic, of course, there is no way that he can express his own experience, let alone enable his audience fully to share it in re-created form through the literary medium that links the mystical writer to his readers. The author of *The Cloud of Unknowing* makes this very clear towards the end of his work:

> Alle þoo þat redyn or heren þe mater of þis book be red or spokin, & in þis redyng or hering þink it good & likyng þing, ben neuer þe raþer clepid of God to worche in þis werk, only for þis likyng steryng þat þei fele in þe tyme of þis redyng. For parauenture þis steryng comeþ more of a kyndely coriouste of witte þen of any clepyng of grace (ch. 75).[1]

The distinction is firmly made: the frisson of interest quickened by the literary effectiveness of the book as art is not the same as, not to be confounded with, the soul's movement towards the mystical life. The literary impact of the text is something distinct again from its spiritual design in appealing to the reader's soul, over the head as it were of any susceptibility to the impressions achieved by literary effects. Yet the *Cloud*-author is only the most striking of many instances where the very inexpressibility of the mystical theme stimulates—paradoxically, perversely—the most original artistic effects.[2]

Among the medieval English mystics, the purpose in writing of Julian of Norwich is least apparent in her text, the *Revelations.* On the one hand, she is not at all so directly autobiographical as Margery Kempe, but nor on the other hand does she adopt so openly didactic, so instructional a role as Hilton, Rolle, or the *Cloud*-author can do. Although Julian is often conscious of those who will see her work,

---

† From *The Medieval Mystical Tradition in England: Papers Read at the Exeter Symposium, July 1980*, pp. 55–71. Reprinted by permission of the author.

1. *The Cloud of Unknowing*, ed. P. Hodgson, Early English Text Society, OS, 218, London, 1944, pp. 130–31.
2. Cf. J. A. Burrow, 'Fantasy and Language in *The Cloud of Unknowing'*, *Essays in Criticism*, 27 (1977), 283–98. Cf. also Frederick J. Streng, 'Language and Mystical Awareness' (in) Steven T. Katz (ed), *Mysticism and Philosophical Analysis*, London, 1978, pp. 141–69; and W. M. Urban, *Humanity and Deity*, London, 1951, ch. 13.

and although her texts reveal that she appreciates the possibilities of literary effects, she does not declare an aim on her reader, and her work is without a persuasive, didactic rhetoric.

Julian's book has a combination of purposes and this produces the distinctive nature of the *Revelations*. It first aims at recording an account of the 'shewings' that happened to Julian, but it further aims to understand those visions, an attempt that extended over many anxious years.[3] In the text this is reflected by a juxtaposition of narrative report and of meditation, of event and interpretation. The book is not written from one established viewpoint in time both on the visions and their meaning. The state of Julian's inner life is not always something different from her writing, unlike Hilton or the *Cloud*-author, who write from an achieved viewpoint on their material in order to instruct a known individual. But Julian is not instructing others in how they can prepare in detail to gain for themselves the illumination that she achieved. Her own experience is the reverse of that long preparation about which mystics often write. For it is after her sudden visionary experience that Julian's own long preparation begins—in the task of interpreting what she has been shown. For Rolle, in his account of himself in his *Incendium Amoris*, a single overwhelming revelatory experience—feelings of fire, song, and sweetness—also underlies his subsequent life and writing. But although Rolle's is an experience that can and does recur, it does not develop.[4] In both respects this contrasts with Julian's experience. Hers is a momentary vision in her history, not recurring as such, but the beginning of a learning process ('In this mervelous example I have techyng with me, as it were the begynnyng of an ABC, whereby I may have sum understandyng of our lordis menyng', ch. 51).[5]

Because Julian's role as a writer springs out of an autobiographical event, her work retains a core of recorded autobiographical experience which she is trying to extend through interpretation.[6] In her book Julian is writing from within this experience of learning and

---

3. Two states of the text survive, shorter and longer, probably reflecting Julian's development as a contemplative. The shorter text survives in a 15th-century MS., B. L. Add. MS. 37790. (For a description, cf. *The Chastising of God's Children*, eds J. Bazire and E. Colledge, Oxford, 1957, pp. 9–10). The longer text survives in later copies of non-extant medieval MSS: Bib. Nat., Paris, Fonds Anglais No. 40 (late 16th century); B. L. Sloane MS.2499 (17th century); B. L. Sloane MS. 3705 (late 17th or early 18th century). On the relation of the two versions, cf. John Lawlor, 'A Note on the *Revelations* of Julian of Norwich', *Review of English Studies*, N.S. 2 (1951), 255–8, and B. A. Windeatt, 'Julian of Norwich and Her Audience', *Review of English Studies*, N.S. 28 (1977), 1–17.

4. *Incendium Amoris*, ed. M. Deanesly, Manchester, 1915, ch. 15. Cf. also Margaret Jennings, 'Richard Rolle and the Three Degrees of Love', *Downside Review*, 93 (1975), 193–200.

5. Cf. further: 'Of which gret things he will we have knowing here as it were in one ABC: that is to seyn, that we have a litill knoweing, whereof we shall have fullhede in hevyn' (ch. 80). All quotation of the longer version is from *Julian of Norwich: A Revelation of Love*, ed. Marion Glasscoe, Exeter, 1976.

6. On Julian's visions, cf. P. Molinari, *Julian of Norwich*, London, 1958, and A. Ryder, 'A Note on Julian's Visions', *Downside Review*, 96 (1978), 299–304.

understanding. The form in which her interpretation has developed
embodies in its own shape a record of how Julian's response has
grown in her contemplative years. She is still seeking her point of
view, a unity of perception, and the disunities in her text reflect her
difficulties *en route*.[7]

I

It is this devotion to a spiritual quest, and the structure of exploration
and enquiry that results in her book, which produce patterns in common between Julian's writing and some of the dream-poems of her
own times. Such parallels are useful to us in providing some contemporary literary correlative which can help locate what is most individual in Julian's text, highlighting the way in which autobiographical
conditions have been transmuted into literary effects, and so helping
toward some critical understanding of what the mystic achieves as
an artist.

Because the impetus of Julian's book stems from her urgent search
for understanding of her showings, her own position as the first-
person within her work has come through autobiographical pressures to resemble the literary questing roles of the first-person
narrator-characters in *The Pearl* or *Piers Plowman*.[8] There is a comparably troubled experience of questioning and doubt for the 'I' of
the poems and for Julian, although despite its autobiographical roots
Julian's book is no more simply autobiographical than the sophisticated contemporary poems with their use of a narrator *persona*, for
Julian expresses through her individual voice a concern for all Christians. Just as the narrative of the dream-poems tends to advance by
means of the progressive education of the dreamer away from the
original limitedness of his outlook—and involves the artistic expression of his experience of disorientation and readjustment—so in Julian's text the experience of interpreting her experience produces
some parallel literary effects.

These resemblances in the place within their works of Julian and
the dreamers are part of the comparable way in which the structures
of such essentially exploratory works have developed. In *Piers Plowman* the dreamer's attempts to understand his dreams produce a
loose structure of successive searching held together by the
dreamer's persevering enquiry. Both progress and aimlessness are

7. For the *Cloud*-author disunities of approach are contained within a larger unity of instruction (cf. *The Cloud*, p. 2/9–17). His sense of didactic responsibility emerges in his anxiety
   that the text can thus be misinterpreted by quotation out of context, an anxiety shared
   with Eckhart (cf. *Magistri Eckardi Opera Latina* II, *Opus Tripartitum*, ed. H. Bascour,
   Lipsiae, 1935, p. viii).
8. On the literary persona in Langland, cf. George Kane, *The Autobiographical Fallacy in
   Chaucer and Langland Studies*, London, 1965.

contained within the overall structure as necessary parts of the dreamer's educative experience. In the *Revelations* the highly distinctive structure and procedure of Julian's text similarly springs from her attempts to understand her showings. The manuscripts show that *Piers Plowman* is not one literary work but a body of ideas in flux over a certain period of the author's life.[9] The three successive writings of the 'same' poem express through a fictive self-projection in the dreamer the development of Langland's obsessing interest with the material of his poem. In short, the reiterative, searching pattern within any one of the extant *Piers* versions itself has an autobiographical model in the external, historical evidence of Langland's recurring attention to his material. The existence of Julian's text in several forms comparably suggests that her interest in her material also developed over a period of time, and that the reiterations in her text have an autobiographical model. The body of these ideas being the text in both authors' minds has a markedly independent existence from the particular literary forms in which the writer attempts to embody it. With Langland this is because of the range of what he is driven to include in his enquiry; with Julian it is because of the infinite suggestiveness of her original visions which she is driven to interpret.

The comparable effect of these circumstances on Langland and Julian is that both authors' most creative writing represents the transcending of an original, somewhat intractable germ or core of material. With his *B* and *C* texts Langland moves beyond the initial visionary experience of *A* into more far-reaching enquiry and abstract speculation. So with Julian, the spiritual superstructure of her book develops beyond the original core of visionary material which, however, like Langland's *A* vision, still constitutes very substantially the earlier part of the work.

Some analysis of the structure of Julian's text will make clear why it eventually resists and confuses a modern reader's expectation of an integrated work written from a single point of view. The text apparently maintains a relatively straightforward narrative for roughly its first half, although already in the thirteenth showing Julian is moving into digressive reflection and losing the thread of her narrative of a single experience. But after the fourteenth of the sixteen revelations has been recounted the text departs from expectations. That the form of the book, as it has developed under pressure of Julian's contemplations, moves beyond an account of a particular chronological experience is illustrated by Julian's insertion here of a relatively enormous expansion, consisting of her vision of the lord-and-servant and the ensuing meditation (ch. 44–63). All this mate-

9. Cf. George Kane, *Piers Plowman. The Evidence for Authorship*, London, 1965.

rial Julian interpolates between her fourteenth and fifteenth showings. The continuity of her original narrative account of experience is decisively broken by this inserted section of meditation. Although Julian describes the sixteenth showing as occurring separately in time from the other showings and performing a distinct confirmatory role (ch. 66), the pressure of her concern with matters arising makes Julian instead break the narrative frame after her fourteenth showing. The showing of the lord-and-servant (which does not occur in the earlier text and presumably was not part of the first experience recorded there) is distinct in kind from the other showings, and Julian's insertion of this later reflective vision within the continuum of her original account represents (even more extremely than some of Langland's digressions) an exploration of problems as they suggest themselves, regardless of self-conscious artistic constraints of form, symmetry and narrative continuity. Julian has simply prized apart the existing descriptions of her fourteenth and fifteenth showings and then—as if nothing has happened—abruptly resumes after the inserted chapters with the unaltered opening of her fifteenth showing and its by now quite dislocated time reference (Aforn this tyme I had gret longyng, ch. 64).

Like Langland's art, Julian's writing here is more concerned with her feeling for truth to perception than with a smoothly consistent narrative. In *Piers Plowman* the framework of first-person narrative can re-establish itself after the digressions. But in Julian's text a narrative of her experience of her showings can scarcely re-establish itself after such a relatively enormous expansion as the lord-and-servant showing, which comprises some quarter of the volume of the whole book. However, Julian briefly returns to narrative to describe her fifteenth and sixteenth showings, before entering on the final meditative section of her text to discuss the general spiritual issues that trouble her, including the balance between love and dread of God (ch. 70 ff.). The structure that results from Julian's meditations can consequently be represented as follows:

ch. 2–63:   Account of first to fourteenth showings;
ch. 44–50: General meditation;
ch. 51:   Lord-and-servant showing, and interpretation;
ch. 51–63: General meditation;
ch. 64–69: Account of fifteenth and sixteenth showings, and attacks by devil;
ch. 70 ff.: Final phase of meditation.

With contemplation on the timeless import of her showings Julian has become correspondingly less interested in the narrative consistency of her original record. Divergence between the two texts shows

how she comes to accept the essential *betweenness* of her situation.[1]
In the thematic range of her text this same betweenness is reflected
by Julian's interest not only in God's endlessness but by her stress
on his *beginninglessness* (ch. 58, 59, 86). Interpretation rather than
simple chronology has become the organizing principle, although
Julian still tried to maintain the framework of narrative events that
originally give rise to her contemplations. ('And *whan* I saw all
this . . .' ch. 48; 'But *yet here* I wondrid . . .' ch. 50; 'And in *this tyme*
I saw . . .' ch. 64, etc.). But as her vision of the lord-and-servant
shows, the questions implicit in Julian's initial account have, with
intervening contemplation, provoked such an amplified response at
the centre of the work that the narrative framework has been pushed
outwards from within towards either end of the book by the pressure
of meditation. A sense of its own narrative continuity no longer con-
trols the book, for the first text has been turned inside out by those
pressures in its implications which have impelled Julian's development as a mystical writer. Instead, the narrative of the original one-
day's visionary experience is held in fractured form within what is
now the real continuum of the meditations on the visions. This continuum is itself unconnected with specific time or space, since it is
the product of Julian's whole intervening period of contemplation.
The expression of her accumulated perceptions does not of itself
need a narrative context, just as Langland's dreams dislocate him
more and more from his acceptance of the waking world. But Julian
still attempts to maintain the semblance of a narrative account of a
single day's experience, even though she works into that narrative
her reactions and responses to the original visions which are
acknowledged to stem from twenty subsequent years of thought.

Her narrative on one day ends up almost splitting at the seams
with the exploration of its own implications, but this is the paradox
of Julian's approach and the special effect of her text. On one hand,
by including all her subsequent reflections within the one-day
account, an impression is created that her response to the showings
was more spontaneously thoughtful than her first text would suggest.
On the other hand, the text explicitly acknowledges itself as but the
latest in a series of layers when it mentions that different parts of
Julian's understanding were achieved at widely different times in the

---

1. In the twelfth showing MS. Add. 37790 reads:

> And in this was I lerede that ilke saule contemplatyfe to whilke es gyffen to luke and
> seke god schalle se hir and passe vnto god by contemplacioun (f. 106r).

(For the shorter text, cf. Frances Beer, *Julian of Norwich's Revelations of Divine Love*,
Heidelberg, 1978). But the longer text here reads instead:

> Wherin I was lernyd that our soule *shal never have rest* til it comith to hym (ch. 26).

The confident promise is postponed in the longer text by a newly-explicit stress on the
restlessness of the soul in this life. (All italics in quotation of Julian are mine).

period since the showings occurred. Julian attributes her understanding that 'love was our lords mening' (ch. 86) to more than fifteen years after the revelations happened. But understanding of the
lord-and-servant showing proved so difficult that it was not until 'XX
yeres after the tyme of the showing save iii monethis' (ch. 51) that
Julian says she received 'techyng inwardly' as to how to interpret it.
These acknowledged gaps in time between the states of understanding represented by Julian's text recall that disconcerting perspective
Langland gives to his narrative by telling how forty-five years of
wasted life have dropped out of account since the time Will has just
been describing in his youth.[2] Julian's and Langland's texts are trying
to convey a sense of their protracted and interrupted development
towards spiritual awareness. Julian is not trying retrospectively as an
artist to conceal the mystic's periods of frustration and doubt after
which she has reached the point from which she now writes. The
visionary, experiential core of the work would have prevented this.
Since the material itself was divinely given, the whole sequence of
her reaction to it could help in its interpretation.

In this way Julian's acknowledgement of problems comes to
resemble the dramatization of the narrator's misunderstanding and
education in *Pearl* and *Piers Plowman*. In discussing her fourteenth
showing Julian admits there are points where understanding cannot
proceed beyond a breaking down into blessings on Jesus (ch. 41);
other contexts show this happening, where her meditations reach a
certain stage and then dissolve into benediction (e.g. ch. 42; ch. 60).
With her lord-and-servant showing Julian first describes the vision,
then admits her difficulty in interpreting the vision, then tells how
she was taught to understand it, and finally proceeds to analyze the
showing according to the instructions (ch. 51). The structure of
interpretative effort within which the showing is presented preserves
in itself the record of Julian's repeated, frustrated, and eventually
more successful attempts to understand, as does a comparable
acknowledgement of difficulty over the second showing. Julian
admits that she has since been troubled whether she should believe
this a showing at all ('I was sumtime in doute whither it was a shewing. And than divers times our gode lord gave me more sight whereby
I understode treuly that it was a shewing', ch. 10). But she goes on
to explain how she eventually came to understand the significance
of this showing of the dark colouring of Christ's face in the passion.
The problematic nature of the interpretation becomes part of the
interest of the showing as it is meditated by Julian, and the vision is
seen not only in itself but in the context of Julian's spiritual development. Because Julian leaves within her text these traces of the

2. *Piers Plowman: The B Version*, eds. G. Kane and E. Talbot Donaldson, London, 1975, XI,
45–9.

interrelation of her book and her life, her problems in interpreting the recorded experience reflect from the inside the processes of Julian's developing inner life. The work has something of the effect, if not the aim, of a spiritual autobiography, which is all the more fascinating for being unconscious and uncontrived. In its unself-conscious inwardness nothing could be further from the self-vindication of Margery Kempe, or from the attempted historical coverage of a life by Margery or by the *Life* of Suso, itself an instance of 'unwitting' autobiography.[3]

The struggle for contemplative understanding itself becomes the principle of Julian's narrative, and one that is not artistically smoothed: Julian returns to some issues more often than would be necessary in an ideal form of her visions and meditations.[4] These repetitions reflect Julian's real difficulty with certain problems, most particularly the thirteenth showing's teaching on sin and its optimistic message that 'all shall be well'. Comparison of the earlier and later texts reveals that this showing is the one that has been more interpolated by subsequent additions than any other. Even if the earlier text had not survived, the heavily glossed nature of the showing would have suggested that it had caused its author concern. But the problems, although apparently settled within the showing, continue to trouble Julian. She returns to the issue of sin and blame over again in the chapters before the lord-and-servant showing:

> I saw him assigne to us no manner of blame . . . yet only in the beholdyng of this *I cowd nowte be full esyd,* and that was for the dome of holy church (ch. 45). . . . And notwithstondyng al this I beheld and *mervelyd gretly* what is the mercy and forgivenes of God (ch. 47). . . . I knew be the common techyng of holy church . . . that the blame of our synne continuly hangith upon us . . . than *this was my marvel,* that I saw our lord God shew- and to us no more blame. . . . And atwix these ii contraries *my reason was gretly traveylid* by my blyndhede (ch. 50).

Even after the showing of the lord-and-servant Julian does not seem completely confident ('In this that I have now seyd was my desire *in partie answerid,* and myn grete awer *symdele esid',* ch. 53). Again, after her showings are complete she relates how she was assailed by the devil and tempted with disbelief, and this autobiographical account leads on to her more general discussion of the proper balance between love and dread in our approach to God, a theme

---

3. The *Life* was originally written by a nun, who recorded the mystic's reminiscences to her without his knowledge, but it was later revised by Suso (cf. *Heinrich Suso: Deutsche Schriften* ed. K. Bilmeyer, Stuttgart, 1907).
4. For Julian's concern with sin, cf. Deryck Hanshell, 'A Crux in the Interpretation of Dame Julian', *Downside Review,* 92 (1974), 77–91.

reflecting an uncertainty in the mystic's spiritual life which takes some working out in the text.

II

It is not far to seek for the autobiographical roots of these returning interests in Julian's text. It is a question of authority, of what to believe among contradictory teachings, and in this Julian's position resembles the quests of Langland's dreamer. For Julian the question of authority was peculiarly intense, since the validity of her experience of revelation underpinned her writing and—very probably—her commitment to the anchoress's life. But as she had meditated an alarming gap had apparently developed between the two supports of her world, the unique showings given *individually* to her and the *general* teaching of the Church. She finds it agonisingly difficult to reconcile her own showing's swelling optimism that 'all shall be well' with Church teaching that heathens will be lost (ch. 32). In particular, this recalls Langland's own nagging concern over the unbaptized,[5] but more generally, the procedure of Julian's text recalls that of *Pearl* in representing the experience of learning for oneself that such apparent inconsistencies we perceive in God lie in the nature of our perceptions.

While Julian's text of course has no interlocutor-figure to guide the mystic, unlike the *Pearl*-poet's maiden who guides and corrects the muddled dreamer on his way, Julian's book does nevertheless chart the contemplative's comparable move towards realisation that seeming paradoxes are unified within God. Julian's reconciling of contraries is achieved by patterns of language which recall *Pearl*, for just as the nature of the Virgin is expressed in *Pearl* by her queenship of courtesy (11.432 ff.), so Julian recurrently finds in her visions and meditations both *homeliness* and *courtesy*, which are distinct yet complementary aspects of God. A broadly discernible pattern emerges: the showings themselves are seen as instances of his homeliness (just as the incarnation itself was an instance of his homeliness towards mankind) which encourage reciprocal homeliness from us. But the theme of God's courtesy characterizes the meditative passages, where Julian strives to understand. The thirteenth showing shows a strong concentration of Julian's references to God's courtesy but has only one reference to his homeliness (ch. 38), for the mysteries by which justice will be done yet 'all shall be well' can for Julian only be expressed as an instance of his courtesy. It is characteristic of the sense of God's workings which Julian achieves that these ideas of homeliness and courtesy are not kept apart but are more often

---

5. Cf. G. H. Russell, 'The Salvation of the Heathen: The Exploration of a Theme in *Piers Plowman*', *Journal of the Warburg and Courtauld Institute*, 29 (1966), 101–16.

found together, especially in the confident acclamations of God's courteous lordship towards the end of the text ('For our lord himselfe is sovereyn homleyhede, and as homley as he is, as curtes he is; for he is very curtes', ch. 77). This recalls the accumulated sense of just but merciful lordship in *Pearl*. The impression given by Julian's text, that its patterns of repeated themes represent a growing understanding by the mystic of God's deeds, receives support from a number of divergences between the MSS, which reveal how contemplation has deepened Julian's awareness of the way that God surpasses what we can understand from within our limited conceptions of number and time.[6]

Similarities between the *Revelations* and some dream-poems—by providing certain parallels and contrasts for Julian's own effects— can help in the critical assessment of the aims and achievements of the mystical writer. For these very similarities serve to emphasize how Julian's text is also profoundly different in its assumptions as a piece of writing, especially in its attitude to time and chronology, and to the relationship between writer and reader. However much Julian's text has been written up into a narrative, it does not have all the normal presuppositions of a narrative text, just as its often seemingly private and personal nature as writing means that it does not have predictable didactic attitudes. *Piers Plowman*, like *Pearl*, is often described as being circular in structure, which usefully conveys how the poems (after exploring the issues they raise) return essentially to their starting point, leaving the reader better equipped to start again. Julian's text can also be described as circular, but in a more radical way. By contrast the dream-poets have relatively normal, linear assumptions about narrative: they narrate a sequence of events which they reasonably assume their readers do not know about until they are told of them. But Julian does not hold herself bound by the constraints of such assumptions about her readership. In the centre of her work, when expounding her idea of our mother Jesus, Julian makes many references to her sixteenth showing of God seated within our soul.[7] But at the time of this discussion, in the interpolation between the fourteenth and fifteenth showings, Julian

---

6. *To her third showing* ('I saw God in a poynte') Julian later adds 'if it be happe or adventure in the sight of man our blindhede and our onforesight is the cause . . . but to our lord God thei be not so' (ch. 11); *to her ninth showing* on Christ's willingness to suffer more pain for us Julian later understands 'how often he would deyn if he myght; and sotly the noumbre passid myn understondyng and my wittis so fer that my reson myghte not, ne coude, comprehend it' (ch. 22). *To her sixth showing* on reward for service Julian recalls *Pearl* by later adding: 'Whan or what tyme a man or woman be truly turnid to God, for on day service and for his endles wille he shall have al these iii degres of blisse' (ch. 14).

7. Cf. 'For God is never out of the soule in which he wonen blissfully without end. And this was sen *in the xvi shewing*, wher it seith 'The place that Iesus takith in our soule he shall never remov it' (ch. 55) . . . if we wil have knowlidge of our soule . . . it behovith to sekyn into our lord God in whom it is inclosid. And of this inclos I saw and understode more *in the xvi shewing as I shall sey*' (ch. 56).

has not yet *reached* her description of the sixteenth showing. For the linear 'first time' reader of her text these references are allusions to a showing that has not yet 'happened' for him by being described in the chronological narrative. There are other such anticipatory references to showings, made in contexts where they have not yet been seen to happen for the reader (to the eighth shewing in ch. 10; to the fifteenth in ch. 41). This is deeply contrary to 'normal' expectations of narrative and reveals Julian's distinctive attitude to her text and its readers. Julian has here apparently forgotten what a reader working through her text in the linear way does and does not know, and she is not operating on that level of didacticism where an author is always conscious of the state of his reader's knowledge and ignorance.

Julian is sometimes assuming her readers already share her own memories, for her attitude to her material has long ceased to be linear and narrative, as her very individual use of self-quotation in her text shows. Sharing again Langland's greater concern for truth than narrative consistency, Julian makes cross-references and allusions that resemble those that can be made in a diagram. Julian's text moves forward by remembering itself, by quoting itself from earlier or later contexts in a way that criss-crosses between present and past and overrides a simple narrative. Julian's discussion of the motherhood of Jesus is supported by such self-quotation (ch. 60), first from her twelfth shewing:

> The moder may geven hir child soken her mylke, but our pretious moder Iesus he may fedyn us with himselfe and doith . . . with the blissid sacrament. . . . *And so ment he in this blissid word wher that he seid 'I it am that holy church prechith the . . .'*

then Julian recalls the striking images of her tenth shewing:

> The moder may leyn the child tenderly to her brest, but our tender moder Iesus, he may homley leden us into his blessid brest be his swete open syde, and shewen therin party of the Godhede . . . and that shewid in the X [shewing].

Such a texture of later cross-references to earlier showings embodies in literary form the way in which Julian's text has undergone a superimposition of later layers of understanding while it still depends on being seen entire. Memory of the past visions is both maintained and modified in a present of continuing meditation. In the way that it carries the authenticating visions forwards within itself by cross-reference to their words and details, striving to pierce beyond them spiritually while acknowledging the essential limits of contemplation, Julian's text presents a state of understanding which is now a whole complex state of mind no longer suceptible to the constraints of linear narrative expression.

III

For in its structure and procedure Julian's text reflects the very individual emphases of what—in meditating—she found important. Written at different times in different parts, it resembles those Gothic works of art that do not presume the single viewing-point that produces perspective and a sense of the relative proportion of parts. It is precisely the strangely individual selectivity of what Julian observes with her painterly eye in her showings, which gives a personal emphasis not only to the visions but to the overall structure of meditation that they provoke in the *Revelations*. That Julian possibly found inspiration in the contemporary visual arts is not unlikely. Julian's passion descriptions are distinctively stylised pictures and her response to the revelations (with her artist's eye not just for colour, but for *relative* colouring, contrast, and the juxtaposition of parts) resembles a response to painting. This very discriminating way of observing is part of the selectivity implied in the idea of 'shewings', which allow some individual access to universal truths.

But Julian's true creativity, as a mystical artist with an intense visual imagination, lies not only in what she sees but in how she sees it. Julian's achievement as a writing mystic lies not simply in being a vividly pictured writer but a mystic whose artistic expression of the achievement of mystical understanding lies in the way in which she seeks to convey through the resources of language how an inspiration received and initially represented in picture-like form is developed into a broader contemplative understanding. The most individual creative impulse represented by Julian's text is consequently the movement from image to syntax, from 'shewings' to understanding.

Comparison with Margery Kempe's attitude to the passion helps to focus Julian's distinctive approach to her own visions. Margery's response to Christ is to wish herself back in time, back into his lifetime, and back into the pictures of Christ's life and passion in her mind's eye. She impulsively lives herself back into the biblical scenes by imaginatively representing herself as present with Christ and Mary and helping them in their troubles. She thus fulfils her warmly personal devotion, and Margery's sense of the continuing presence of Christ's passion in our lives expresses itself, somewhat superficially, through a readiness to be moved by such people and things as put her in mind of biblical events.[8]

8. *The Book of Margery Kempe*, eds. S. B. Meech and H. E. Allen, Early English Text Society, OS, 212, London, 1940, ch. 6–7; ch. 35; ch. 79–81. On Margery's career, cf. M. Thornton, *Margery Kempe*, London, 1960, and L. Collis, *The Apprentice Saint*, London, 1964.

But for Julian, as the complementary roles of her showings and meditations reveal, an awareness of the ongoing spiritual relevance of the passion is combined with a sense of the distinct pastness of the historical event. Margery confuses and overcomes the pastness of the passion by going towards it actively in her imagination envisaging what she already knows, and is reminded of by the visual arts of her time. By contrast, Julian's impressions come upon her strangely, challenging her ability to see meaning in them. And through the process of composing her text, so that showings lead on into meditations, Julian is concerned to escape from the confines of human perception of time. For although, like other meditators on the passion, Julian graphically records the outward signs of his suffering, she noticeably avoids much attempt to enter into Christ's feelings in the passion. Julian's interest lies not so much with the 'historical' mind and feelings of Christ-in-passion as, more ambitiously, with what man can grasp of God's eternal mind and purpose. Julian's showings do not admit her to the mind of Christ, but they do confront her with the image of a crucifix, as if a painted image is running and dissolving strangely into a film. This stylised fragmentedness of what Julian first sees with such force in the showings drives her on to create the rest of the picture spiritually rather than visually, by moving on from his passion to his compassion.

The way in which Julian's visual memories of her showings are held within a continuum of more general contemplation itself reflects through literary form the spiritual truth that preoccupies Julian as mystical artist, who is conveying in her *Revelations* how the significance of the historical passion recreates itself to man throughout time. The showings are recorded in the past tense, but the meditations are expressed in a present tense that is timeless and opens out into infinity to reflect in syntactical patterns the purposes of God.

One striking divergence between her two texts reveals how Julian—with time and contemplation—has come to put the emphasis in the growth of love not on its purgative but on its transforming effects on the individual, and this offers a clue to her text's idiosyncratic combining of passages of marvellously assured prose within a structure of overall strain. The carefully revised and embellished descriptions of her showings—together with the precision of Julian's definitions of God's manner of working in her extended meditative passages—are instances of the mystic's artistic control over her material but the sense of how the showings have given rise to the meditations, which can only be partly reflected within the text, maintains within the work the tension of an impetus which cannot be completely satisfied. Other mystical artists, after representing periods of exploration and difficulty, could adumbrate some achievement of understanding by moving finally into imagery, into visionary forms. But since visions and images are Julian's starting point, she cannot use them as both spiritual and artistic climax as some other mystical artists do. The developing structure of the text itself becomes self-revealing of the developing spirituality of the author, and the movement between the two levels of the text, shewing and interpretative meditation, crystallizes in literary form—and so carries its reader through—a change in plane of perception that has become itself artistically expressive of the attainment of contemplative understanding. But of this process the reader is not so much a pupil in the presence of a teacher, any more than he is expected to be the admirer of artistic effects as such. In the modest manner of the *Revelations* he simply becomes—like Julian herself within the autobiographical structure of her text—a witness.

Selected Bibliography

EDITIONS

•indicates works included or excerpted in this Norton Critical Edition.

Beer, Frances, ed. *Julian of Norwich's Revelations of Divine Love: The Shorter Version, ed. from BL Add. MS 37790*. Middle English Texts 8. Heidelberg: Carl Winter, 1978.

Colledge, Edmund, OSA, and James Walsh, SJ, eds. *A Book of Showings to the Anchoress Julian of Norwich*. 2 vols. Studies and Texts 35. Toronto: Pontifical Institute of Mediaeval Studies, 1978. [Includes both short and long texts, the latter based on Paris.]

Julian of Norwich. *A Revelation of Love*. Ed. Marion Glasscoe. Rev. ed. Exeter Medieval English Texts and Studies. Exeter: University of Exeter Press, 1993. [An edition of the long text based on Sloane 1.]

Julian of Norwich. *Revelations of Divine Love* (Short Text and Long Text). Trans. Elizabeth Spearing. London: Penguin Books, 1998. [A translation of both texts; long text translated from Glasscoe's edition of Sloane 1.]

Crampton, Georgia Ronan, ed. *The Shewings of Julian of Norwich*. TEAMS Middle English Text Series. Kalamazoo, Mich.: Medieval Institute Publications. 1993. [An edition of the long text based on Sloane 1.]

Julian of Norwich. *Showing of Love: Extant Texts and Translation*. Ed. Sister Anna Maria Reynolds, CP, and Julia Bolton Holloway. Florence: SISMEL, Edizioni del Galluzzo, 2001. [Descriptions and transcriptions of the Westminster, Paris, Sloane 1, and Amherst manuscripts and translations of W and P.]

Julian of Norwich. *Showings*. Trans. Edmund Colledge, OSA, and James Walsh, SJ, Classics of Western Spirituality. New York: Paulist Press, 1978. [A translation of both texts; long text based on Paris.]

STUDIES

Abbott, Christopher. *Julian of Norwich: Autobiography and Theology*. Studies in Medieval Mysticism 2. Woodbridge, Suffolk: D. S. Brewer, 1999.

•Aers, David, and Lynn Staley. *The Powers of the Holy: Religion, Politics, and Gender in Late Medieval English Culture*. University Park: Pennsylvania State University Press, 1996.

Baker, Denise N. "The Image of God: Contrasting Configurations in Julian of Norwich's *Showings* and Walter Hilton's *Scale of Perfection*." In *Julian of Norwich: A Book of Essays*. Ed. Sandra McEntire. New York: Garland, 1998.

———. *Julian of Norwich's Showings: From Vision to Book*. Princeton, N.J.: Princeton University Press, 1994.

Barratt, Alexandra. " 'In the Lowest Part of Our Need': Julian and Medieval Gynecological Writing." In *Julian of Norwich: A Book of Essays*. Ed. Sandra McEntire. New York: Garland, 1998.

Bauerschmidt, Frederick Christian. *Julian of Norwich and the Mystical Body Politic of Christ*. South Bend, Ind.: Notre Dame University Press, 1999.

Beer, Frances. *Women and Mystical Experience in the Middle Ages*. Woodbridge, Suffolk: Boydell Press, 1992.

Bradley, Ritamary. *Julian's Way: A Practical Commentary on Julian of Norwich*. London: HarperCollins, 1992.

———. "Mysticism and the Motherhood Similitude of Julian of Norwich." *Studia Mystica* 9 (1985): 4–14.

Bynum, Caroline Walker. " ' . . . And Woman His Humanity': Female Imagery in the Religious Writing of the Later Middle Ages." In *Gender and Religion: On the Complexity of*

Symbols. Ed. Caroline Walker Bynum, Steven Harrell, and Paula Richman. Boston: Beacon Press, 1986.

•————. *Jesus as Mother: Studies in the Spirituality of the High Middle Ages*. Berkeley: University of California Press, 1982.

Gillespie, Vincent, and Maggie Ross. "The Apopathic Image: The Poetics of Effacement in Julian of Norwich." In *The Medieval Mystical Tradition in England: Exeter Symposium* 5. Ed. Marion Glasscoe. Cambridge: D.S. Brewer, 1992.

Glasscoe, Marion. *English Medieval Mystics: Games of Faith*. London: Longman, 1993.

Heimmel, Jennifer. *"God Is Our Mother": Julian of Norwich and the Medieval Image of Christian Feminine Divinity*. Elizabethan & Renaissance Studies 92:5. Salzburg: Universität Salzburg, 1982.

•Jantzen, Grace. *Julian of Norwich: Mystic and Theologian*. New edition. Mahwah, N. J.: Paulist Press, 2000.

————. *Power, Gender and Christian Mysticism*. Cambridge: Cambridge University Press, 1995.

•Johnson, Lynn Staley. "The Trope of the Scribe and the Question of Literary Authority in the Works of Julian of Norwich and Margery Kempe." *Speculum* 66 (1991): 820–38.

Kempster, Hugh. "A Question of Audience: The Westminster Text and Fifteenth-Century Reception of Julian of Norwich." In *Julian of Norwich: A Book of Essays*. Ed. Sandra McEntire. New York: Garland, 1998.

Lichtmann, Maria. " 'God Fulfylled My Bodye': Body, Self, and God in Julian of Norwich." In *Gender and Text in the Middle Ages*. Ed. Jane Chance. Gainesville: University of Florida Press, 1996.

McAvoy, Liz Herbert. " 'The Moders Service': Motherhood as Matrix in Julian of Norwich." *Mystics Quarterly* 24 (1998): 181–97.

McEntire, Sandra, ed. *Julian of Norwich: A Book of Essays*. New York: Garland, 1998.

•————. "The Likeness of God and the Restoration of Humanity in Julian of Norwich's *Showings*." In *Julian of Norwich: A Book of Essays*. Ed. Sandra McEntire. New York: Garland, 1998.

McInerney, Maud Burnett. " 'In the Meydens Womb': Julian of Norwich and the Poetics of Enclosure." In *Medieval Mothering*. Ed. John Carmi Parsons and Bonnie Wheeler. New York: Garland, 1996.

McNamer, Sarah. "The Exploratory Image: God as Mother in Julian of Norwich's *Revelations of Divine Love*." *Mystics Quarterly*, 15 (1989): 21–28.

Newman, Barbara. *God and the Goddesses: Vision, Poetry, and Belief in the Middle Ages*. Philadelphia: University of Pennsylvania Press, 2003.

•Nuth, Joan. *Wisdom's Daughter: The Theology of Julian of Norwich*. New York: Crossroad, 1991.

Pelphrey, Brant. *Christ our Mother: Julian of Norwich*. The Way of the Christian Mystics 7. Wilmington, Del.: Michael Glazier, 1989.

————. *Love Was His Meaning: The Theology and Mysticism of Julian of Norwich*. Salzburg: Institut für Anglistik und Amerikanistik, Universität Salzburg, 1982.

Riddy, Felicity. "Julian of Norwich and Self-Textualization." In *Editing Women*. Ed. Ann Hutchison. Toronto: University of Toronto Press, 1998.

————. " 'Women Talking about the Things of God': A Late Medieval Sub-Culture." In *Women and Literature in Britain, 1150–1500*. Ed. Carol Meale. Cambridge Studes in Medieval Literature 17. Cambridge: Cambridge University Press, 1993.

Riehle, Wolfgang. *The Middle English Mystics*. Trans. Bernard Standring. London: Routledge & Kegan Paul, 1981.

Robertson, Elizabeth. "Medieval Medical Views of Women and Female Spirituality in the *Ancrene Wisse* and Julian of Norwich's *Showings*." In *Feminist Approaches to the Body in Medieval Literature*. Ed. Linda Lomperis and Sarah Stanbury. Philadelphia: University of Philadelphia Press, 1993.

Staley, Lynn. "The Man in Foul Clothes and a Late Fourteenth-Century Conversation About Sin." *Studies in the Age of Chaucer* 24 (2002): 1–47.

Warren, Ann. *Anchorites and Their Patrons in Medieval England*. Berkeley: University of California Press, 1985.

Watson, Nicholas. "The Composition of Julian of Norwich's *Revelation of Love*." *Speculum* 68 (1993): 637–83.

————. "Julian of Norwich." In *The Cambridge Companion to Medieval Women's Writing*. Ed. Carolyn Dinshaw and David Wallace. Cambridge: Cambridge University Press, 2003.

————. "The Middle English Mystics." In *The Cambridge History of Medieval English Literature*. Ed. David Wallace. Cambridge: Cambridge University Press, 1999.

————. "The Trinitarian Hermeneutic in Julian of Norwich's *Revelation of Love*." In *The Medieval Mystical Tradition in England, Exeter Symposium* 5. Ed. Marion Glasscoe. Cambridge: D.S. Brewer, 1992. Rpt. in *Julian of Norwich: A Book of Essays* Ed. Sandra McEntire. New York: Garland, 1998.

———. "Visions of Inclusion: Universal Salvation and Vernacular Theology in Pre-Reformation England." *Journal of Medieval and Early Modern Studies* 27 (1997): 145–87.

———. " 'Yf Women Be Double Naturally': Remaking 'Woman' in Julian of Norwich's *Revelation of Love*." *Exemplaria* 8 (1996): 1–34.

•Windeatt, B.A. "The Art of Mystical Loving: Julian of Norwich." In *The Medieval Mystical Tradition: Papers Read at the Exeter Symposium, July 1980*. Ed. Marion Glasscoe. Exeter: University of Exeter Press, 1980.

———. "Julian of Norwich and Her Audience." *Review of English Studies*. n. s., 28 (1977): 1–17.

———. " 'Privytes to Us': Knowing and Revisions in Julian of Norwich." In *Chaucer to Shakespeare: Essays in Honour of Shinsuke Ando*. Ed. Toshiyuki Takamiya and Richard Beadle. Woodbridge, Suffolk: D.S. Brewer, 1992.